Material Culture and Authenticity

Materializing Culture

Series Editors: Paul Gilroy and Daniel Miller

Material Culture and Authenticity

Fake Branded Fashion in Europe

Magdalena Crăciun

B L O O M S B U R Y

LONDON · NEW DELHI · NEW YORK · SYDNEY

Bloomsbury Academic
An imprint of Bloomsbury Publishing Plc

50 Bedford Square	1385 Broadway
London	New York
WC1B 3DP	NY 10018
UK	USA

www.bloomsbury.com

Bloomsbury is a trade mark of Bloomsbury Publishing Plc

First published 2014

© Magdalena Crăciun, 2014

British Library Cataloguing-in-Publication Data
A catalogue record for this book is available from the British Library.

ISBN: HB: 978-0-85785-450-6
PB: 978-0-85785-451-3
ePDF: 978-1-47251-713-5
ePub: 978-1-47251-712-8

Library of Congress Cataloging-in-Publication Data
A catalog record for this book is available from the Library of Congress.

Typeset by Apex CoVantage, LLC, Madison, WI, USA
Printed and bound in Great Britain

Contents

Acknowledgments

My doctoral fieldwork in Istanbul (2006–2007) was made possible by financial support from the Romanian Cultural Institute. I also wish to acknowledge the support I received for writing the dissertation from the Ratiu Foundation and the Royal Anthropological Institute. Much of the present book was written while I held a post-doctoral fellowship from the British Institute at Ankara.

From the beginning of my interest in fakes I have benefited from the unflagging energy and support of my supervisor, Daniel Miller. I am deeply indebted for his comments. The book draws on material I first analysed in my dissertation (Crăciun 2009). I would like to thank my examiners, Catherine Alexander and Annelies Moors, for their valuable comments. The Department of Anthropology at University College London has been generous when it mattered most. I received warm assistance and advice from my UCL colleagues, and I thank especially to Janine Su, Besim Can Zırh, Ivana Bajic-Hajdukovic and Julie Botticello. I would also like to thank my family and friends in Istanbul and Romania for their patience and support.

Parts of this book have appeared in a somewhat different form in Crăciun 2012 (with acknowledgements to the Journal, Royal Anthropological Institute and Blackwell Publishing) and Crăciun 2009 (with acknowledgements to Berg).

–1–

Introduction

AN ORDINARY DAY IN THE LIFE OF AN ISTANBULITE

It is mid-afternoon, the time when business hits a lull in the bazaar. Kerim,[1] a sturdy, middle-aged man, busies himself with putting his shop in order, the one thing that never seems to bore him. In the morning new stock arrived, but he could not find time to open the large plastic bag and pushed it under the counter. Now he dusts and tidies up the shelves and rearranges the table he keeps in front of the shop, making sure all the brand names are visible. Most of his goods are branded Armani, Dolce & Gabbana, and Björn Borg, but he also offers Calvin Klein, Ralph Lauren, Dsquared, Gucci, Versace, and, under the counter, Hugo Boss and Diesel.[2] Then he empties the carrier, unwraps a few packages, places the new models on the counter, and piles up the rest under the shelves. Every now and then he stops, lights a cigarette, and invites other shopkeepers to come and have a look at these new products. They do come, swinging by amidst the packages spread inside and outside the shop, looking at the products, drinking their glasses of tea, smoking their cigarettes, listening to him talking up his merchandise, and bringing up other topics of conversation too. This time, Kerim is particularly proud of the color combinations he himself chose. The new arrivals are microfiber seamless men's boxer briefs with thin and wide waistbands in white and crimson, white and dark forest green, burgundy and ash grey, and brown and dark blue. His visitors express their sincere admiration. A few select some of these new models for themselves, while the others speculate about what lady will get to see these fancy briefs first. These men often hear Kerim speaking about his business, torrents of words about the high-tech factory, the clever way his business is organized, the quality of the products, the new models, the brand names, his numerous customers, and his reliability and honesty. Upon finishing with the tidying up, Kerim stands motionless for a few seconds, as if nailed to the spot, and scrutinizes the shop. The satisfaction he feels at what he sees is so evident that a fellow shopkeeper who passes by cannot help but congratulate him on having such a tidy shop. Smiling, he replies: "I guess I can say that I put my life in order too."

Kerim is an established trader in the business of legally fake branded garments. He occupies a relatively stable position on the market, somewhere in the middle, between the "big players," who invest millions in this business, and the insignificant participants, who stitch poorly cut labels onto cheap clothes. His current arrangement includes this shop, a workshop he equipped with high-tech automated Italian machines, several stable partnerships with other manufacturers, and a few secluded storage depots. The manufacture of most of his goods starts as after-hours production in his workshop. Subsequent manufacturing operations, such as dyeing, printing the brand names, sewing the logos and labels, and packing, are performed in his partners' workshops. All the places through which these goods are moving, including storehouses and the bazaar, are strategically placed in various parts of the city. However, from a different point of view, this is a normal production chain in the local clothing industry. Moreover, he increases his stock by placing orders with other manufacturers and by purchasing export surpluses and rejects that can be transformed into imitations or used for manufacturing good-quality products. He runs a successful business, and his shop is always full to the brim with merchandise and is constantly visited by customers, friends, and business partners.

He was in his mid-twenties when he entered this trade. At first he traded in rubber goods. He did nothing but work and build capital. His days were long, sometimes very long, longer than he thought he would be able to bear. They began early in the morning when he drove his van to manufacturing sites across the city, haggled with workshop owners for every penny, and carried the goods to the shop on his own to avoid spending money on the porters. He spent long hours in the shop, where he tried hard to please his customers and convince them to return or spread the word about his merchandise, his good prices, and his honesty and reliability. When business was bad, he worked during the night as a taxi driver. Then bad luck hit him. In his rush to serve a customer, he left his half-burnt cigarette in the attic. Most of his rubber goods melted in that fire. One second of inattention and, after months of work, he was back to square one. However, things made more sense to him after that disaster. He gave up the rubber goods and entered the trade in fake branded garments. He did nothing but work. He learned about clothing manufacture; how to distinguish between different materials; what quality meant; where he could find suppliers of fibers, fabrics, and accessories; what sources of excess products and leakages from the local clothing industry were available; and how to evaluate which brand sold well, which colors were preferred, which models suited the taste of local and foreign clients, and what technologies were most effective and where he could buy them at a reasonable price. He got to know who else was in this trade and built his network of contacts. During all those years, Kerim made an effort to carve a place for himself in the market and eventually succeeded.

After the brief visit from one of his business partners, the most important moment of this quiet afternoon, Kerim remarks, more for himself than for his companions: "I love this business. I have given it many years of my life." He plays absentmindedly with a pair of bright orange boxer shorts, stretching them, checking the seams and stitches, rubbing the fabric between his fingers and against his chin, evaluating their quality, muttering away to himself that it could have been even better if his partner had used higher-quality thread. He will have to tell him again what his "Russian" customer told him: "You Turks know everything about good cotton, but nothing about good thread." To an occasional customer, Kerim offers not only the well-rehearsed speech—"please, come and have a look. I have sixteen colors and many brands. I have everything you want. You cannot find such good things in the whole bazaar, trust me"—but also a detailed description of the manufacturing process of these quality goods, which are "just like the originals you can buy for forty euros a pair."

Kerim worked hard. As he put it, "effort must be put into making fraud too. If your products are good and you are an honest man and a cautious businessman, then you stay on the market." His golden rule was to divide his money into money for everyday life, to be put in the right pocket, and money for the business, to be kept in the left pocket. This rule always allowed him to remain on the market even in times of financial difficulties. His attitude was to ponder carefully over business propositions and to trust more in his own ability to evaluate materiality and his own knowledge of clothing manufacture, available technology, and excess materials and products than in the exalted stories of his potential business partners.

He went through many difficult moments, for blows and betrayals are frequent in this trade. In time, the local competition for harnessing a brand's agency became tougher and tougher, this profitable business attracting crowds of newcomers who had no scruples about betraying other traders, had no principles, and respected no rules. He also had his share of the other type of troubles that are an inevitable concomitant in this business. Kerim was caught several times, but never jailed, for manufacturing and trading in fake branded goods. He was first caught in 2001 because of a careless mistake. The number of the apartment in which he had a depot and the number of the building were the same. A team of lawyers was looking for the ground floor shop to make a routine inspection. His employee happened to smoke a cigarette in front of the entrance at the wrong time and answered candidly to their question, indicating that number fifty-six was on the fifth floor. The lawyers entered the paradise, a flat filled to the brim with fake branded goods. Kerim faced a heavy fine and years in jail. The sentence was, however, suspended for five years, as this is the period after which the files are cleared, a legal loophole for whose application he generously bribed his lawyers. Consequently, he took more precautions, changing more often the location of his production sites, hiding the depots even better, arranging for the bank to sequester some of his properties, and strengthening his ties with politicians, lawyers, and underworld figures. In the following years, police raided the bazaar numerous times, lawyers paid impromptu visits to his shop, judges spoke harsh words about this business and lectured him on business ethics, but each time he managed to keep himself out of trouble, half-bribing, half-threatening the law.

He experienced moral disapproval outside the court of law too. Encounters with his rich and educated relatives often reminded him that not only lawyers and the law thought of him and his business in disparaging terms. Kerim pointed out in vain that the so-called originals were rather ordinary mass-manufactured objects and their high price was unjustified, that his goods were fairly priced objects of good quality, that he invested in materials and technology, that he was dedicated to his work, that he knew very well how clothing manufacture works, and that they themselves could see, as he did, the actual clothes behind the shiny wraps of advertisement and fancy stores. They turned a deaf ear to these arguments. They did visit his shop and did buy his merchandise, but refused to talk about their reasons for buying these objects. They made no secret of their opinions. They regarded counterfeits as debased objects and they always insisted on calling Kerim's products so, although he called them imitations. They considered him an uneducated man who did an unethical business and disobeyed the normative order. One of his paternal uncles always went further and accused him of pretending to be who he was not and could not be, that is, a businessman.

This afternoon, the uncle shows up to while away time in his nephew's shop. As usual, at an opportune moment, the uncle launches into one of his lectures about the immorality of copying and counterfeiting and urges his nephew to invest his heart and money in something of which he can be proud. The uncle uses a banal example to support his argument, namely the manufacture of the table Kerim keeps in front of the shop. He states that an honest man produces this table and he can be proud of his work and product. In contrast, his nephew just copies other people's work and there is nothing rewarding about this. This is not a profession, as no particular skills are required to do this kind of work. This is not a business, as no risks are taken and success is guaranteed through the reproduction of popular products. Upon hearing this example a thousand times and knowing that next on his uncle's agenda is the criminal aspect of this business, Kerim rolls his eyes and addresses his standard question: "Isn't it a crime to sell what cost you two euros for forty euros? Or is it a crime to sell it for three euros?" He for his part long ago decided this is not a crime and he is not a criminal. They both shrug their shoulders, as if to say there is nothing more to add, and move on to other topics of conversation.

A thought that Kerim later shares with his companions, after his uncle leaves, demonstrates that the speech has had some effect on him, either this afternoon or sometime in the past. He bitterly remarks: "I heard that nowadays, if you type a name on the Internet, all the lawsuits of that person will pop up. I have many, so many. One might think I am a bad person. But I do imitations." To disperse such a gloomy thought, Kerim says, more to himself than to his companions, that those who are eager to condemn him seem to conveniently forget that the moral police officers, lawyers, and judges take bribes from the immoral criminals like him. Moreover, he reasons that it has been worth taking these risks and dealing with this harsh criticism. All the way. As he puts it, "I became like this for I wanted to. Life too made me like this. But I am happy with the way I am. I live by my own rules and I will stay like this until the end...I will drown not in a lake, but in the ocean. I will be eaten up by sharks or whales in the ocean, but I will not die in a lake." Looking at his shop and flipping through the notebook where he records his transactions, Kerim emphasizes once more that it has been worth entering the trade in fake brands.

In his youth, Kerim had walked on a dangerous path. "As a child, I was so afraid of my father. He seemed such a hulk of a man to me. He had a hoarse voice and shouted all the time. But then I grew stronger," he recalls. His father was a conservative Macedonian Turk, who settled down in Istanbul in the 1950s, entered the industry for leather goods, and owned and ran several bazaar shops. This severe man, whom Kerim sometimes describes as a conservative person and, at other times, as an uneducated individual, mistrusted his family members' ability to execute important decisions. He tried to make his children dependent on his judgment and sought to imbue them with his own traits and values.[3] His children had had a harsh upbringing. "I grew up in this bazaar. I know it like the palm of my hand. I know the owners of many of these shops. I was a kid playing on these alleys when the current president of the bazaar began to work in a shop next to ours," Kerim points out. He started coming to the bazaar at about the age of five, together with his brothers, and spent many hours in the bazaar alleys, running errands, playing with other children, getting bored and hungry, and longing to go home. His father wanted his boys there, almost every day, to earn their pocket money and learn the trade. Kerim alone was sent to an Imam-Hatip school.[4] His father wanted him to become an imam. Kerim thinks this was a choice motivated less by interest in education in accordance with Muslim beliefs and more by the positive evaluation of the school in terms of parental prestige and social mobility. He studied four years in an institution characterized by an atmosphere of discipline, where the duty of the students was to obey, and the task of the teachers was to compel them to be adherents to and practitioners of Muslim teachings. He remembers the long, painful hours he spent reading and memorizing passages from the Quran. He, the youngest among the six children in his family, had grown up trying to understand why he was treated in a manifestly unfair way and reached the conclusion that he was an unwanted child.

Upon finishing the Imam-Hatip school, Kerim left home. He knew how heartbreaking it had been for his mother and little sister, who loved him dearly, when he left home for good. Still he could not help but suspect that his parents had also been relieved deep down, for he was not going in the direction they wanted; he was not fulfilling the role they envisaged for him, for he was often rebelling against his father and causing troubles at home. He had to leave the house and pursue his own life of self-fulfillment. For six years, he lived a colorful life on the streets, encountered all manner of experiences, and made the most of doing everything that was previously forbidden. His father knew nothing about him getting arrested at the age of sixteen and again at the age of eighteen. He knew nothing about him being political, that is, actively involved in the turbulent events of the late 1970s, when leftists and ultranationalists clashed violently all over the country. He had become a *delikanlı*, literally meaning one who is crazy-blooded.[5]

His bold manners helped him rise to the challenges of a conscript's life. Hard as it was during that time, he managed and became the personal driver of a high-ranking officer. Upon finishing the military service, he embarked on new adventures, far beyond the streets of his neighborhood and rarely in the company of his old friends. He met new people; drove trucks around Turkey, Eastern Europe, and the Middle East; smuggled watches, chewing gum, jeans, gold, and silver; bartered with the "Russians"; and rested in jail. He availed himself of the opportunities that came his way and accumulated years full of all kinds of adventures that made him feel life was worth living. He stopped the day it dawned on him that he had taken the path of marginality. The bazaar was the place where he returned to start anew at a time when he was yearning not only for adventure, but also for a purpose. After a brief engagement in the trade in rubber goods, he oriented toward something that better corresponded to his understanding of the world and better served his aim of carving a place for himself within it.

Late in the afternoon, Kerim recalls that once an acquaintance told him a foreigner was interested in Calvin Klein men's underwear. This happened a few months before he was due to leave for the military service. The foreigner was looking for someone who could not only take care of the entire manufacturing process, but also help him ship the merchandise to his country. He liked that challenge. As he puts it, "I had already had the tendency, so I dived right in." Gesturing toward the shop full of fakes, Kerim adds: "And I still have not surfaced."

AN ISTANBULITE AND HIS FAKE BRANDS

I met Kerim while I was conducting research on the manufacture and trade in fake branded garments in Istanbul. He, at the time recovering from his most severe blow yet, a lawsuit that forced him to hide his goods and that reduced the rhythm of his business, gradually welcomed the inquisitive anthropologist and the opportunity this encounter presented for self-reflection and self-presentation.[6] For about six months, I went to his shop nearly every day and kept him company throughout the day. I also visited him during later stages of my research, while I was writing up the fieldwork and still living in Istanbul. During the many hours I spent in his shop, I often had the chance to talk with him about his life and profession and to learn about his business.[7]

Kerim called his goods *imitasyonlar* (imitations).[8] He openly declared he sold imitations, but proudly insisted that his goods were of good quality. He relentlessly tried to convince his customers, partners, and visitors that his products were not notably distinct from what they (were told to) consider originals. He taught them what quality felt and looked like and told them they too could learn how to understand garments. In the case of mass-manufactured garments, anyone could learn how to differentiate between objects of various qualities. He assured them that he produced these goods with the same care and with the same or similar materials as the originals. He explained that his goods were manufactured either in workshops caught up in the official production or equipped with similar technology. In so doing, Kerim, like many other manufacturers, sellers, and consumers I encountered during my research, rejected the assumption that imitations or fakes were necessarily of bad quality, and that their manufacturers cheated consumers and their consumers were cheated.

His business strategies and his reflections on the nature of clothing and the nature of brand are illustrative of the interest in and the importance accorded to the materiality of garments, brands, and fake brands that I discovered during my fieldwork. However, there is something different about this man, and for this reason his story is singled out here.

Kerim called himself an *imitasyoncu,* a rarely used Turkish word, translating as a maker and seller of imitations, thus clearly stating this was his profession. He legitimized his business through his honesty, reliability, and hard work, against the common assumptions that dealing in fake brands did not necessitate personal and professional investment and that his sole intention was to cheat his customers. He resisted the assumption that he cheated himself by copying and stealing other people's work. Moreover, Kerim described himself as being *kaşarlı. Kaşar* is a type of hard dark yellow cheese. The longer it is kept in molds, the harder and better it becomes. *Kaşarlı,* literally meaning "with *kaşar,*" is slang for a sexually experienced woman. A man can be *kaşarlı* too. However, in this case the adjective indicates experience in illicit activities. This was his way of declaring that he was experienced in an activity that, for many, fell outside the boundaries of conventional morality and legality.[9]

This man committed himself to fakes because they permitted him to be who he wanted to be and because they were true to the nature of the world as he saw it. Kerim started his life under strict rules, but responded by systematic rejection and the embracing of illegality to confirm himself as an individual rather than the mere product of these rules. Later he entered the trade in fake brands. These objects provided him with a mirror through which he came to understand the contradictions and juxtapositions in his life. They guaranteed a life full of exciting experiences. They enabled him to have a profession, earn a living, accumulate expertise in clothing manufacture, and take pride in trading valuable objects. They allowed Kerim the possibility to construct himself in terms of a morality he was comfortable with, which had much smaller oscillations between conventional morality and illegality and expressed his own moral position. These objects became central to the way this man reflected on and practiced the world. However, Kerim often had to legitimize this commitment and to authenticate himself. He made claims about himself, his products, and business ethics. And they had always been similar claims. He created an understanding of himself as an individual and ran a business in fake brands. And they had always been mutually constitutive processes.

These fake brands materialized the position Kerim carved for himself. These objects were simultaneously marginal and not so marginal. So was Kerim. Through his close identification with these objects, he came to see himself as authentic. Despite adverse reactions to his engagement with these objects, Kerim constantly celebrated the fullness of life to which this commitment gave rise. Although people of similar social and cultural background to that of Kerim, whom I encountered during my fieldwork, shared some of his opinions and concerns, engagement with fake brands played a more central role in his project of self-construction. In his case, engagement with fake brands allowed for the possibility of living authentically.

This is a paradoxical juxtaposition. In their modern cultural conceptualization, the notions of inauthentic object and authentic self seem incompatible and irreconcilable. The notion of inauthentic object implies an intention to deceive. Inauthentic objects are fraudulently introduced to the world through various acts of deception, such as falsification, theft, imitation, and impersonation. However, these acts affect not only others, but also those who practice them. By falsifying, stealing, imitating, and impersonating, an individual pretends he or she is someone else and, consequently, is not true to himself or herself. This individual attenuates, if not erases, his or her self. Engagement with the inauthentic object erodes the possibility of articulating an authentic self. Therefore, the juxtaposition at the center of the life of this Istanbulite ought to be incommensurable and contradictory. Nevertheless, he lives with and through this paradox.

This man and this paradox get to the heart of what is at stake on the issue of authenticity. In our modern world, we often struggle with this problem: How can we come to see ourselves as authentic rather than inauthentic beings? This man has a modest lesson to teach us. He discovers the solution to this problem through his close identification with fake branded commodities. The centrality of these objects in his life makes his case a paradigmatic example that best supports one of the main arguments of this book, namely that the authenticity of selves can be maintained in relation to the acknowledged inauthenticity of objects.

For these reasons, this book begins and ends with descriptions of ordinary days in the life of this Istanbulite. These vignettes illustrate ethnographically all the arguments about authenticity, brand, and materiality that this book contains.

THE BOOK

This is an ethnography of engagements with fake branded garments on a European periphery, more specifically Turkey and Romania. This book aims to illuminate the significance of fake branded commodities and the ways these objects are entangled within economic imaginaries and notions of good working lives and within projects of identity construction and notions of true self. To achieve this aim, this book critically engages with and contributes to theoretical perspectives on key concepts pertaining to the topic of fake branded commodities, that is, authenticity, brand, and fake.

This book builds on a material culture perspective and exemplifies an "anthropology engaged with the material world as entry into the most pressing concerns of what it is to be human" (Geismar 2011: 4). In this book, objects are not reduced to "other relations or meanings in which they are embedded" (Thomas 1999, quoted in Keane 2005: 2), but they are treated in their own right. "Their qualities, the practices they mediate and the interpretations to which they give rise" are placed within a "world of causality" (Keane 2005: 7). Moreover, in this book, the relationship between people and objects is conceived as an ongoing dialectical process of objectification. "Everything that we are and do arises out of the reflection upon ourselves given by the mirror image of the process by which we create form and are created by this same process...We cannot know who we are, or become what we are, except by looking in a material mirror" (Miller 2005b: 8). People make objects and objects make people. Furthermore, in this book, garments are not treated as mere representations of inner selves and social relations, but considered in their own right as constitutive of subjectivities and socialities. Clothing is not mere appearance, "a form of representation, a semiotic sign or symbol of the person," but plays a "considerable and active part in constituting the particular experience of the self" (Miller 2009: 40). The material culture perspective allows the particular contributions to the study of brand and authenticity this book proposes.

Brand has been theorized as an "unstable conjunction of tangible, material things (products, commodities) with 'immaterial' forms of value (brand names, logos, images)" (Moore 2003: 334). In this perspective, the branded commodity is "partly a thing, and partly language" (Moore 2003: 334), and the connections between these two components are under constant negotiation. However, it has been pointed out that, in the interested discourses of brand professionals and cultural theoreticians, the inherent instability of brand is often ignored or hidden and signification and semiotics are privileged. In the brand discourse, this move reflects a practical concern with the vulnerability of brand, which "comes into view when the semiotic ideology of brand is confronted with the contingent world of its materializations" (Moore 2003: 336). Keane can be invoked here to elaborate on this concern, for he argues that "part of the power of material objects in society consists of their openness to 'external' events and their resulting potential for mediating the introduction of 'contingency' into even the most hegemonic of social orders" (2003: 416). Brand professionals recognize the power of materiality to destabilize the carefully constructed meanings of brands. The solution for this problem is what Moore calls the "dematerialisation of brand" (quoted in Manning 2010: 35). In the brand discourse, brand is no longer conceived as the "symbolic extension" of the product (Arvidsson 2006, quoted in Manning 2010: 36), but is rather defined against the product. Brand leaves behind the "dull, passive, generic, inert utility and materiality of the product" (Manning 2010: 36), takes on a quasi-spiritual dimension, and becomes a "floating signifier" and "self-referential sign" (Beebe 2004, quoted in Manning 2010: 36). In the academic discussion of postmodernism, this tendency to ignore the inherent instability of brand reflects a theoretical predisposition to focus on signification. Brand is turned into a privileged locus of the postmodern condition, and its analysis has little to offer regarding the interplay of materiality and the "intangible" in the actual form and function of brand (Moore 2003: 332). Newell approaches this inherent instability of brand ethnographically and argues that the way brand value is enacted in social life closes the gap between materiality and semiotics. "Like masks, brands overcome the gap between image and its unstable link to authentic materiality through public secrecy" (2013: 151). Like the audiences of masking ceremonies, people know, but pretend not to know, because they are not supposed to know. This book also explores ethnographically the inherent instability of brand. The result is an alternative theory of the significance of brand. Through an ethnography of engagement with fake brands—objects whose value is usually reduced to the brand name they illegally carry—it demonstrates that the gap is recognized on this European periphery, but interpreted in a particular way. This interpretation permits the following argument: the significance of brand is related not to the brand itself, but to the attendant materiality that accompanies the brand.

Authenticity has been theorized as a construction. The garb of authenticity has been pulled aside to reveal projects of distinction, prestige, domination, and profit. The quest and need for authenticity within and without has been shown to be marked by ironies, perplexities, vicissitudes, excesses, and even atrocities (Bruner 2005; Gable and Handler 1996; Handler 1986; Lindholm 2008; Lowenthal 1992). One consequence of this deconstructivist stance is the denial of the possibility of authenticity and the disregard for the continuous significance of the experience of authenticity in ordinary people's lives. As Gable and Handler emphasize, "the critic's dream is that once already anxious natives are exposed to the constructedness of authenticity, they will stop buying it" (2007: 568). A second consequence is the disregard of the materiality of objects central to various projects of authenticity. As Jones points out, "having situated authenticity as a cultural construct, it is as if layers of authenticity can be simply wrapped around any object irrespective of its unique history and materiality" (2010: 183).

Against an objectivist understanding that sees it as inherent in materiality, authenticity has been presented as a quality that is socially, culturally, politically, and economically constructed and that varies according to who is observing and engaging with particular objects and in what circumstances. This book is developed from an instance of anthropological respect: it recognizes the contemporary importance of the ideal of living authentically and focuses on ordinary people's capacity to reflect on their projects of self-articulation and self-presentation and convince themselves and others that they live authentic lives. Through an ethnography of engagement with fake brands—objects usually situated outside the realm of material forms that allow for the possibility of articulating authentic selves—this book argues that the materiality of the objects with which people engage plays a crucial role in processes of self-authentication and that the authenticity of selves can be maintained in relation to the acknowledged inauthenticity of objects. Through an ethnography of engagement with fake brands, this book brings to the foreground a "good enough" relationship to authenticity and, consequently, a particular form of authenticity, called here *authenticity writ small*.

This book also argues that fake branded commodities in particular and inauthentic objects in general are an ideal addition to material culture studies. Inauthentic objects form a peculiar category. They are considered not to be what they are claimed and presumed to be, and, subsequently, are believed to betray both their makers and users. They are culturally and legally marginalized. In museums and courts of law, their inauthenticity is seen as an objective and measurable attribute inherent in their inferior materiality. They are extraordinary objects, and people are socialized (or coerced) not to engage with them. To repeat the main proposition of material culture studies, things make people just as much as people make, exchange, and consume things.

However, in the case of inauthentic objects, this proposition takes a twist. What if these things are, in the eyes of the others, *only* inauthentic objects? What kind of material mirror are people looking into? Are their real selves actually reflected in this mirror? Starting from Kerim's insistence that he is true to himself and lives an authentic life, and further building on an ethnography of people's engagements with objects deemed inauthentic in Turkey and Romania, this book demonstrates that people might see such objects as both extraordinary and ordinary. They manufacture, retail, and consume these objects. They legitimate and distance themselves from these objects. However, they also see themselves as they truly are in this peculiar material mirror.

To make these arguments, this book begins with excursions into cultural history, brand theorization, and legal theory. Chapter 2 unpacks the notion of fake brand and illustrates the complex assortment of concepts, interests, and concerns at work in this notion. The law plays a major role as an arbiter of what is authentic and what is not. Interrelated discourses surrounding originals, copies, fakes, brands, fake brands, and intellectual properties provide the ground on which engagements with fake brands become moral lapses. People who engage with these objects are derided as self-deceivers and condemned as deceivers of others. The conceptualization of the inauthenticity of objects as inherent in their materiality further legitimizes these discourses through the mantle of scientific objectivity. These excursions permit a better understanding of the points Kerim so passionately emphasized in his daily encounters with fellow traders, in stories about his interactions with the authorities, and in his conversations with this anthropologist. Toward the end of the chapter, these discussions are contrasted with studies that detail engagements with these objects in various ethnographic locations. The third and fourth chapters focus on the manufacture, distribution, and consumption of fake branded garments in various locations in Turkey and Romania. These chapters show how ordinary people acknowledge or deny the characterization of objects as fake brands, attribute to these objects various meanings, and integrate or separate them from their lives according to a variety of mundane preoccupations and locally significant practical and moral considerations. Chapter 5 begins with another excursion into cultural history and demonstrates that a potential to provoke existential questions is inscribed in the modern conceptualization of the inauthentic object. Engagement with authentic objects is believed to guarantee the articulation of an authentic self. In contrast, engagement with inauthentic objects is presented as eroding, if not erasing, the possibility to articulate an authentic self. This chapter describes the circumstances in which people in these ethnographic locations confront accusations of inauthenticity and analyzes the similar ways they deal with them in order to authenticate their selves. The materiality of these objects is the foundation that determines certain courses of action and supports particular arguments. This chapter demonstrates that people of similar social and cultural backgrounds to that of Kerim approach these objects in comparable ways and switch, just like this man, between seeing them as extraordinary and ordinary objects, depending on the circumstances and interlocutors. The final chapter contains an ethnographic vignette as well as concluding remarks. This vignette describes another day from Kerim's life and, thus, adds more ethnographic material before the presentation of the main arguments of this book.

THE FIELDWORK

The ethnographic material that forms the substance of this book was collected during nineteen months of doctoral research in places where fake branded garments abound. In a commercial area on the outskirts of Bucharest, I found a T-shirt on which a popular brand name was printed. A label indicated it was manufactured in Turkey. This object was legally a fake. Between October 2005 and April 2007, I followed the thing (Marcus 1995). I conducted a research project that took me to places in Turkey where this thing might have been produced and sold and to places in Romania where it might have been sold and consumed. I carried out fieldwork in three distinct locations: Istanbul, a major regional producer of fake branded garments; a commercial area in Bucharest, a destination point for goods produced in Istanbul and the main source of counterfeited brands in Romania; and Turnu Măgurele, a provincial Romanian town, where goods from this area predominate. In a way, I traveled one of the myriad routes of an informal transnational trade. Since the fall of communism, traders from the former socialist countries have traveled to Istanbul in search of merchandise. In the 1990s, this was a hectic "suitcase trade." Today it is mainly carried out by "big players," with goods transported by cargo companies and sold in warehouses. An example of the later manifestation is the commercial area where I found my thing.

I translated into a multisited research project Appadurai's insight that "from a *methodological* point of view, it is the thing-in-motion that illuminates their human and social context" (1986: 5, emphasis in original). Each site was conceived as a vantage point from which to consider and compose a picture of people's engagement with fake brands. My intention was to contribute to an emerging body of anthropological work that focused on the much publicized and fiercely combated phenomenon of fake brands (Brandtstädter 2009; Halstead 2002; Lin 2011; Nakassis 2012a; Pang 2008; Pinheiro-Machado 2010; Thomas 2009; Vann 2006). However, by treating production, circulation, and consumption within a single framework, and by focusing on how the proclaimed inauthenticity and inferiority of fake brands and the celebrated semiotic capacity of brands is experienced, negotiated, refuted, and ignored, this project was a pioneering attempt to paint a more nuanced picture of this contemporary phenomenon (Meneley (2007) and Foster (2008a) carried out similar multisited projects in the legal side of brand economy). Together, these places offered a synoptic view of a commodity network and, at the same time, the situated views of people whom the network connected. My research remained close to the classical demand of practicing anthropology through intensive dwelling, for it meant traveling between these places as well as set-tling down in each location (including Bucharest, for a shorter period).

This research topic and design posed particular problems. Researching fake brands proved a challenging experience. People were not particularly eager to talk about their engagements with objects labeled fakes and car-rying negative assumptions about their makers and consumers. In Istanbul, I was told that the act of making an unauthorized copy is like a "spark" (*kıvılcım gibi*). This is a pertinent image, suggesting the ephemeral, the intan-gible, the transient that had been so central to my fieldwork. I was suspected of secretly laughing at and condemning people, practices, and objects. As dif-ficult as it is to explain and carry out an anthropological project under normal circumstances, it became even more so under those in which I found myself. The anthropologist is, almost by definition, transient, and as a result it is at least as difficult for the people she works with to establish ties with her as it is for her to do the same. The anthropological mode of knowing is relational and performative, that is, gained through social relationships and through liv-ing and performing our role(s) in a social world. However, there are cases in which being allotted a role or the role one wants is less likely to occur. The an-thropologist who realizes this is not always in a comfortable position. I strove to objectify my status, bringing to the foreground whatever I had in common with my interlocutors, ranging from clothing preferences to common back-ground or non-Western identity, "in the hope that a sort of complicity/spon-taneous empathy will make the outsider the desired anthropological insider" (Marcus 1997: 89).

I not only attempted to immerse myself in social worlds, but also tried other ways of doing fieldwork. I hung around, being here and there, grasping knowledge as it appeared, but also provoking its appearance in glimpses. I looked at things from one side, discreetly. I rarely recorded conversations verbatim and seldom took notes in the presence of my informants. I gleaned most of the information from low-key interactions and collected ethnographic details by dropping by here and there, strolling into markets, memorizing ges-tures, and witnessing single events. These were methods of capturing some-thing that was not always discussed straightforwardly in the presence of the researcher, something that quickly turned from visible to invisible. In addition, it was an attitude in which respect blended with diffidence and discretion.

In addition, I conducted multisited research, moving between sites, shifting affinities for, affiliations to, finding myself with "all sorts of cross-cutting and contradictory personal commitments" (Marcus 1995: 113). I despaired many times that my method of hanging out and catching events and opinions as they appeared was sending me in a wrong direction, toward a lack of commitment and detachment. I constantly pondered the dangers of "understay" and "overstay." My mood kept vacillating between "I am not committed," "I am too committed," and "I should not look too committed." Nevertheless, there were instances in which commitment was something that I felt I accomplished, some people believing in my sincere academic interest in their lives. Moreover, this strategy allowed me not only to become aware of issues of ethics, stakes of research, and the position of the researcher, but also to carve a position at the margins of illegal practice.

Two main questions guided me in this research. What is a fake brand? What does it mean to engage with something that is considered a fake brand? These different locations and methods provided an illuminating experience in terms of the range of encounters with people who engaged with fake branded garments as producers, traders, and consumers. They permitted an ethnographic study of the complex field through which people reflect on the nature of clothing and the nature of brand. They allowed an ethnographic study of the relationship between the way objects were considered inauthentic and the way people were accused of being inauthentic. They enabled an ethnographic study of the sense of the degree to which people feel they are true to themselves and the world they inhabit. They allowed an ethnographic study of the role of materiality in the consolidation of opinions about self and life. They had been almost ideal locations for developing an intuition that the presence of fake brands might also say something more profound about the world. They complemented each other in the light that it sheds on this deeper issue: production highlighted the ambiguity intrinsic to objects and trade in these objects and this, in turn, pointed to the way the fake brand was used as an instrument by which individuals thought through their own achievements, contradictions, and compromises; the market was used to set the limits of what was acceptable given that the world of fake brands led us into areas that were clearly problematic in terms of their ethical implications; in consumption, the choices people could make with these relatively inexpensive items resulted in quite a range of stances on the issues of what was truthful about who they were and how the world around them was. Therefore, these three areas of inquiry do not simply form the trajectory or are not simply episodes in the story of the fake brand I originally intended, but they are hopefully valuable in giving the wider range of possible encounters with the fake brand.

My search for what legally are fake brands brought me to places where their existence is relatively visible and put me in contact with people belonging to the social groups that, from a sociological point of view, seem more inclined to engage with such objects. It is worth mentioning from the beginning that, although my search took place on the periphery, I often heard stories about the presence of the inauthentic object in the center, that is, rumors that important formally operating companies also mix the black and the white and secretively take part in the lucrative business in fake branded garments, as well as rumors that well-to-do people also consume fake branded commodities. More to the point, in portraying these people's engagement with inauthentic objects, my intention is to complicate the sociological picture by pointing out the variety of individual reasons for and strategies of engaging with these objects. A dialectic between how far engagement in the manufacture and trade in fake branded garments situates the person and how far the person has a propensity for this manufacture and trade given his or her social and economic background becomes visible in the self-presentations of these manufacturers and traders from Turkey. A multiplicity of strategies of integrating or rejecting the inauthentic object becomes visible in the self-presentations of these consumers from Romania. The fake branded article is more than an affordable piece of clothing. The affordability gives rise to different implications and translates into various associations, which are taken into consideration when deciding whether to purchase a fake branded article and, simultaneously, in reflecting if this garment objectifies who one is in relation to the wider context of one's life. Emulation is far from the most significant element in these clothing decisions. Therefore, this is an attempt to demonstrate that there is more about the topic of fake brands than mere economics, which, nevertheless, account for the manufacture of and demand for this category of material culture. Moreover, this is an attempt to illustrate the ways these objects mediate, affect, and alter both the experience and sense of the self. My intention is not to turn these individuals into representatives of certain social categories, but to bring them and their reflections and concerns to the foreground. This is a response to Miller's (2005b: 38) appeal for ethnographies that focus on how people's sense of themselves as subjects is created.

−2−

Fake Brands

This chapter situates the fake brand at the intersection of discourses on fake, brand, and fake brand and of cultural, legal, and economic logics. The chapter shows how these discourses reinforce each other and attempt to constrain objects into certain categories, to define and/or erase the material presence of certain objects, to command people's apprehension of certain material forms as inferior and even dangerous, and to socialize, or coerce, people not to engage with certain objects. The chapter also points out the contradictions and paradoxes these discourses and their articulations contain and, at the same time, emphasizes that these contradictions and paradoxes tend to be glossed over as powerful groups and institutions mobilize substantial resources to cover them up.

FAKE

In the common understanding, a *fake* is something other than that which it is claimed or presumed to be. "To deem an object inauthentic is to assert that it is not, despite claims to the contrary, an example of an identified class of objects, or not the creation of an identified person or group" (Handler 2001: 964). This understanding implies an intention to deceive: this object is produced and displayed with the intention of making someone believe it is indiscernibly identical with another object. Fakes have presumably always existed (Benjamin [1936] 1999; Schwartz 1996). Moreover, the existence of these objects has probably never been regarded with moral indifference (Grafton 1990; Johns 2009).[1] However, with the advent of modernity—and in response to various cultural conceptualizations, epistemological developments, technological changes, commercial interests, and legal elaborations that gained prominence during this period—their presence has become even more problematic.

This section disentangles the complex set of concepts, interests, and concerns that operates within the common understanding of fake. It also points out that the ways authenticity and inauthenticity are intimately bound up in each other's histories are rarely mentioned in this common understanding.

Another set of assumptions within this common understanding of fake is presented in the fifth chapter. That chapter shows that location, more specifically center and periphery, plays an important role in the conceptualization of fake. Moreover, it demonstrates that deception, the presumed reason behind the fake, takes another meaning with the advent of modernity: it is understood not only as deception of others, but also as self-deception.

ORIGINAL, COPY, AND FAKE

The fake is the opposite of the original, that is, a unique work produced by an inspired, solitary, creative, and unique author. The powerful cultural figure of the author is a Romantic creation. Romanticism attributed substance to certain persons and things, at the expense of other persons and things. The received history of the notion of the author locates its first articulations in Wordsworth's self-presentation as a poet who exercises his genius and produces an original work and Young's theoretical emphasis on originality as the defining element of literary composition and his criticism of the mere mastery of composition rules that predominated in classical literature (Woodmansee 1984). The original works the author creates owe their individuality solely to their creator. The source of inspiration is located in the author's inner reality. Authored works are creations ex nihilo, entirely new matter brought into being by the genius of the creator, endowed with the same unique qualities their creator possesses (Trilling 1972). The notion of the author transcends the cultural boundaries of Romanticism: the author becomes the "agent of original self-definition" and the "paradigm case of the human being" (Taylor 1991: 62). This history tends to forget episodes that demonstrate the way the Romantic notion of author is constructed with reference to its shadow, the forger. In eighteenth-century Britain, for example, in a period when literary forgeries proliferated, the Romantic idea of the author as the originator of a work was also articulated in response to the practice of forgery (Russett 2006). Moreover, Romantic writers used these literary productions as sources of inspiration and even modeled the figure of the Romantic poet upon the tragic life and death of a young forger, Chatterton, whom they nevertheless condemned and placed on the very margin of the literary canon (Groom 2007). Partial as it is, this received history carries the Romantic component of the common understanding of fake.

In the Romantic understanding, an *original* is a singular work that expresses an author's unique inner reality. In contrast, a copy, even a perfectly imitated copy, is an empty, soulless thing. What is lost is the sense of a direct connection with the author's inner being. A copy is similar to a translation, that is, "something of the original is both added to and erased in the copy" (McClean 2002: 22). A copy resembles a quotation, that is, it shows "what we are to respond to rather than being what we are to respond to" (Danto 1973: 13). A copy has no value of its own and exists only because the original has value and is, therefore, worth copying. Moreover, copies are incomplete, inaccurate, crude, and clumsy versions executed in inferior materials. In this way, copying, a venerated tradition especially in the education of artists, is reconceptualized to fit the Romantic emphasis on originality and authenticity (Baudrillard 2001). The act of copying is considered a second-rate activity, a failure of creativity, a mere demonstration of technical proficiency and imitative ability, and a "simple repetition without any addition of personality or work that would deposit the trace of an original self" (Frow 2003: 59). Therefore, in this Romantic understanding, the original and the copy are placed in a hierarchical relationship, with the original as the valorized term and the copy as the discredited term.

There have been numerous attempts to eliminate the conceptual distance between the original and the copy. Much of twentieth-century art was marked by such disputes, and its exemplary moments involved "radical renunciation(s) of originality" (Frow 2003: 59). Different artists questioned the notion of original and experimented with copying, appropriation, ready-mades, pastiche, paraphrase, parody, and homage (McClean and Schubert 2002). Intentional or not, forgers also brought their contribution to this critique. The ideological message of forgery was conveyed by forgeries that were indiscernible from the original to the naked eye. These objects undermined the belief in the artist's ability to create unique works. Even after they were disclosed and removed from collections, these objects continued to raise the question of whether authenticity mattered aesthetically (Dutton 1983; Jones 1992; Radnóti 1999).[2] These practices aimed to demonstrate that the copy was the "*underlying condition of the original*" and that the original and the copy "mutually sustain each other" (Krauss 1981: 58, 64; emphasis in the original). Nevertheless, "despite the elite artist's loss of belief in the artistic myth, the conventions of authenticity have not been dispensed with" (Lindholm 2008: 24) and remain at the core of contemporary culture.

Moreover, there have been numerous instances in which the proclaimed aesthetic and material distance between the original and the copy has been questioned. As modernity became the "age of mechanical reproduction" (Benjamin [1936] 1999), and as modern individuals began to embrace the "culture of the copy" (Schwartz 1996) and to delight in the deluge of copies, these developments conspired to blur the line between the original and its copy. However, the somewhat paradoxical response to the development of modern reproductive technologies is a preoccupation, if not obsession, with the original. Latour and Lowe state, for example, that "paradoxically, this obsession for pinpointing originality increases proportionally with the availability and accessibility of more and more copies of better and better quality…No copies, no original" (2010: 278). The Romantic distinction between the original and the copy has remained at the center of contemporary culture.

In the dominant understanding, the mutual constitution of these concepts is not mentioned. In this understanding, original and copy are caught up in a hierarchical relationship, with a yawning gap interposed between them. The culturally and materially inferior copy stands as "the discredited part of the pair, the one that opposes the multiple to the singular, the reproducible to the unique, and the fraudulent to the authentic" (Krauss 1981: 58).

The fake is placed on an even lower position. In the Romantic understanding, the author is the sole origin of his or her works. In contrast, the faker copies someone else's work or imitates someone else's style, signs his or her work with that author's name, and tries to pass it off as an original. The fake conceals its biography, mimics the biography of the original, and attempts to replace it. The fake simultaneously draws on and subverts the authority called upon to authorize its existence and to give it value. This intention to deceive has always been condemned. However, the fake becomes an even more serious threat when it is understood as prejudicing a right.

The criminalization of the fake begins with the conceptualization of knowledge as property. The notion of intellectual property was articulated during the disputes between authors, publishers, and book pirates that raged in the book trade in the early modern period. Rose (1994) points out that the notion emerges through the articulation of the Romantic theory of authorship and Locke's theory of labor. Locke argues that an individual, as the proprietor of his or her own person, is also the owner of the products of his or her labor. The right of property in the products of one's labor is declared a just reward for one's labor and a natural right, prior to any social regulation. During these disputes, Lockean ideas about real property were translated to the cause of literary property. Woodmansee (1984) and Gaines (1991) stress that this articulation is not an inevitable theoretical outcome: it was realized, at that time and later, not so much through logical affinity, but interested rhetorical shifts. These disputes served as a background against which an agreement was reached: artistic and literary works were to be understood as intellectual properties owned by their individual originators. The law recognized and granted rights in this new type of property. A consequence of this legal elaboration was the criminalization of fake, because this prejudices the right of the author and, therefore, owner of the original. In this way, the hierarchical opposition between original and copy/fake has been not only culturally defined, but also legally regulated.

AUTHORED AND AUTHORIZED OBJECTS

The legal notion of intellectual property was further refined to serve a wide range of interests, not only in the domain of culture, but also in the realm of commerce. As a consequence, the notion of fake was enlarged to refer to not only fraudulently authored objects, but also unauthorized copies.

This pragmatic reformulation was articulated around two crucial notions in the Romantic thinking, that is, the notions of original and copy. Intellectual property law began to operate with a particular notion of originality and an enlarged concept of original. Romantic theory distinguished between the original and the copy. Intellectual property law maintained this distinction; however, it protected creative efforts of many types and recognized many works as originals, regardless of whether they were unoriginal, banal, or even imitative. "A kind of doubleness" was put at work in the legal concept of originality. "[T]he law retained the connotations of artistic creativity and the ideal of the singular work. [However] 'creativity' came to refer simply to the work's point of origination, not to the unique, soul-invested nature of the work itself" (Gaines 1991: 58). This reduction of originality to the blunt fact of origin was realized through a tautological shift in the discourse: "[A]ll works of authorship are original. Why? Because they originate with authors" (Gaines 1991: 63). The uneasy coexistence of these partially overlapping notions of authenticity has ever since been concealed in the legal discourse (the interested oscillation in the brand discourse between authenticity as origin and authenticity as originality will be discussed in a different section of this chapter).

Moreover, intellectual property law began to use a nuanced category of the copy. Romantic theory discredited copying, in any form, licit or illicit. Intellectual property law encouraged and, simultaneously, policed copying. In the legal context, an authored work was conceived as the source of its authorized copies. In the accusatory legal context, the unauthorized copy was presented as the outcome of a clandestine act of intellectual trespassing carried out for base motives. A copy needed not be identical to amount to an infringement. In this way, intellectual property law provided generative conditions for sanctioned processes of duplication and prohibitive obstacles for unauthorized processes of reproduction (Geismar 2005). This legal framework has ever since distinguished between authorized, legitimate and, thus, authentic, and unauthorized, illegitimate and, therefore, inauthentic copies.

This pragmatic reformulation was a response to the growth of trade and the development of more integrated, dynamic, and commoditized economies in which the implementation of novel ideas and technologies became crucial. "The Romantic image of the individuated author as creative genius, autonomously creating works characterised as embodiments of personal originality, provided ideological support for the legal institution of fictions that denied and obscured market forces" (Coombe 1998: 255). "Intellectual property is justified on the basis that it provides an incentive for future productive activity, or that it acknowledges and represents the sovereignty of the individual over their thoughts and ideas" (Moor 2007: 96). Intellectual property claims, rights, and restrictions were developed in different European countries and the United States beginning in the eighteenth century. These laws aimed to construct authors and owners and regulate reproductive activities. They offered (limited) monopoly rights over knowledge to its primary or "entitled" producers. They granted the rights to materialize and, thereby, control knowledge and to capitalize on the attendant profit that the circulation of this knowledge and of the products that materialized it could afford. These laws also ruled that the unauthorized reproduction of the products that materialized this protected knowledge could potentially pose an economic threat to its primary or "entitled" producers and, as a consequence, criminalized the unauthorized duplication and the resulting unauthored and unauthorized objects. These laws "constitute a political economy of mimesis in capitalist societies" (Coombe 1996: 206). The forms of abundance that industrial development made possible have been locked into this particular conceptual framework.

Today these laws are hegemonic in markets and courts of law around the world. The major vehicles for protecting intellectual property—and for deciding which objects fall outside the legitimate domain and are, thus, fakes—are patent, copyright, and trademark. Patents are applied to inventions, copyright is used to protect literary and artistic creations, and trademark is used to protect the qualities that distinguish the products of a company from those of others. Copyright and patent promote profits generated from new works and inventions, whereas trademark protects and perpetuates existing monopolies (Moor 2007). This legislation has spread to virtually any country with aspirations of taking part in the global economy. International pressure is so strong that countries that refuse to enact such laws or fail to enforce them find themselves on the receiving end of serious trade sanctions. Moreover, the introduction of this legislation is often portrayed as a matter of democracy and progress, and countries that refuse or lag behind are frequently described as politically and culturally "backward" states (Lippert 1999).

In this pragmatically refined conceptualization of intellectual property, authored and authorized objects materialize knowledge over which individuals and corporations are given property rights. Fraudulently authored and unauthorized objects infringe on these rights and are consequently criminalized.

THE MATERIALITY OF INAUTHENTICITY

In the modern period, anxieties about the authenticity of objects have found resolution in an objectivist understanding of authenticity as inherent in materiality and in the development of scientific methods for the investigation of materiality.

In other periods, the authenticity of objects was evaluated through different methods. Relics, for example, were evaluated in relation to the biography of the person who offered the object or the biography of the object itself. In the first case, it was important to know who this priestly individual was, for he or she could transform certain objects into sacramental artifacts through specific invocations. The substance and methods of creation of these objects were completely irrelevant. In the other case, the connection with a saint and the story of the acquisition were important. The value of these objects lay precisely in their substance. However, relics were not man-made, but recuperated from the cadavers and possessions of venerated saints (Geary 1986; Lindholm 2002).

In the modern context, when man-made objects became so important, the craze for collecting spread throughout society, and technologies for multiplication began to develop, the identification of objects as authentic or inauthentic became crucial as regards their financial value. In this period, when objective observation and experimentation were increasingly valorized over received opinion (Jaffé 1992), the authenticity of objects began to be conceptualized as an objective and measurable attribute inherent in their very materiality. Consequently, it could be established scientifically through an investigation into the essence of these objects in terms of date of creation, materiality, authorship, workmanship, primary context, function, and use.

The development of this understanding was not only a response to the practical problems that confronted especially the market for art and antiquities, but also an extension of the notion of individualism. With the advent of modernity, the medieval worldview of a cosmic order ordained and encompassed by God was replaced by individualism. This was a worldview that allowed individuals to locate ultimate reality within themselves. They were conceived as fixed and bounded entities, each with its own unique internal essence (Handler 1986). Their truth could be discovered through an investigation or self-investigation of their inner beings. This way of conceptualizing the individual was extrapolated to the material world. Artifacts were also conceived as stable, fixed, and self-contained entities, autonomous from their context and audience (Jones 2010). Their ultimate reality, that is, their authenticity, was inherent in their materiality. The truth of objects could be discovered through a scientific investigation into their essence.

In this way, the fear that objects could no longer be guaranteed by their authors, owners, or authorizing institutions was countered by the theory that deception could not be denied forever, inscribed as it was in the very materiality of the object. The fake could always be identified. Something in its materiality eventually betrayed its true nature. Inauthenticity was declared an attribute of materiality. This objectivist understanding of the authenticity of objects remains hegemonic in contemporary institutions such as the art market, museums, markets, and courts of law, that is, in institutions in which authenticity has commercial value (Handler 2001).

However, the materiality of inauthenticity is not always brought to the foreground. Depending on circumstances and interests, it might be very well be pushed to the background. There are instances in which materiality must be investigated. In this case, the aim is to denigrate an individual object. Inauthenticity is inscribed in materiality, but it is not necessarily inferior. There are other instances in which materiality ought to be rejected a priori as inferior. In this case, the aim is to create and denigrate a category of objects. A discursive strategy through which this aim might be achieved involves lumping together all types of inauthentic objects as the same kind of immoral thing.

There is a huge variety of inauthentic objects, ranging from forgeries of art and luxury objects, themselves extraordinary objects, to the ubiquitous fake brands of today, unofficial copies as banal as the official ones. There are significant differences between these objects, in terms of knowledge, craftsmanship, and technology that go into their production. There are also significant differences in terms of the morality associated with their presence: art forgeries, fake branded garments, and fake medication do not pose the same moral dilemmas. However, there are instances in which these differences are played down. The following exhibition illustrates this tendency. In 1990, an exhibition entitled Fake? The Art of Deception was mounted at the British Museum. An impressive range of objects from different periods and locations, including medieval relics, paintings, sculptures, enamels, metalwork, manuscripts, printed books, newspapers, and fake branded commodities, were brought together as "material evidence of the myriad deceptions practiced by men upon their fellows over three millennia" (Jones 1990: 11). The following opinion exemplifies this line of reasoning: "there is no reason why art-forgery should not be punished as severely as cheque-forgery, larceny, counterfeiting or fraud, since there is no moral difference between any of them" (Savage 1976, quoted in Haywood 1987: 114). "All of the house of forgery are relations" (Baines 1999: 162). This idea—which was uttered by an eighteenth-century observer at the time when the process of cultural and legal marginalization of inauthentic objects began—is still with us.

In the dominant discourse, the different types of inauthentic object are often treated interchangeably. Ideas elaborated for the condemnation and exclusion of a type of inauthentic object are used for the condemnation and exclusion of other types of inauthentic objects. The reasoning behind this is that all types of inauthentic objects represent transgressions against identity, property, morality, and the authority of the law (Baines 1999; Haywood 1987;

Malton 2009). Therefore, all types of inauthentic objects are—and should be—equally condemned as inferior products of dubious morality.

To link this with the discussions in the previous and following pages, in brand discourse the inverse of this strategy is the lumping together of all types of authentic objects, be they art objects or branded commodities, in one category. This is achieved through interested omissions of the conceptual difference between authenticity as originality and authenticity as origin and of the material differences between various types of authentic objects. In this discourse, brand is the equivalent of a signature (Frow 2003).

This section has focused on the proclaimed conceptual and material differences between authentic and inauthentic objects at work in the common understanding of fake and, at the same time, has pointed out how the praised authentic object was constructed against the inauthentic object. The more the authentic object became virtuous, the more the inauthentic object had to become vicious. In this way, this section has shown that inauthentic objects were first conceptualized as things that matter less than others, then as things that do not matter at all and later, when the need to reject them grew stronger, as things that should not exist at all.

BRAND

In the simplest understanding, *brand* is a mode of mediation between producers and consumers. Brands are usually associated with the development of modern capitalism (Carrier 1995). However, Wengrow argues that theoretically they can appear in any large-scale economy, for they represent a way of coping with the "reality of living in a community…formed and sustained through the circulation of impersonal objects," a reality specific not only to modern capitalist societies (2008: 21). Earlier discussions of brand tend to focus on the more traditional function of brand, which approximates the function of the trademark in legal discourse. Brand identifies the origin and/or ownership of the commodities to which its name and logo are affixed (Manning 2010). At the same time, brand functions as a guarantee of quality and consistency, and an index of the goodwill associated with the source of commodities. Names and logos are, therefore, "visible or materialised goodwill" (Foster 2008b: 79). More recent discussions of brand present it in financial terms—as an "intangible asset," a "wealth generator" whose value increases, or at least does not decrease, with use—and in legal terms—as a protected form of intellectual property (Moor 2007). Moreover, almost all recent accounts see brand as incorporating far more than a name and a logo and proclaim that brand embodies "relationships," "values," and "feelings" (Fournier 1998; Nakassis 2012b). They focus, to use Foster's (2005) words, not only on trademarks of production, but also on lovemarks of consumer loyalty. In the present account, the notion of brand is further unpacked through a focus on production and consumption, and the complex set of concepts, interests, and concerns that link them, and through an analysis of brand as a legally protected form of property. This account mirrors the way the ethnographic material is organized in the next chapters of this book.

For a long period in the modern history of brand, branded commodities organized the processes of production: developments and improvements in printing, papermaking, packaging, and manufacturing technologies of various sorts have been linked with the requirements of standardization and presentation (Moor 2007). More recently, the brand itself organizes production. Lury points out that brand has acquired a new *productive* role in the contemporary global economy. Brand has become "a mechanism—or medium—for the co-construction of supply and demand . . . an abstract machine for the reconfiguration of production" (2004: 27–28). Innovation in product design as well as the management of corporate extension are organized around the brand. This change is related to the recognition of brand as a valuable intangible asset, whose already existent reputation diminishes the risks associated with product innovation and corporate growth. To make her point clearer, Lury employs the punning opposition between brand as logo ("the sign or slogans that mark brands") and brand as *logos* ("the kind of thought or rationality that organizes the economy") (2004: 5).

This shift has coincided with a more general transformation within developed economies, in which the creative components of the production process of branded commodities are carried out and organized in the company and the manufacturing components are outsourced to smaller companies, usually from less developed economies (Gereffi 1999). The mass production of branded clothes incorporates millions of workers from all over the world (and in many cases forces them to work in appalling conditions) (Klein 2001; Schneider 2006). Among the many consequences of this way of organizing the production of branded commodities, two are mostly relevant for the present discussion. The first regards the ability of the brand to index the product. In the contemporary economy, brand acts as a transferable form of property that can operate entirely through licensing and without any involvement or regulation of product quality. Manning points out that in this context "it becomes debatable whether trademarks indicate any specific source at all or whether they even act as guarantees of quality relative to, for example, the actual locus of production" (2010: 37). Beebe is even more categorical, entirely rejecting this possibility: "the modern trademark does not function to identify the true origin of goods. It functions to obscure that origin, to cover it with a *myth* of origin" (2008: 52, quoted in Manning 2010: 37). Although authenticity (as origin) remains a constitutive element of brand discourse, as corporations increasingly produce their commodities in poorer parts of the world, the brand is increasingly distanced from the site of production and cannot entirely guarantee the product. The second consequence regards the capacity of brand to index the producer. Throughout the modern and contemporary history of brand, its actual producers have been almost always erased from sight. This is more the case today, when branded commodities are "worldly things" (Foster 2008a), produced in locations with cheap and docile labor forces, circulated through complicated commodity chains, and consumed in another, more affluent place. The actual places of production, and the working conditions, are often a matter of secrecy (Klein 2001). Brand has not been so much an index of a producer, but rather a means to create, consolidate, and unify a prosthetic personality, that is, the modern corporation (Mazzarella 2003).

Brand does not only organize production, but also harnesses consumption. "The creation of value for many consumer products...depends not only upon the extraction of surplus value from the labour of the producer, but also from the meaningful use to which the consumer puts the product" (Foster 2005: 10). Brand is designed to perform not only a functional, but also a symbolic role. Brand singularizes commodities and adds a touch of extraordinariness to what is, in many cases, an ordinary mass-produced object. In the brand discourse, this aim is often achieved through an overlapping of the notions of authenticity as origin and authenticity as originality/uniqueness. However, uniqueness is often claimed at the level of brand, and not of the product, in many cases mass-produced commodities similar to those produced by other companies. Moreover, brand capitalizes on human propensity for forging deep or, equally valid, shallow affective connections with things. Furthermore, brand appropriates people's social productivity, that is, their production of themselves and of their social relationships. Finally, brand makes use of culture in the sense that it works with people's imaginaries and practices of common social worlds and insinuates itself into these webs of meanings. Brand management is a concerted effort to shape and control consumers' associations with and uses of brands. Arvidsson argues that the purpose of brand management is to guide consumers' investment of affect and to make sure this guidance unfolds in a way that guarantees the reproduction of a distinctive brand image and, thus, strengthens brand equity. In his words, "for consumers, brands are means of production...For Capital, brands are a means of appropriation" (2006: 93–94). This belief in the importance of brand-consumer relationship as a site of value creation is at the core of contemporary brand management.

However, this is how brand *ideally* functions. Despite considerable efforts to cultivate brand identities and to keep consumers' associations within the boundaries of these carefully crafted identities, brand may not always work in the ways intended. In practice, there are instances in which the desired re-attachment of objects to people is achieved, and consequently, capitalized upon. In these cases, consumers "pay [monopoly] rent for the use of a brand that has become entangled with their particular biographies and passions" (Foster 2008a: 19). There are also instances in which consumers invest brands with meanings and put them to uses not conceived by their owners.

Consumption plays a crucial role in the determination of what brands come to represent for consumers. Miller (1987) argues that consumption is a form of human creativity in industrialized societies through which individuals appro-priate commodities and pursue projects of self-fabrication denied to them in the realm of production. Various studies have illustrated this theoretical prop-osition in relation to the consumption of branded commodities and the articu-lation of individual and social projects. Miller (1998a) shows that food brands are mobilized to define and enact particular relationships within a family. These brands might become so entangled into these relationships that they are finally rendered essential and indispensable. They come to objectify family values and relationships. Skeggs (1997) describes ways in which knowledge of brand names and of their class connotations as well as actual consumption of branded garments are used in processes of social distinction. Brand becomes a means that people of lower background employ to construct "respectability." In their study of secondhand consumption practices, Gregson and Crewe (2003) present the profound dislike of more middle-class consumers of branded commodities and their derision of the attempts of other consumers to acquire cultural capital in objectified forms through brands. Rausing (2002) points out that Estonians consume expensive foreign branded commodities to demonstrate that they have returned to "normality," that is, they are no lon-ger forced to be citizens of the Soviet Union. Appadurai (1996) emphasizes that deterritorialized populations might use brands from their places of origin to acquire a sort of ontological security and brands from their new locations to demonstrate to themselves and others their successful integration into their new home.

Other studies have focused on the different meanings with which people imbue brands. Miller (1998b) argues that in Trinidad Coca-Cola is a "black sweet drink," which, in combination with rum, represents the most popu-lar alcoholic drink for most people of this island and conjures up images of the past. The corporate brand identity is if not disrupted, at least ignored in a place where this drink is embedded in ethnic and national imaginaries. Coombe (1998) brings to the foreground the struggles over signification in cases when the meaning of brand is appropriated and contested in the form of product names and images that are themselves legally protected. On the whole, this approach emphasizes the role consumers themselves play in constituting the meanings of brands, meanings that may or may not correspond to those projected by brand owners and managers.

Moreover, there are instances in which brand itself is harnessed by the unauthorized producers of fake brands, a process brand owners try to control through the legal apparatus of intellectual property laws. Brand is a legally protected form of property, mainly under trademark law. This is a late addition to the intellectual property legislation. Initially, the trademark was not considered a form of intellectual property, as it did not involve the creation of something new, but the use of preexistent linguistic and material forms. Sherman and Bently (1999) argue that in the premodern period creative labor was the organizing principle of intellectual property laws. Copyright, designs, and patents were distinguished in terms of the quality and, later, quantity of the creative labor embodied in the works in question. Toward the end of the nineteenth century, in the context of rapid economic development and in response to a growing preoccupation with objectivity, calculability, and stability, this organizing principle was no longer appropriate. Registration became a prerequisite for the protection of nearly all forms of intellectual property. This eliminated the necessity to distill and measure elusive creativity, offered indisputable proofs of origin and ownership, and "ensured that intangible property was placed in a format which was stable yet indefinitely repeatable" (Sherman and Bently 1999: 182). Copyright, designs, and patents were "still differentiated in terms of their relative 'value.' The main difference was that value now tended to mean the economic value of the property rather than, as had been the case previously, the quality or quantity of the mental labour embodied in the property in question" (Sherman and Bently 1999: 194). The early claim that the trademark could not be included in the intellectual property system because it was noncreative became therefore obsolete. Its economic value allowed the trademark to be conceptualized and protected as a form of intellectual property.

The law prevents the "dilution" of the brand's semiotic distinctiveness, protects investment in design and marketing, and safeguards the brand owner from unfair forms of competition. The law also protects the consumer from being "confused" or deceived as to the origin, ownership, and quality of branded commodities. However, in the past decades, there has been a growing tendency in the law to favor the "dilution" rather than the "confusion" definition of trademark infringement, therefore to protect the companies rather than the consumers' interest in the identification of the origin and content of the branded commodity (Lury 2004). In addition, the brand owner has been redefined as a "quasi-author" who "creates" the meanings attached to the brand (Coombe 1998). This emphasis on the trade-related aspects of trademark law is evident in the recent agreements on international trade, for example the Agreement on Trade-Related Aspects of Intellectual Property Rights (TRIPS) and the Anti-Counterfeiting Trade Agreement (ACTA) (Blakeney 2009; Grosse Ruse-Kahn 2008). These changes reflect legislative efforts to respond to, and simultaneously support, the growing importance of brands in the global economy. "All commentators agree that a brand consists of much more than a brand name—but they also agree that without a protected brand name, a brand does not exist" (Moore 2003: 336). Trademark law is particularly important in the present context, when names, signs, and designs are believed to play a greater role in identifying the brand in the minds of consumers and, therefore, in carrying the values the brand is supposed to contain. This law protects a company's profits by excluding other individuals or companies from using these names, signs, and designs and, consequently, capitalizing on the value they are expected to produce.

FAKE BRAND

In the legal understanding, a fake brand is the outcome of an act of counterfeiting, that is, the "unauthorized copying of the trademark, labels or packaging of goods on a commercial scale, in such a way that the get-up or lay-out of the cover, label or appearance of the goods closely resemble those of the original" (Sodipo 1997: 126). Infringement is judged on the basis of substantial similarity, but is often a question of degree, as an infringing object need not be literally identical to a protected object. Nevertheless, the law draws a sharp line between the authentic and the fake, the genuine and the counterfeit. Authentic commodities are those whose brand names and logos truthfully signify a corporate origin. In contrast, fake brands are inauthentic because they "misrepresent the relationship between an object and its creator or producer. Corporations and international IPR organizations argue that, because counterfeits misrepresent that proprietary relationship, their production and sale violate companies' intellectual property and damage their good names. Further, they claim that counterfeiters deceive consumers into buying goods that are not what they appear, and, more seriously, cause consumer injuries and deaths" (Vann 2006: 287). The disruptive potential of fake branded commodities is objectified in their very materiality. The slipshod versions, the so-called obvious fakes, diminish the exclusive appeal of branded commodities and affect carefully constructed brand identities. The higher-quality versions, the so-called real fakes, which might have been produced in the same factories and/or with the same materials as the originals, reveal the size of the premium the brand owner charges. These objects undermine claims of authenticity, originality, uniqueness, and quality in the brand discourse and dissipate the value of brand itself, not only of particular branded commodities.

"These brazen simulacra...expose a conceit at the core of the culture of Western capitalism: that its signifiers can be fixed, that its editions can be limited, that it can franchise the platonic essence of its mass-produced modernity" (Comaroff and Comaroff 2006: 13).

Different factors might have contributed to the production of counterfeits. One factor is the nature of branded commodity. Counterfeiting might be seen as "a natural outgrowth of the fact that intellectual property law seeks to create a false scarcity in categories of things which, by their very nature, are relatively cheap and easy to produce" (Moor 2007: 101). Another factor is the nature of brand economy. Counterfeiting might be seen as an inevitable consequence of the current divisions in the global economy. In many cases, this illegitimate production shadows the legitimate production of branded commodities as an unwanted consequence of the outsourcing of the manufacture of branded commodities in low-wage countries. Badly paid manufacturers harness the value of brand and use the infrastructure of the global brand economy. Moreover, counterfeiting might be interpreted not only a pragmatic response to present conditions, but also as a defiant response that reflects past and present realities. Sodipo (1997) points out that many of the regulations contained in the current intellectual property legislation were originally imposed in the colonies to protect the interests of the colonizers. In addition, in the former colonies, economic and social exclusion, access to technologies of reproduction and authentication, and lax legal systems have prompted many to engage in daring and dangerous activities. These places have become manufacturing sites for fakes of every conceivable sort. In these places, deception has become a means of production. However, this is not so much about defying authority, but about "creating a sort of authority for oneself" (Siegel 1998: 57, quoted in Comaroff and Comaroff 2006: 14). In brief, when the focus is on its production, a fake brand conjures up either an accusation or a "badge of honour" (Dent 2012).

The consumption of counterfeited commodities might be explained in different ways too. It is linked to the perceived inability of brand/trademark to indicate origin and to guarantee quality and consistency. The counterfeit is just a commodity like any other for consumers who ceased to believe in this promise of brand and have few rights to redress should the branded commodities change or deteriorate. Another explanation relates the consumption of fake brands to unsatisfied demands. Branded commodities are desired by many consumers, but hard to acquire because of their prohibitive prices. In these conditions, the social value of branded goods is met by their unauthorized versions. However, their consumers are rarely the "confused" or "deceived" individuals portrayed in intellectual property legislation. The dominant perspective on the consumption of fake brands adds a pejorative dimension to this explanation and is largely indifferent to the issue of confusion.

This links the consumption of fake brands to status emulation and dispar-ages it. Envious consumers do not have the means to emulate and go for the fakes. At work here is the cultural denigration of the copy/fake and the social derision of the person of lesser means who imitates the taste of his or her social superiors. In brief, when the focus is on its consumption, a fake brand is conceived either in appreciative terms, as savvy consumption, or in derisive terms, as emulation.

In the past decades, counterfeiting seems to have proliferated tremen-dously. However, official reports might exaggerate the dimensions of this phe-nomenon. When reading the alarming statistics, one should also keep in mind the ways corporations and governments estimate the dimensions of this phe-nomenon. The assessment of the amount of money lost to business through these illegal activities is rather peculiar, for there is no guarantee that the consumers of the unauthorized copies, if not tempted with commodities at a much lower price, would have otherwise bought the authorized versions at the original price (Blakeney 2009; Grosse Ruse-Khan 2010; Sodipo 1997). This logic is more illustrative of corporate greed at the prospect of how much money can be made if everyone buys a company's legitimate products and is used to justify corporate demand for drastic intervention from national govern-ments and international organizations.

The fierce battle against counterfeiting is mainly carried out in the poorer parts of the world (Comaroff and Comaroff 2006) (as well as in poorer parts of the Western world) (Stoller 2002). To naturalize a muscular response, coun-terfeiting is often equated with illicit activities such as banditry, drug traffick-ing, and terrorism, in a rhetoric that effortlessly brings economic security and national and international security together on the basis of vague allegations rather than concrete proofs.

CONCLUSION

The chapter has unpacked the notion of fake brand and has demonstrated why we are encouraged to think about fake branded commodities in a particu-lar way. This has developed in relation to the notions of fake, brand, and fake brand and the attendant interests and concerns that shaped their conceptu-alization. Moreover, this unpacking has revealed the importance of the law as arbiter of what is a fake brand. Furthermore, it has emphasized the role ac-corded in these elaborations to the materiality of objects placed or forced into the categories of fake, brand, and fake brand.

This conclusion spells out what we are encouraged to think about fake brands and the people who engage with them. These objects are consid-ered inferior material forms. The people who engage with them are derided as self-deceivers and condemned as deceivers of others. The fake-ness (criminal activity) of the fake brand is pushed to the forefront and vigorously condemned; its brand-ness (materiality) is declared insignificant. Powerful institutions, from courts of law to governmental agencies and international trade organizations, circulate this basic set of assumptions all over the world and attempt to command people's apprehension of materiality and to social-ize people not to engage with these objects and in these activities.

The ethnographic material with which this chapter ends brings back in a different manner the complex territory covered throughout this chapter. It demonstrates that ordinary people are accustomed to or are getting accus-tomed to think about fakes in particular cultural, economic, and legal ways. It shows that they are inclined to criticize the claims about brands because of their participation in the production of branded commodities and their mun-dane experience with objects. It offers examples of how and why people all over the world engage with objects labeled as fake brands, how and why they legitimize persons, practices, and objects, and how and why this conceptual framework unevenly affects ordinary people's thoughts and actions. The com-plex assortment of ideas, interests, and concerns behind the understanding of fake brand resurfaces in these ethnographic vignettes. In this way, this sec-tion serves as an ethnographic conclusion to the discussion of this chapter as well as an ethnographic introduction to the following chapters.

ETHNOGRAPHIC CONCLUSION

The anthropological record offers examples of mundane engagements with objects that legally are fake brands. These studies exemplify the kind of is-sues these objects raise for those who make, trade, and consume them. They depict reasons and moments in which elements of this framework are employed by these people or those in their vicinity to legitimize or delegiti-mize objects and practices. They show there is more to the topic of inau-thentic objects than mere economics, which, nevertheless, accounts for the manufacture of and demand for this form of material culture. They offer ex-amples of engagements that are not necessarily ideological responses to this conceptualization of objects, but rather mundane practices of individu-als who try to benefit from the flow of ideas and goods that characterize the contemporary world.[3] They show that diverse cultural understandings of authenticity, originality, and ownership guide production activities and con-sumption habits and complicate the implementation of intellectual property rights (IPR) legislation. The following pages present a selection of studies from this growing anthropology of fake brands, with the aim of preparing the ground for the next ethnographic chapters and of pointing out how the book draws on and advances the anthropological thinking about mundane engagements with objects labeled fake brands.

A point often raised in this literature is that the definition of fake brand under the intellectual property regime, although circulated all over the world, might hold little value for people who use other conceptual frameworks and base their actions and thoughts on their mundane engagements with objects. Vann demonstrates this is the case for Vietnamese consumers. Although the intellectual property legislation was introduced by the Vietnamese state under international pressure, these people use their own way of categorizing the goods available on their markets. This classification includes "model goods," which set the market standards, and "mimic goods," which fail to fully attain the standards of the goods on which they are modeled. Moreover, these consumers are guided by a different understanding of the relationship between those who copy products and those whose products are copied. The "mimic goods" are considered inevitable elements of a market economy. Their producers try not to deceive consumers, but to carve a place for themselves in a highly competitive market by offering products of some degree of similarity to popular commodities. The materiality of "mimic goods" plays a crucial role in this understanding. The closer the "mimic goods" approximate the "model goods," the better they are. Furthermore, these consumers also experience anxiety about deceptive products, for the market is full of this type of products. However, their anxiety reflects different market logics. In this case, the "terms *real* and *fake* call into question not the authenticity of a product, but its existence: whether a product is actually a product at all" (Vann 2006: 286). None of these categories entirely overlaps with what the intellectual property laws define as authentic and inauthentic goods. Vann emphasizes that "what is at stake with mimic and model goods and with fake and real goods is not simply an alternative understanding of authenticity" (2006: 294). For people in Ho Chi Minh City, the very notion of authenticity is unfamiliar.

Other studies demonstrate that the legal understanding of brand might circulate in parallel with and only occasionally and circumstantially affect local understandings of brand and/or style. Nakassis shows that this is the case in Tamil Nadu, India. Brand names adorn people's clothes. However, these are not only proper brand names, but also distorted, hybridized, and refashioned versions. The garments are locally made in factories that produce authorized branded clothing for foreign companies and workshops that have mushroomed in their vicinity, taking advantage of the infrastructural and material excess of brand economy. These garments are avidly consumed by nonelite youngsters. The classificatory principle that brings together all these material and stylistic elaborations as branded forms is what Nakassis calls "brandness as an aesthetic category." For the local producers, brand represents an aesthetic assemblage: its constituting parts can be disassembled and reassembled with other brand and design components and with whatever new element the producer believes will increase the salability of garments. Nakassis focuses on the various factors that play a role in the production of these diverse forms. Inventiveness plays a role in the duplication, hybridization, and recombination of elements, but so do the availability and affordability of materials. Moreover, producers assume their customers are not necessarily brand knowledgeable, but rather interested in brandness as such, thus a fictive brand might do just as well. Furthermore, awareness that the identical reproduction of the logo, name, and slogan of a brand might get one into trouble determines the alteration of brand names. "From this point of view, local Tamil producers aren't counterfeiting brands, but reanimating them, citing them, refashioning them, simulating them" (Nakassis 2012a: 717). For these producers, to carve a place on a competitive market means to navigate a complex terrain, in which the legal status of the brands occupies a place, although not the important place foreign companies, international organizations, and national authorities would want.

Somewhat similarly, Mayan entrepreneurs in Guatemala understand the material semiotic apparatus of foreign brands as design elements and not as markers of identity for the right-holder companies. Thomas (2009, 2012) shows that these entrepreneurs take inspiration from or entirely copy the design of foreign garments. They use logos, labels, size stickers, and tags reproduced with varying degree of similitude in local workshops or smuggled out of the assembly factories that work for the global clothing industry. Moreover, brands and design patterns are not seen as unique creations, but as temporal manifestations in a continuous creative process that involves borrowing and imitation. These practices are seen as problematic only in certain cases, for example when a manufacturer reproduces another local manufacturer's design, more or less exactly, and sells the products at a lower price. Their ethics of imitation and condemnatory remarks echo elements of intellectual property legislation. Intellectual property discourse is employed by parties interested in further distinguishing themselves from these entrepreneurs. The few local brand owners, who abandoned these practices and registered their own brands, relate their commercial success to their moral superiority. Their class position allows them access to resources such as formal distribution channels, business services, and educational opportunities in the capital city. However, this uneven distribution of resources is covered through the moral discourse that separates those who obey the law from those who do not. Maya entrepreneurs are portrayed as shady characters who engage in unethical activities and produce low-quality goods. In addition, in the national media they are depicted as lawbreakers who participate in an underground economy that threatens the integrity of the national economy and the state's modernist aspirations. In this way, intellectual property discourse becomes a resource for various local actors.

Other studies show that fake brands are embraced or rejected not so much in response to this cultural and legal marginalization, but rather according to local reasons and moral logics. In China, a lesser-known development, as Brandtstädter emphasizes, is that of an urban-based consumer movement that rejects counterfeited goods and demands "truth," that is, quality products and services for the Chinese consumer-citizen. This movement employs a Maoist ideological vocabulary: the consumer becomes an agent of social progress and the discovering and "beating" of counterfeited goods stands for a patriotic act that facilitates the formation of quality in the Chinese economy and society. Counterfeited goods are nevertheless embraced by other Chinese consumers, who use them as means to (re)construct a valuable self. These consumers, many of rural origin, are more or less aware that the consumption of counterfeits is taken as a sign of backwardness. They know that, in the eyes of the urban middle classes, peasants, especially those who move to cities and become workers, are "at worst, a source of chaos...and, at best, fake citizens...just like the masses of counterfeit goods" they produce and consume (Brandtstädter 2009: 147). Acceptance or rejection of counterfeits takes place in a post-Maoist context marked by anxieties about the authenticity of people and objects. Under Mao, value was objectified in the work point system that publicly accounted for labor in its quantity and quality. Under the current circumstances, value is accounted for in money, namely in what was historically perceived as the sign of a regime of inauthenticity and self-interest. The anxieties of urbanites and peasants mirror each other: urbanites deplore the deluge of fake goods and citizens that might derail the country's development; peasants lament their lost status as the backbone of the revolution and struggle to find a place for themselves in the new market-oriented society. As Brandtstädter points out, "in the Shanghai market, local stalls owners catered to both—contrasting—desires for fakes and for true value by producing Gucci bags that not only looked like the 'real thing,' but also came with a fake certificate of authenticity" (2009: 142).

Another case study reveals other particularities of the presence of fake branded commodities in China. The fake indexes relationships between real self, real life, and the foreign as more real than the real. Pinheiro-Machado (2010) compares consumption practices in Brazil and China, both developing economies in which the signs of income and consumption polarization have become increasingly visible. She argues that, in both countries, consumption of fake brands creates the person. Emulation represents an identity process through which people give themselves substance, empower themselves, and place themselves in the world. They pretend "to have and to be," for what one has objectifies who one is. At a more general level, the personalized nature of power, captured in the Brazilian concept of *jeitinho* and in the Chinese notion of *guanxi,* is the common cultural characteristic that explains the avid interest in fake branded goods in both societies. One must materialize power to convince oneself and others that one possesses it. The cultural significance of brands turns them into a material form that best suits this purpose. This common general cultural trait has specific forms, developed in relation to very different local and historical contexts. These particular understandings of power further determine the value of fake goods, so that, for example, in southern China, these objects play their role in defining a Chinese person and distinguishing him or her from someone from Hong Kong.

In contrast, in Guyana, as Halstead emphasizes, fake brands are embraced as temporary manifestations of the authentic. Fake branded sportswear imported from neighboring Brazil are called "Jarvex bottles," after a bleach product marketed in bottles of poor quality that get crumpled quickly. Fakes are believed to "mash up" rapidly too. These goods represent the very opposite of the quality branded commodities of American origin. In the postcolonial context, migration to the United States has generated an inward flow of goods in relation to which people that remain construct their identity. This process draws on the colonial understanding of foreign commodities as representing superior quality and reinforces the idea of perfection as accessible through the foreign. People who dream of emigrating consume the inferior fakes, but not because these goods are marketed as the real thing or consumers are fooled into believing they are buying the real thing. For these Guyanese, the "brand is a visible marker of the *other they could become* in the desired migratory destination" (Halstead 2002: 274). The relation between the fake brand, as an affordable product, and the real brand, as an expensive foreign product, objectifies a specific conceptualization of the real self as something attainable only by living a real life in the imagined elsewhere as land of opportunities. Until they settle in such a place, people's lives are somewhat fake. The fake branded goods are acceptable as a temporary means of accessing the foreignness. Their consumption is not derided, but recognized as an index of the anticipated journey. In other words, the real is accessed through the fake. The fake indexes relationships between the real self, the real life, and the foreign as more real than the real.

The last set of case studies I include in this section shows that the original and the copy/fake might be just the two ends of a continuum, in between which different notions and material forms proliferate. Sylvanus presents a context in which original copies, copies of copies, and fakes of copies are placed in competing hierarchies of value and consequently embraced or rejected. In Togo, copies of Javanese batik cloth, which have long been produced in Europe for African markets, are central elements in processes of identity construction and social distinction. This fabric of modernity originally reached the Togolese market in different quality versions. Those at the top of the social hierarchy displayed their status through the consumption of the expensive quality "original copy." The rest made do with the inferior quality copy of the copy. Though they were legally counterfeits, these objects were not presented as the original copy. They were consumed as "good enough" copies. Togolese took pride in their ability to discern different fabric qualities. This hierarchy of value has been disrupted by the state's attempt to lure its citizens into consuming "fakes." Since the mid-1990s, after being cut off from international aid, the Togolese state has accommodated any business that could potentially bring income. The free port has become the key site of profit extraction. Chinese manufacturers have eagerly embraced this opportunity to export their counterfeited commodities to the West African markets via the Togolese *entrepôt*. Local consumers' first reaction was panic. For them, the new forms were fakes of a dangerous nature. They pretended to be something other than what they truly were. They robbed them of their ability to apprehend materiality. Sylvanus notes that "Togolese, across socio-economic class divides, felt they were tricked out of their agency" and demanded the intervention of the state (2010: 9). The moral discourses they used came very close to the rhetoric of intellectual property regime. The state did intervene, but not in the way the consumers anticipated. A faction of the regime launched its own branded cloth manufactured in China. The legitimizing discourse of this brand stated that the Togolese people had the right to take ownership of the European designs that owed their reputation to them and to become the authors of their own history. Nevertheless, the consumers soon rejected the branded cloth, for its materiality was judged inferior to other Chinese counterfeits available on the market. Instead they developed skills to distinguish between the different qualities of the new fakes and reactivated the old hierarchy of distinction.

The discourse of the original and the copy might be put to different uses than those specified in the mainstream culture. Luvaas (2010) analyzes the art of fashion remix in Indonesia. Local indie designers appropriate various elements from the global commercial iconography and assemble them in novel and daring combinations. They clearly distinguish their "cut and paste" practice from the wholesale copying and downright stealing of other people's designs. It is the counterfeiters who just copy branded commodities. In sharp contrast, their work is based on careful deliberation and, in many instances, open acknowledgment of their sources. The resulting compositions have their own aesthetic and semiotic independence. Moreover, these designers claim that for the counterfeiters this is a pragmatic choice that does not involve personal investment, critical intent, or creative vision. In contrast, the designs they produce reflect their subjectivities. They do not use random elements of the consumer culture, but choose those that allow them to express who they are and what worldviews they hold. The other figure from whom these designers differentiate themselves is the designer as portrayed in the Romantic imagination, an individual whose unique genius is mirrored in the uniqueness of his or her creation. Designers attempt to restore sociality to the act of production. Luvaas argues that these practices and reflections make sense in light of the middle-class position these designers occupy in Indonesian society and the marginal place they inhabit on the global scene. Their middle-class status allows them access to some things, but also makes them acutely aware how few these things are, in comparison to what people of similar social status have elsewhere. This frustrating position pushes them to do what they do. However, this appropriation is not so much about rebellion or resistance. These designers do not have a coherent political agenda. They mess with the corporate imaginary, but their work is rather a playful criticism. They are less concerned with subverting global commercial culture than working with it and finding a place for themselves within it. This practice of aesthetic appropriation becomes therefore an act of social and existential positioning in the wider world.

These studies illustrate the impact the dismissive and condemnatory understanding of fake brands might have on ordinary people's thoughts and actions. This impact might be insignificant, as in the case of Vietnamese consumers. It might be occasional and circumstantial, as in the case of Indian producers of branded garments. It might be significant, as in the case of Maya manufacturers of fake branded clothes in Guatemala, who are portrayed as shady characters and lawbreakers. Moreover, the conceptual framework itself might take an unexpected form, when combined with the Maoist ideological vocabulary to justify the rejection or consumption of fake branded commodities by Chinese consumers of different social backgrounds, or it might find an unexpected echo in the moral condemnation of copying by Maya manufacturers of fake branded clothes. Engagements with objects deemed fake brands might be accepted or rejected according to local reasons and moral logics. For some Chinese, rejecting the inauthentic objects becomes a means to be progressive citizens. For other Chinese, consuming the inauthentic objects becomes a means to construct a valuable self. For Guyanese youngsters, the fake brands are good enough until they move to the United States, where they can live an authentic life. Furthermore, central notions at work in the cultural and legal understanding of fake brands only partially guide people in their attempts to make sense of and legitimize or delegitimize the proliferation of certain material forms. In Togo, hierarchies of value include original copies, copies of copies, and fakes of copies. In Indonesia, indie designers distinguish between copying and creative copying. Therefore, these studies bring to the foreground nuances that exceed the realm of the possible envisaged within this dismissive and condemnatory conceptual framework. Moreover, they demonstrate that materiality plays an important role in these engagements, as ground on which to justify production and consumption, as base on which to choose to produce and consume these objects, and as evidence on which to contest and reject mainstream claims that these objects ought to be neglected as material detritus.

In short, these studies demonstrate that we live in a world unevenly circumstanced by this dismissive and condemnatory conceptual framework. Perhaps against the pretention of universalism with which this conceptual framework, especially in the form of intellectual property legislation, is circulated around the world, anthropologists seem more preoccupied to analyze instances in which the assumptions about objects and people encapsulated in this framework are not recognized, or they are contested or simply ignored. On the whole, this body of literature concurs with more general theoretical insights into the multiple and contradictory articulations between global and local in the modern world (Miller 1995; Sykes 2009).

The present book builds on these insights, but it also distances itself from them in the way it highlights the significance of materiality and argues for a particular form of authenticity. The following chapters offer detailed ethnographic material about the impact of the mainstream cultural and legal understanding of fake brands on the lives, practical choices, and senses of self of people who engage with these inauthentic objects. These chapters delve into mundane engagements with fake branded garments and bring to the foreground the multifaceted presence of these objects in places of manufacture and distribution in Turkey and place of distribution and consumption in Romania. These chapters show how this conceptual framework, which attempts to command people's apprehension of certain objects as inferior, even dangerous, and to prevent people from engaging with these objects, is acknowledged or disregarded, matters or does not matter, and affects or does not affect objects and people. In addition, the fifth chapter focuses particularly on those moments and contexts in which such assumptions are recognized and in which their implications for one's sense of self are confronted or refuted.

–3–

The Elusiveness of Inauthenticity, The Materiality of Brand: Fake Branded Garments in Turkey

In Istanbul, branded garments can be purchased in locations other than brand stores and authorized outlets. These might be improvised stands— a cardboard box, a piece of cloth, or a plastic sheet—placed on the pavement on busy streets, piers, and underground stations, and guarded by men who keep a studious lookout for authorities. On these stands, garments are neatly folded, with brand names and logos visible, so that any passerby can spot them in the blink of an eye. These alternative locations might be shops on backside alleys, booths in passageways, and stalls in the weekly open-air markets. In these neighborhood markets, sellers cry "brands," "originals," "world brands," "export excess," "come, sister, come! these are real, sister," in all sorts of keys, running up and down strange scales of notes. They stand on top of piles of garments, throw them in the air, shout, clap their hands, pause to take a breath, and begin again with renewed energy. They might be shops in the Grand Bazaar, crammed to the brim with merchandise by shopkeepers who nowadays capitalize on the desire for garments bearing global brand names. These locations might be fancy shops in Laleli, the center of the transnational informal trade with Eastern Europe and the former Soviet Union. Shopkeepers try to please the "Russian" taste for flamboyant outfits, not only by overly decorating their shops, but also by offering branded garments with an extra layer of glamour in the form of heavy embroidery, gold, silver, sequins, and the like. They might be shops in Merter, a peripheral neighborhood refashioned as the newest center in this informal trade. Its central area was reconstructed to accommodate new shops with their fancy billboards, mannequins, and a huge quantity of clothing, export excess, brands, fakes, anything. In front of its main mosque, a traffic sign reads "Western fashion," proclaiming the new identity of this place. The city is literally flooded with fake branded garments and the overflow from export-oriented manufacturing sites. The underbelly of the local clothing industry is, thus, exposed.

Many of these garments fall into the category of counterfeits. In Turkey, laws for the protection of different forms of intellectual property have long been promulgated. In the nineteenth century, in its efforts to integrate in the new world economy created by industrialization, the Ottoman Empire introduced legal instruments for the protection of trademarks and patents modeled on French legislation (e.g., the first law regarding trademarks was promulgated in 1871, and the first law concerning patents was put into effect in 1879) (Keyder, V.B. 1997; see also Kayaoğlu 2010 on the spread of Western legal categories and practices in the Ottoman Empire). In the late twentieth century, in its efforts to meet criteria for participation in the Turkey-EU Customs Union and accession in the European Union, Turkey adopted or approximated European legislation, including intellectual property laws. Another incentive for harmonizing its existent intellectual property legislation with the international legal system came from participation in the TRIPS Agreement (Keyder, V.B. 1997; Togan 1997).

This chapter demonstrates that inauthenticity is an elusive attribute: it might be recognized, negotiated, and refuted when it refers to objects; it might be recognized, negotiated, and feared when it refers to the activities that bring into existence and circulate these objects; it might be recognized and challenged when it refers to the people who engage with these objects and who are, consequently, marginalized and criminalized. Moreover, this chapter shows that the realization of brand depends on the materiality of the branded commodity and illustrates why this matters for people who build their professional lives and extract their notions of good working lives from their short- or long-term engagement with fake brands.

Two analytical strategies are employed here to respect the local nature of these objects: the first strategy is to situate these objects within the political economy of their manufacture and distribution; the second strategy is to present the ways a few Istanbulites speak about objects whose characterization as inauthentic they are occasionally forced to acknowledge. Some of the opinions voiced by Kerim—the Istanbulite introduced at the beginning of this book and who is himself a manufacturer and trader in fake brands—will also be encountered in these ethnographic vignettes.

The fieldwork this chapter draws on was carried out in manufacturing and trading places in Istanbul. The first months of fieldwork had been rather disconcerting. Fake branded clothes, footwear, and accessories of different degrees of similitude and quality were ubiquitous. However, getting in touch with those who manufactured and retailed them was not an easy thing to do. Many a time I boarded a bus and went to peripheral areas, wherever my fancy or my feet happened to take me. There was a high probability of ending up in a clothing manufacturing area, anyway. Every now and then, a colorful bundle of waste material, job announcements glued on the walls, and workshop/factory outlets confirmed I was in such an area. Workshops were located on the ground floor or in the basement of residential buildings and, from outside, looked like ordinary apartments. Many a time I hung about bazaars and weekly markets, experiencing not only aesthetic delight in front of the exuberant touches added to original models and sympathy for those who trembled next to piles of poorly made copies in side alleys and on cold quays, but also despair and touches of alarm, when I fully acknowledged the danger of being too curious and the dark side of counterfeiting. Several times I traveled between Istanbul and Bucharest by bus, in the company of petty traders, unobtrusively observing ways of crossing the borders with (decent) quantities of fake branded goods and engaging my fellow travelers in casual conversations.

Everyone seemed to know what was going on—even common people were in possession of bits of information—everyone but the anthropologist. I talked about my research agenda with everyone, hoping to forge connections. The mediators of my encounters claimed that those they introduced me to were producing fake branded clothes. Whether they were certain or assumed they manufactured because, as a rule, anybody could do it, I could not know. The following fragment is an example of the negotiation that took place before such encounters: "Could you please introduce me to a producer of fake branded clothing?" I would try my luck. "Well, this is a very simple question, but, at the same time, a very difficult one. For you cannot simply approach these people with such a blunt question! I know a factory owner, you could interview him. You could also ask him about fakes, but . . . Here everyone can produce fakes, without being really specialised in this area. They can get involved only for a brief period, because this business is very profitable," my acquaintance replied. "I will ask about their businesses, daily concerns, general views on the local clothing industry," I rephrased my research interest. "This sounds better," I was told. Some people were offended by my research interest. Others whispered that such and such manufacturer was producing fake branded garments, but insisted I could not include this information in my study, for suspicion was already in the air and foreigners seemed inclined to the view that counterfeiting was a well-spread activity in the Turkish clothing industry. "Do you really want to expose dirty linen? Do you really want to dirty clean linen?" I was asked. I defended myself by reminding my interlocutors that Turkey was, despite such suspicions, a significant manufacturing site in the global clothing industry. "Nobody can compete with us! We produce quality stuff. Even our fakes are very good," was the usual prompt reply. The problem lay in convincing my acquaintances I was conducting a study, in explaining what use this would be to others, and in gaining their trust. My position as a non-Western student from London on her own in Istanbul, struggling to speak Turkish had its advantages, diluting some of this suspicion and, more important, impressing my interlocutors.

I was introduced to people and scoured textile districts in search of acquaintances of my acquaintances. Sometimes, I and my companion(s) could not find the persons we were looking for, as the industry was very dynamic and a person could enter this business easily, but could also go bankrupt quickly. At other times, we were able to engage workshop owners in short conversations, most of them recounting personal reasons for mixing "white and black" in their production and mentioning strategies for avoiding being caught, while stressing that many others were doing the same to earn a living. In a workshop, the owner directed my attention to a white sheet of paper saying "quality first." "We make the fakes in that corner," he joked. A few owners ventured to show how a counterfeit was made in the workshop. I found myself in the awkward position of asking questions in a milieu where people did not ask each other too much, for a trusted acquaintance was enough to put them in contact (ironically, I was always asked to have precise questions; several times when my interlocutors stopped in the middle of a conversation and wondered if I really found what they were telling me of any use, a reply of "anything is fine, for I do not know many things anyway" was the worst answer!). Then, one day, I felt the fieldwork started, in a bazaar shop crammed full of fake branded underwear, where I spent day after day for many months and learned about the manufacture and trade in fake branded garments. "Do not be shy, come whenever you want, I have nothing to hide, *kardeşim* [my brother/sister, Turkish being a genderless language]," Kerim told me.

FAKE BRANDS

In Istanbul, many of the people I encountered claimed fake branded garments could be produced everywhere, in any of the myriad locations of the local clothing industry. In addition, they pointed out that in certain cases the official and unofficial manufacture were carried out on the same premises.

The city is one of the manufacturing and trading sites within an uncontrollable alternative economy of value that has very likely spread by now all over the world. China is considered the unrivalled manufacturer and the world's number one perpetrator, closely followed by other Asian countries such as Taiwan, Singapore, Malaysia, or Hong Kong (Chang 2004; Hung 2003; Yao 2005). Turkey is believed to be a major exporter of counterfeited products to the European markets, some reports mentioning it among the three most important manufacturers of fake branded garments, alongside China and Taiwan (Santos and Ribeiro 2006; Waite 2004).

Istanbul accommodates a well-developed clothing manufacturing sector and different national and international factors can be invoked here to explain its growth. In the mid-1980s, during the Özal period (called so after the prime minister under whose leadership many liberal economic measures were introduced), Turkey opened itself to the world and set off on the road to the free market. The government offered various incentives to encourage domestic producers to orient themselves toward export and, simultaneously, allowed massive intrusion by multinational firms and foreign goods (Şenses 1994).

During this period, a global clothing industry began to operate across the world and Turkish companies became part of it. Companies in the developed countries concentrated on the high value-added parts of clothing production— design, branding, marketing, and advertising—and outsourced the other parts of production to less developed countries, which could offer cheap labor forces and low manufacturing costs (Gereffi 1999). In outsourcing production, buyers were looking not only for price competitiveness, but also for reliable product quality, punctual delivery, and flexibility in coping with small high-quality orders and changes in large orders (Schmitz and Knorringa 2000). Turkey became an important partner in such business arrangements because of its proximity to the European market, its tradition in textile and clothing manufacture, and the large-scale cultivation of cotton. Moreover, the European Community's objective to establish a customs union with Turkey prompted Turkish companies to secure partnerships with European counterparts, an essential condition, they imagined, for becoming more competitive in a national economy about to be reshaped by this agreement (Tokatlı and Boyacı 1997). The opening to the European market was reciprocated, with European companies establishing assembly plants in Turkey and signing franchising and licensing agreements with Turkish firms (Tokatlı 2003). In addition, tariff cuts and the progressive lifting of quotas that limited imports of textile and clothes from less developed countries to the United States created favorable conditions for Turkish manufacturers interested in entering the American market (Tokatlı and Kızılgün 2004).

Another factor that influenced the development of the clothing industry in Istanbul is an "unexpected" form of globalization (Keyder 1999), that is, the huge informal trade that since the fall of communism has linked Istanbul with Eastern Europe and the former Soviet Union. Inhabitants from all over this region have been pouring into the city in search of commodities, with garments among the most sought-after things. At its high point in the mid-1990s, this trade was estimated at US$9 billion per annum, a significant amount in comparison with Turkey's official exports, which ranged between US$13 billion and US$27 billion per annum (Yükseker 2004: 49).

In this favorable context, enticed by export incentives, international demand, and low labor and investment costs, many Turkish businessmen entered this sector. By 1999, for example, Turkey had become the world's sixth largest clothing exporter, exporting approximately US$6.5 billion each year, and its industry—still primarily concentrated in Istanbul— had grown to include over 5,000 exporting firms, according to the 1998 statistics of the Istanbul Textile and Clothing Export Union (Riddle and Gillespie 2003). Therefore, in a short period of time, the clothing industry has become the country's leading export sector and Istanbul's largest manufacturing sector (Keyder 2005).

Many of the economic actors that operate within this huge clothing industry are small- to middle-scale firms (older actors are large companies established during the import-substitution period). The smallest ones have up to ten employees and are usually family enterprises. Then there are the medium-scale firms that employ up to thirty workers. The middle- to large-scale companies have up to 100 workers. Thousands of clothing manufacturing workshops mushroomed on the outskirts of the city, taking advantage of the resources these peripheral places had to offer, that is, low rents and unemployed internal migrants. In 2005, the unofficial number of workshops of various sizes operating in the city was estimated to be around 80,000 (Yörük 2006). Most of these small- and middle-scale workshops straddle the line between formal and informal economy and use all possible means to keep themselves above the water and maximize their chances amidst the tough competition for contracts and skilled workers that characterizes this level of the clothing industry (Dedeoğlu 2008).[1]

In addition, many of these companies act as assembly sites in the global clothing industry. The clothing industry is "a cascade of operations, each of which can be, and in practice is at one time or another, partitioned off and subcontracted, creating a near continuum of firms arranged in a hierarchy of skill, power, and profitability" (Peters, Duran, and Piore 2002: 229). At the bottom of this hierarchy, there are simple assembly firms, which do the sewing and assembly on the cheapest garments. These firms seem to be trapped in the role of simple manufacturers for companies that collect the real rents. Subcontracting has for a long time been an intrinsic characteristic of the clothing and fashion industry. Given the high degree of unpredictability in this market, no player wants to be left with garments that have gone out of fashion, so the risk is passed down to the smallest subcontractor and, eventually, the poorly paid worker (Howard 1997). Moreover, "globalization truncates industrialization instead of deepening it, encourages simple assembly, prevents the industry from becoming a sustainable industrial base that could contribute to long-term economic development, and does not automatically give birth to domestic industry leaders that evolve into global competitors" (Tokatlı and Kızılgün 2004: 225). However, in recent years, Turkish firms have upgraded their production, moving from industrial subcontracting to commodity subcontracting and becoming full-package producers. Moreover, several companies have developed their own brands, with Mavi Jeans as an outstanding example.

This enormous clothing industry operates as a factory without walls. The interconnections between manufacturing sites of different dimensions are multiple and intricate. Subcontracting relations are not only vertical, but also

horizontal, some factories and workshops specializing only in certain parts of the production process. Subcontract-offering and subcontract-receiving firms prefer to have as many partners as possible: the former because in this way they can have a wider network to rely on in case of delays and disagreements and can better negotiate production costs, the latter because in this way they can increase their chances to obtain good payment for their work (Kaytaz 1994). The relationships between workshops and exporting companies are short lived, with poor-quality work, bad timing, and a constant preoccupation with lowering costs accounting for this volatile nature (Dedeoğlu 2008). Moreover, the firms targeting Western markets and those manufacturing clothing for the informal trade with Eastern Europe and the former Soviet Union are not completely separated segments of this industry (Çınar et al. 1988; Eraydin and Erendil 1999).

In brief, in Istanbul, the clothing industry is a well-developed sector that targets different domestic and international markets. Although no exact data is available because of the large number of firms that operate informally, useful indicators of its enormous dimension include Turkey's position among the top ten major clothing exporters in the world and the high number of export companies officially registered in Istanbul, up to 70 percent of the total number of clothing exporters in the country (Dedeoğlu 2008; Riddle and Gillespie 2003).

Fake branded garments of different degrees of similitude and various qualities can be manufactured in a myriad of locations in this clothing industry. However, everywhere they are produced "under the stairs," that is, secretively. As one of my informants put it, making a fake must be an activity "like a spark." A spark happens and dies out. It leaves no traces. This image is also meant to suggest the danger inherent in this activity. A second of inattention and this spark might have disastrous consequences: equipment and goods can be confiscated, businesses can be shut down, fines have to be paid, and those caught involved in this illegal activity can go to prison.

The following examples illustrate how and why this illegal activity might take place in typical locations in this clothing industry. The first example discusses a successful factory caught up in the global clothing industry. The second example presents a workshop close to bankruptcy, which drags out a miserable existence through executing whatever orders its owner can secure. This ethnographic material focuses on the ways the owners of these manufacturing sites describe their work and demonstrates that in one case the manufacture of fake brands is a matter of business savvy and in the other case it is a survival strategy. In both cases, the manufacturing of fake branded garments was a topic that appeared during conversations about the clothing industry in Istanbul and the competitive local and global environment.

The first sign that the factory was thriving were the two trucks parked in its courtyard and the cardboard boxes some men kept loading. Ömer proudly pointed out that the boxes contained finished products for a famous foreign company. Ömer's father established this factory in the early 1990s, at a time when the clothing industry was booming in Istanbul. Now the family ran a prosperous business and planned to expand in other manufacturing sectors too. Plunged in a comfortable chair in his spacious office, Ömer explained what it meant to be a subcontractor. He spoke at great length about the effort, excitement, and anxiety that were integral parts of this work. The manufacturer who wished to become a subcontractor had to invest a significant amount of money in equipment, an attractive showroom in which to exhibit his products, and the entertainment of brand representatives in fancy restaurants. A serious investment was bound to bring contracts with well-known brands. Upon signing the contracts, the hard work began. So did the factory owner's insomnia, for there were many things to worry about, such as manufacturing details, measurements, quality standards, and delivery deadlines. It was even worse if work was outsourced to workshops, for they occasionally disregarded delivery terms and quality specifications. Ömer emphasized that clothing manufacturing was a demanding activity and a subcontractor had to deal with all these problems in an efficient way, otherwise his future in this business was compromised.

To elaborate on this idea, Ömer focused on the last decisive moment in the production, that is, quality control. This was usually carried out by a representative of the foreign contractor, who would visit the factory and evaluate the products. However, things might go wrong exactly around that time. For example, not long before that person's arrival, the factory owner was informed there were problems with the execution of the order. The most common problem was the size of the contracted products. This usually occurred because an employee misread an e-mail or misunderstood product specifications communicated over the phone in a foreign language. Ömer insisted that a realistic factory owner would come up with a solution to this problem. He recounted a story that he heard from someone in this business. In that case, the contracted T-shirts came out smaller than they were supposed to be. The simplest way to correct the size was to unpack, iron, enlarge with hot steam, iron again, and repack the products. Anyone in this business knew that this was a temporary solution, for after a while the fabric would return to its initial shape. However, by that time, the products would be already on the foreign market. Ömer pointed out that every producer knew such tricks. Nevertheless, the best subterfuge was the quality inspector's complicity. Social networks were mobilized to get around that person, for he was a Turk, "one of us," and, thus, an individual with whom an agreement could be reached. The factory owner could pay, for example, US$1,000 to solve a problem, and that was far better than paying compensations and ruining his future in the chains of the global clothing production.

Upon emphasizing the responsibilities and difficulties of this work, Ömer moved on to other opportunities that a subcontractor in the global clothing industry might benefit from, not before emphasizing that in this business one just needed to be careful and know the right people (and at this point it was up to the listener to decide if he spoke about his own experience or not). He began with the beginning, that is, export excess. There were many instances in which export quotas were exceeded or the foreign company changed its order during the production process. In such cases, the factory owner was left with an overstock. He tried to sell this overstock either in his shop or to a third party. The foreign firm could not forbid him to do so, especially because he was not spoiling the brand's good reputation by selling these products in weekly markets or other less prestigious locations. Moreover, as these products sold well, this owner decided to supplement the initial stock. He continued to manufacture this product in his factory, without informing the brand owner. He knew all the suppliers and had the necessary technology as well as the design specifications. One could easily claim these products were originals: the same fabrics, patterns stitches, and packaging were used for these garments as for the originals. Furthermore, this person also produced lower-quality items. He modified product parameters and combined overstock parts from the official production with inexpensive articles bought from the local market. He could easily find buyers for these products too, for there were plenty of buyers catering for those less discerning customers that still come from the former socialist countries in search of fashionable but cheap garments. Then our owner began to multiply a brand in high demand using materials from suppliers other than those he dealt with for the official production. He tried to pass these goods off as originals and found a buyer. In his turn, this buyer too tried to sell these products to yet another party, claiming they were originals, but recounting their story in his own way. "And so on and so forth," Ömer concluded his story about the fortunes and misfortunes of a subcontractor working in the global clothing industry.

Ahmet, the owner of the workshop, had his own story of fortunes and misfortunes, except that in his case the fortunes were things of the past. This workshop was situated on a narrow back alley in a residential area. Broken buttons on the pavement in front of its main door was the only indicator that there was a manufacturing place there. The workshop had five sewing machines and employed nine workers. Its owner, Ahmet, first called my attention to the dirtiness and messiness around us and then, in his most serious expression, began to talk about his misfortune. The appearance reflected his sad situation. Time had begun to flow with painful slowness and business had being going from bad to worse. He was always tight for money, orders were hard to find, maintenance prices were growing up, and workers were quitting their jobs. When he was at his wits' end, when the money he got for a jacket was less than what he got five years ago, he was seriously considering the possibility of closing down the place. Had it not been for his reputation, his high-quality Japanese and German machines specially designed to perform the complicated work demanded in a jacket, he would have long ago closed the atelier. Having said this, Ahmet leaned against a table, hands deep in his pockets, a cloud hanging over him.

He opened the workshop in the late 1980s, after he spent a few years working as an apprentice in his uncle's tailoring workshop. The uncle helped him buy two sewing machines, get his first work orders, and establish himself as a workshop owner. The atelier was located in a neighborhood renowned for its small- and middle-scale workshops producing high-quality clothes in boutique style for domestic and foreign markets. The neighborhood also hosted various agents in the clothing business, contract intermediaries, and purveyors of different goods and services. For almost twenty years, Ahmet had produced jackets and occasionally accepted orders for trousers and shirts. He was himself a skilled machinist, specializing in some of the most difficult parts in the production of a jacket, such as attaching the collars or arms to the main body of the jacket. He established his network of contacts not only by mobilizing whatever social resources he had, but also by knocking on factory and shop doors in search of orders, showing sample pieces and giving the particulars of his atelier, such as details about machines, garments, and the quality of execution. He earned a reputation on the local market and managed to expand his business by buying three sophisticated machines. For many years, orders kept coming, and patterns and materials kept piling up on his tables. He often worked for companies targeting the domestic high-end market, executing sophisticated models that required skillful use of the machines and complicated hand stitching. At one time, he received a visit from the representative of a German company, himself a German, who came to oversee the quality of the subcontracted jackets. Ahmet covered half of the floor with plastic sheets and then spread out the garments for inspection, deeply touching the German with his manners.

Today he gladly accepted any order. Shrugging his shoulders, Ahmet described some of the orders as coming from "unregistered firms" whose representatives knocked at his door and did not say much, except for the date when the products should be ready. They delivered everything he needed: materials, patterns, labels, and logos. He learned not to ask questions, not to discuss these materials, and not to suggest suppliers for the other materials he needed. On the day the products were due, a truck came, loaded the garments, and they were gone, people and objects alike. Ahmet got his money and hoped more orders of this sort would come. And they did. Sometimes he was asked to manufacture simple products such as T-shirts. At other times, he produced more demanding garments. Such orders pleased him, for he could demonstrate his skills, even if only to himself and not to his unknown buyers and customers. "Anyone with some money in his pocket can produce imitations. He visits a workshop, says he would like this and that, and makes an offer. Let's say five dollars for a T-shirt. This is a very good price. The workshop takes the order," he abruptly ended the story about his business. The fate of this workshop bespeaks the vulnerability of small workshops in the highly competitive environment of the local clothing industry. To enter clothing manufacture, work experience and skills are not compulsory. Boldness and modest capital are enough to buy inexpensive machines produced in China, for renting a place, and to start a business. Ahmet estimates that a working capital of US$10,000 would be enough to enter this business. Anyone can become a manufacturer. And, more important, anyone can enter the lucrative sector of fake brands production. He does not even need to do the manufacture himself, for there are plenty of workshops in need of work orders, any kind of work orders.

These two examples are illustrative of the fact that in Istanbul any clothing manufacturing place, be it formal factory or informal workshop, is the space of the possible. Fake branded garments can be technically produced in a myriad of locations. This ubiquitous presence reflects the specificity of industrial manufacture. Fake branded garments are easy to produce. Sometimes, all it takes is stitching a label onto a garment. In addition, fake branded garments are easy to produce because standardized (branded) clothes are easy to manufacture. The clothing industry is an "imperfect industry": "compared with other industries, clothing manufacture is much less mechanised; technological developments have not eliminated the basic unit of production, the woman at the sewing machine" (Entwistle 2000: 212). The sewing machine is a relatively cheap, simple, and long-lived piece of equipment and the entry barrier to manufacturing is therefore low. "Cloth and clothing manufacture have remained remarkably resistant to technological change . . . Labour is, has always been, and probably always will be the largest cost factor in making cloth and clothing. Assembly and sewing in particular remain highly demanding of the human hand; most fabrics are simply too fluid to trust the machines alone" (Schneider 2006: 214). The mushrooming of manufacturing workshops in Istanbul since the 1990s supports these statements.

Moreover, fake brands are easy to produce because of the transfer of technology and knowledge that takes place in a manufacturing site in the global clothing industry. To meet the demands for product quality, punctual delivery, and flexibility in production, local subcontractors upgrade and increase their capacity to translate design into technical specifications. In this way, local firms learn how to "do things better" and how to "make better things" (Schmitz and Knorringa 2000). My informants pointed out that, given these favorable circumstances, subcontractors might use the infrastructure for their own benefit in after-hours production and might transfer knowledge through their own social networks (see also Mertha (2005)).

Any discussion about the multiplication of a certain model that I witnessed during my fieldwork began with an evaluation of the equipment necessary for its manufacture. In certain cases, the discussion ended quickly, for neither those taking part in it nor their acquaintances possessed the technology required by those models. In some cases, a compromise was reached, an acceptably similar product, the best that could be produced with the kind of technology they had. In other cases, the discussion moved rapidly to other issues because technology and know-how, even for the production of identical copies, was at their fingertips. However, it is worth noting that the degree of similarity was not just a problem of technology and know-how. It was also considered in relation to the potential customers, for only some were imagined or known to be interested in identical copies, while the majority, even the former socialist citizens, were known to be concerned with the quality of materials and the precision of execution.

Furthermore, fake branded garments are easy to produce because remains of the official brand production can be incorporated into their manufacture. Tokatlı and Kızılgün (2004) estimate that rejects might constitute up to 10 percent of a brand's production. At the global level, communication problems regarding the integration of design components and the quality standards of the final product might result in flawed goods. At the local level of manufacture, human mistakes, technological disruptions, and flaws in the fabrics are the most common factors that account for the appearance of products that cannot pass quality inspection. Rejects might be sold as such. Together with export surplus, refused stocks, and overruns, they circulate in lots sorted not by design and brand name, but by quality, and are traded in the underbelly of the clothing industry. In such instances, Tokatlı and Kızılgün's observation might be useful. As they point out, the trade in rejects "may or may not be considered part of the counterfeiting business...The 'export excess' articles are not necessarily 'fakes,' since they are manufactured at the same factories, together with the items that pass quality inspections, without any intent of counterfeiting" (2004: 228). However, in other instances, this observation loses its validity. My informants stressed that some of these objects could be mended and sold as originals, that they could also serve as models in the production of fakes, and that parts could be used in the manufacture of fakes. In one way or another, these objects might live a second life as fakes, even if they were not intended to pass for brands, but to be brands. There are also the other remains—fabrics, accessories, paint, thread, and so on—which can be combined with generic goods and used to manufacture more branded items. The resulting garments might be included in what I call the category of the "partially fake," as opposed to the "entirely fake."[2]

Besides the specificity of industrial manufacture, another factor could explain the significant presence of legally fake branded garments. The various agents of the state tolerate the presence of fake branded garments because they can take a share of the profits these objects generate. My informants pointed out that they bribed lawyers, judges, municipality employees, policemen, and customs officials to keep their businesses running smoothly. "We all get on marvellously," a producer of fake branded garments summarized this situation.[3] At the time I was doing fieldwork, rumor had it that some of the intellectual property lawyers negotiated the release of every individual caught red-handed. The negotiation started from US$20,000 in cash, paid directly to the lawyer. Studies of the Laleli district, the center of the informal trade linking Istanbul with Eastern Europe and the former Soviet Union, and one of the distribution areas for fake branded garments, demonstrate that state agents take their share of the profit this trade generates (Dedeoğlu 2008; Eder and Öz 2010; Keyder 1999; Yükseker 2004). In this way, intellectual property laws build as well as cut up networks, resulting in protected and unprotected, exclusive and nonexclusive areas (Gaines 1991).

This section has shown that in a manufacturing site in the global clothing industry, fake branded garments proliferate. As I was told or was able to observe many times during my fieldwork in Istanbul, the availability of technology, knowledge, and materials and the possibility of convincing the authorities to turn a blind eye to informal activities translate into a deluge of unauthorized branded objects of different degrees of similitude and various qualities. Moreover, the section has brought to the foreground the particularities of the mass production of garments and, consequently, has illustrated the very thin line that separates the authorized copies from their unauthorized counterparts when both are relatively cheap and easy to manufacture. This brings more light on why the law proclaims itself the only arbiter of the authentic, a claim that was discussed in the previous chapter. Furthermore, this section has illustrated the impact of the legal characterization of objects as fake brands on the way their production is carried out. This throws a different light on why the question of authenticity is important. In addition, this section has painted the background of this discussion, that is, the economic viability of this informal sector. Fake brands can be manufactured, and they are manufactured because they bring profit; the risks involved in their production and circulation are somewhat manageable. The next section takes up again the issue of economic viability, but presents it not as making profit, but rather as earning a living. This section also focuses on the issue of manufacture, but this time the emphasis is on people's preoccupation with the materiality that accompanies the brand, on their reflections on the nature of brand, and on the role of manufacturers and sellers of fake brands in constituting the local meanings of brand. The characteristics of the manufacture of fake brands discussed in this section feed back into these people's reflections on the nature of brand and the advice they occasionally offer to their customers.

ENGAGEMENTS WITH FAKE BRANDS

As demonstrated in the previous pages, in Istanbul there are plenty of opportunities to engage with what legally are fake branded garments. The men introduced in this section took the opportunity the city presented. They invested themselves in this terrain as manufacturers, copyists, peddlers, and retailers; and capitalized on the demand for these commodities.[4] I recount how these Istanbulites—small- to middle-scale actors in the trade in fake branded garments—spoke about the commodities they engaged with and focus on their insistence that materiality is crucial for the realization of brand. Moreover, I show why they disagree with the classification of certain objects as inauthentic and recount how this legal characterization affects their activities. Other individuals I encountered during my stay in Istanbul reflected on the nature of brand and the nature of clothing in similar ways and argued for the importance of substance (of people as well as objects). Moreover, these individuals voiced similar arguments against the classification of certain objects as inauthentic and against the assumptions about objects and the people who engage with them that this classification carried. This might prove that there is a collective effort to problematize engagements with objects labeled inauthentic. Following Hosein, such arguments might be seen as belonging to what she calls "lore," as opposed to "law," that is, "a legitimacy emerging from the conventions of informal life," a consensual construction of "fairness," a form of legitimacy that guides ways of being and, at the same time, acts as a source of power enabling people to take a stance (2007: 10).

ISMAIL

I first met Ismail in a café. By way of introduction, he stated that he knew very well what kind of comments and questions those like me had in their minds about counterfeited products. However, he understood very well what I was trying to do, that is, to hear their opinions too. Therefore he had prepared for this meeting by doing a bit of brainstorming as well as asking for his friends' opinions. I summarize here the ideas Ismail shared with me.

He knew that those like me thought the goods he was selling and imitations in general were of a low quality. Here we were wrong, for that was not always the case. If we had had the curiosity to learn a bit about how the clothing industry operated, we would have better appreciated the wide range of products a peddler like him actually sold. Not all the garments he sold were imitations or, to use the word we and the police employed, counterfeits. Some were selected from the export excess bales. These items had some tiny invisible defects, but they were originals. Other items were manufactured on the same premises and with the same materials as the originals. Companies claimed that there are two types of products: good-quality originals and low-quality counterfeits. These companies used the law to distinguish between their goods and the similar ones that others could easily manufacture in many workshops in Istanbul. Sometimes the other products were so good that even the brand representatives were surprised and experts had a hard time in distinguishing the original from its fake. Ismail related in a mocking voice that in such cases the time of production became the crucial criterion, with the first produced considered the original and all the others labeled as counterfeits. He also heard about the case of a manufacturer whose rival managed to have his goods seized in customs and have their production date modified, so that his own goods became the originals. Moreover, many of our branded clothes were in fact ordinary garments executed in ordinary fabrics. If we had stopped to think for a moment about how the branded garments were manufactured, we would have better understood this point. Companies charmed us with their fancy shops, glamorous advertisements, and nice bags.

Moreover, he knew we thought what he was doing was wrong. His way of earning a living was not necessarily immoral. Trade in imitations could be seen as something good, a way of helping the poor, facilitating their access to products they coveted, but could not possibly afford because of the exaggerated prices practiced by the brands. He for himself was happy to do a good thing and to sell garments of acceptable quality at an acceptable price. Ismail insisted that the companies that owned these famous brands were in fact responsible for this situation. To stop the trade in imitations, they should have sold their products at decent prices. In vain they tried to prosecute people like him. Truth be told, Ismail continued, the trade in imitations could be seen as a problematic activity for a Muslim, for his religion condemned theft. In a way, he, Ismail, a Muslim, was a thief who earned *haram* (impure, forbidden by religion) money. His way out of this moral dilemma was to reconsider his work as a form of free advertisement, thus not harming but actually helping the company. The logic was very simple: a person who bought one of his fake branded hoodies, for example, would not go around bragging about buying a fake; if his friends wanted to emulate him, they would certainly go for the originals. Upon sharing with me his ideas, Ismail relaxed with a glass of tea and a cigarette, pleased with his well-defined position with regard to counterfeits and counterfeiting, frozen in his bravery. I met him on other occasions too,

sometimes randomly while I was wandering around the streets of Beyazıt, and learned more about his life and work.

Ismail, a man in his mid-twenties, is a small player in the underbelly of the clothing industry. In the early 1990s, his family left a town in eastern Turkey and settled down in Istanbul. Ever since, Ismail has contributed to the family's budget. He entered this trade by chance. One day, a friend, taking pity on him, gave him a few T-shirts to sell. They were simple T-shirts for women, in various colors, with a thin red strip sewed on one sleeve. The strip bore a brand name, one he long forgot. To his surprise, he managed to sell them in a relatively short time. Thrilled with the possibility of earning more money, he gave up trading in rubber balls and offered his stock to his younger brothers and children in the neighborhood. Through this friend, he met a supplier of branded hoodies. With the money he borrowed from his uncle, he secured a small stock and started hawking his garments on the busy streets of the historical peninsula. Some friends of his spent small fortunes in a mall for similar hoodies. He would have never done such a foolish thing. As an aside, Ismail told me he still had one of those hoodies at home and cherished it, for it kept him warm during his long walks. He still liked its color and cut, and the way the brand name was clearly written on the front part and the sleeves. He bought many of his clothes from street peddlers, for they suited his taste and budget. Ismail kept expanding his network of suppliers of branded garments. He learned that one needed to move fast: if a supplier called and said he could offer this and that, he had to rush to take the goods before the other hawkers, provided he could afford to pay for them or managed to take the merchandise on credit. He also tried to get his merchandise directly from producers, but failed for he did not have enough credibility and no one to guarantee for him.

For a while, Ismail had a booth in a small bazaar. A friend taught him how to stay out of trouble: he covered the windows with newspapers and stuck a sign that read "place for rent" on the door. It worked for a while—no authorities poked their nose into his business. Unfortunately for him, one day the whole bazaar was demolished, for it lacked any kind of authorization. He could have made a bundle by selling that booth a few days before everything was turned into debris, when someone came and asked if there was any booth available for sale. Rumor had it that the man was working for the police, but he thought he simply missed a chance to earn good money. After that, Ismail was back on the streets.

Street sellers are vigilant, but a seller of legally fake branded garments needs to be extra vigilant. Ismail risks having his merchandise confiscated and being fined or sent to prison. He spreads his clothes on a small blue plastic sheet. In case the authorities show up, he can bundle it up and run away "like a rabbit," to use his words. I never saw Ismail running "like a rabbit," but witnessed by chance such moments on the busy streets in the vicinity of the Spice Bazaar. Each time some unfortunate fellow was caught red-handed. I recounted to Ismail one such event and its most surprising, to my mind, moment. I told him that while many sellers were running down the street, one man stayed calmly in front of his pile of garments. I could not see if they were fake branded garments or not. Ismail smiled and replied that the man could have very well sold fake brands. The point was that his back was assured. That was the reason he remained there, undisturbed. He for one was caught once on one of these streets, but somehow managed to persuade the policemen to let him go. Ismail told them that he normally sold rejects, that it was the first time he had tried to sell those branded hoodies, that they did not harm the brand owner, that no one thought that those were originals, that he had to earn money and feed his family, that he earned an honest living, that he trembled all day long in the cold weather. He told them many things. He talked and talked and talked, until his throat got dry and his tongue got swollen. They must have pitied him. They lectured on how counterfeiting was a crime, but eventually told him he could leave the police section. He stopped peddling for a while, but then returned to the same streets.

Ismail begins each day with the hope that people will buy from him. He waits for customers, goes here and there, each cigarette pushing the day on, each song bringing home nearer. Fortunately, every day he finds at least one customer for his wares. Ismail lives on the edge of respectable society. In a way, he forces himself there, on the edge. The way he entered the café and started interviewing himself is illustrative of his positioning in the world around him. His bold discourse brings to the foreground the distinction between the way those like him are situated in the discourse of the others and the way they attempt to situate themselves in their own discourse.

As this ethnographic vignette shows, Ismail does not only legitimize his involvement in this trade and his position in the brand economy. Like Kerim, he points out that fake brands are not necessarily distinguishable from or inferior to the authorized branded commodities and that brands are not necessarily the extraordinary objects they are claimed to be. Moreover, he emphasizes that the categorization of objects as inauthentic is always negotiable. It is the smaller player in this trade, he one of them, who often pays the price for engaging in an illegal activities. Others have the means to protect themselves from the implications of illegality this categorization carries. Furthermore, Ismail points out the importance of the materiality of these objects. People, he among them, buy these unauthorized versions because of other reasons than the brand names they carry. Abdullah, the man introduced in the next vignette, draws on his experience as producer and consumer of branded garments to present similar conclusions.

ABDULLAH

During one of my walks in Merter, a peripheral neighborhood that had refashioned itself as a center in the trade with Eastern Europe and the former Soviet countries, I entered a basement shop to look at the clothes on offer. Piles of packed garments covered almost the entire floor and pairs of jeans dangled on hooks along the walls. In between these hooks were racks crammed with denim shirts and jackets. Numerous spotlights bathed things as well as people in shades of green, blue, and red. In a corner, behind a bar topped with colored glass, a young man was surfing the Internet. A shop assistant approached and told me in one breath that the shop sold Abercrombie & Fitch, Replay, Energy, Diesel, and Dsquared denim garments at very good prices. Upon noticing my hesitation, he gave me a business card and advised me to visit other shops in the area and figure out for myself that the shop had indeed good-quality merchandise at affordable prices.

I did return. I looked for the man in his early twenties who sat behind the bar during my first visit, and bluntly told him why I came back. I informed him that I was doing research on the clothing industry in Istanbul and was interested in learning what people involved in this industry taught about the presence of fake branded garments. I pointed out that a lawyer told me that it was impossible to find illegal copies of Diesel on the market, and there I was, with a pile of Diesel jeans right in front of me. I asked him how it was possible to run such a business, for even in Turkey there were laws against counterfeiting. The young man, Abdullah, shrugged his shoulders, as he would do many times during our subsequent encounters. With the easy familiarity of someone accustomed to all sorts of chance encounters, he agreed to talk about his experience. I summarize here his ideas and stories.

Abdullah spoke about his trials, a few going on at the same time. The oldest had begun five years ago, the newest three months ago. He emphasized that they were inevitable in this business. At the beginning, he was scared, but then he got used to these trials. Besides, he had a lot of other things on his mind. He had a shop to run. He recounted a meeting with a judge. It was late afternoon. The judge must have been tired and bored after dealing with similar cases all day long. "What's your story, son?" the judge asked him. "Sir, there is not a single lie left for me. The others have told them all, since the first hour of the day," he replied. The judge seemed to like his bold manner, but insisted he speak about the activity that brought him in the court of law. Abdullah repeated one of the stories he heard from an acquaintance of his. He told the judge that he bought the merchandise from abroad and personally sewed the labels on these garments. The judge gave a short speech about the immorality of this business and fined him. The next day Abdullah returned to the shop.[5]

He admitted that brand owners had all the right to accuse people like him of committing the crime of manufacturing or selling counterfeits. These brand owners had struggled. People like him copied their models and used their brand names. However, their business was not as simple as it might have seemed from outside. They had their own problems to deal with, such as rent and maintenance costs, bouncing checks, unreturned loans, and pressures from their suppliers and subcontractors. He and his brothers had known from the beginning that they were setting for a risky business. "Whenever I think of what I am doing, I remind myself of the old proverb: the one who enters the hamam sweats," he concluded.

Moreover, Abdullah insisted that they were forced to do this business. Everyone seemed to be fascinated with brands. He had often had the chance to observe this not only in the shop, but also in everyday life. He believed companies fed this desire. However, many people could not really afford these highly priced products. Customers poured into shops like his and demanded nothing but famous brands. Needless to say, everyone knew these goods were not originals. Abdullah explained that they reproduced the paper tags to please their customers and help them imagine they bought the "real stuff". He recounted that he recently passed by a Lacoste outlet and marveled at the long line out the door and the happy shoppers leaving the place with enormous bags. He had seen Lacoste T-shirts and canvas shoes in the weekly markets too. Although in many cases there was nothing special about these products, people seemed not to grow tired of Lacoste garments. Moreover, the fascination with brands seemed so strong that many people paid no attention to the actual products that bore the brand name. Many of their customers seemed not care so much about the quality of their garments. Brand names and logos, written as clearly as possible, mattered more. As he could gather from his friends' discussions, the material properties were the last element taken into consideration when shopping for branded garments in shops like his or fancy malls. "What would one do with the Nike swoosh if the T-shirt looked like a rag two months after one bought it?" he wondered. He grew tired of telling them this was a wrong approach. He used to tell this to his customers. Then he gave up and let the shop assistants to deal with them.

Abdullah angrily predicted a future in which there would be no small brands left on the market, just the coveted famous brands and their imitations. Then he laughed, for this meant that they got involved in a lucrative business. His elder brothers entered this business a few years ago and took him in at a time when he was sinking, after months in which he could not find work. A relatively large group of backers threw money into this venture. Their duty was to keep the business running so that they could pay back their debts and help their relatives and friends.

He reasoned that people in this business were clever. They managed to keep everything running smoothly, despite the illegality of their deeds. They found ways of dealing with the law, bribing lawyers and policemen who paid impromptu visits, learning in time about raids in their area, spreading the news to their friends, and not engaging in business with strangers. "Do not imagine that any peasant who gained some money by selling two cows can enter this business. You do not put three-five lira in your pocket and come here saying 'I will do this business.' Who are you? I can tell you who you are right away! You are Sarı Çizmeli Mehmet Ağa [i.e., an insignificant person]," Abdullah emphasized. If it had not been for such smart persons, the imitation sector would not have progressed.

For him, however, working in this sector was not only a matter of business savvy. He confessed his passion for clothes. He had worked with garments for many years. Upon finishing primary school, about the age of twelve, he started to work, first in a clothing workshop, then in clothing shops. He had always loved to wander around shops and spot the newest trends, and to stroll into streets and look at how people were dressed. He had whiled away many empty moments looking at brand catalogs and fashion magazines. However, Abdullah thought of himself as more an observer than a participant in the enchanted world of beautifully dressed people. His own wardrobe was lacking. He dressed smartly, but he was still far from his ideal image. He observed clothes for two reasons: he did this for himself, for beautiful clothes allowed him to feel he was in touch with the beautiful side of life, and he did this for their business, for knowledge of trends enabled them to quickly fill their racks and hooks with fashionable denim garments.

Abdullah took pride in selling fancy garments. He claimed that out of the thirty or so models displayed in the shop, only some were copies of original models, the rest were his creations, each a mixture of elements he had seen in shops or on the street. "There is hardly a thing worthy of being called an original, anyway," he reasoned. In fashion, everyone copied or received inspiration from other people's work. Turkish companies were notorious for sending their designers to fashion shows in Italy to catch a glimpse of the latest trends and then to reproduce them at home. Moreover, in many cases, there was nothing special about the models people copied or were inspired by. Had it been, they would have respected that work and paid their humble homages to those brands and designers for their achievements instead of multiplying their designs.

Furthermore, Abdullah took pride in selling garments of good quality. His elder brothers took care of the manufacturing side of their business and ran a workshop that employed twenty-five workers. Unlike other shops in the neighborhood, in which remains of the production for export or products that mixed such remains with other materials were routed, their shop displayed only their own garments.

Abdullah insisted many times that, to understand how a business like theirs was possible, even thriving, one should take into consideration all these various elements. He accumulated these observations over a six-year period, in which he worked in a shop that responded to the unsatisfied demand for branded garments.

As this second ethnographic vignette demonstrates, Abdullah does not only legitimize his involvement in this trade and his position in the brand economy. Like Kerim, he points out that fake brands are an inevitable concomitant in a world bombarded with invitations to consume brands, but also inhabited by people who cannot afford the exorbitant prices of these commodities. However, like Kerim and Ismail, he does not only capitalize on this desire for branded goods, but also looks through it. He criticizes designers and companies for promoting their ordinary products as extraordinary in terms of design and quality. He criticizes consumers for not paying enough attention to the material properties of their branded garments. Yavuz, the third man introduced here, delved more into the nature of clothing than the nature of brand.

YAVUZ

In Zeytinburnu, the oldest shanty town of Istanbul, now a center in the trade with Eastern Europe and the former Soviet Union, I made the acquaintance of Yavuz, a man in his mid-thirties. Although he did not have formal education, he was known in his milieu as a fashion designer. He often copied other people's works. His models were frequently copied too. Our common acquaintance thought he was situated at the heart of the activities I was researching in Istanbul and, therefore, could be an ideal informant for me.

Yavuz met us in his office—a apartment in a residential part of this neighborhood. Still lifes in oil and drawings in pencil decorated the walls of this office. A large desk was covered with finished or half-finished sketches of ornate dresses and jackets, all covered with frills, ribbons, and ruffles. He invited us to have a look at these sketches and spoke briefly about the collection he was preparing for a manufacturer who did business with the "Russians." A typical "Russian" customer earned around US$100 per month, but wanted to dress in expensive-looking garments, something like a US$1,000 dress. He created this illusion by heavily embellishing the garments. He declared that different fashion magazines provided the inspiration for this collection, but he insisted that the models were not simply copies. His drawings would be sooner or later copied by someone else, for this was a common occurrence in the clothing manufacturing sector. Pressed by my companion, he admitted that he also copied, whenever his clients came with samples of branded garments and asked him to help reproduce them. However, he pointed out that these were challenging demands and he considerably improved his designing skills from doing these jobs. The garments for which he was asked to prepare patterns and recommend color schemes and fabrics were complicated products. If they were simple T-shirts, these men would have drawn the pattern themselves. Moreover, he would not label fake brands the resulting garments, for this label completely disregarded the work that went into the production of these clothes, his included. As soon as the tea was served, Yavuz took the lead and presented the aspects he considered most relevant for understanding the ubiquitous presence of fake branded garments in Istanbul and elsewhere.

He first launched into a consideration of the emulation of ancient arts that marked the Renaissance period in Western Europe. The best artist was the one who could recreate the ancient sculptures. The best poet was the one who could rewrite the ancient poems. Hardly mastering his complicated sentences, Yavuz pointed out that there was a time in which imitation was highly valued. During the Renaissance, Westerners imitated the Greeks and the Romans. However, later they forgot how much they valued imitation. From here he jumped to the contemporary world and to a situation in which the rest of the world imitated the Westerners. He himself worked in and for this "market of alienation," to use his words. Non-Westerners wanted to clothe themselves in the garments Westerners wore. This desire had been growing stronger and stronger in the past decades. Their customers, Turks and foreigners alike, familiarized through the global media industry with these fashions and brands, insisted on having them. Someone like him had no choice but to copy Western trends. Turkish manufacturers had no choice but to sew these brand names onto their products.

Yavuz stated that these consumers were right. Clothes had always mattered and, in our times, they were constantly told that brands mattered the most. As people often do in Turkey when they want to emphasize something, Yavuz recounted one of the Nasrettin Hodja stories and drew upon the popular wisdom to make his point. The Hodja went to a wedding, but because of his humble appearance, was seated in a corner and forgotten there. Having enough of being ignored, he left the party, only to return in a short while, wearing his Sunday best and his rich neighbor's fur coat. This time he commanded a great deal of respect. However, people soon noticed his strange behavior. The Hodja kept dipping the sleeve of his coat into the plates and whispering "eat my dear fur coat, eat." When someone rose from his seat and asked for an explanation, the Hodja said that he too did what they did, that is, treated the fur coat with respect. For Yavuz, this story was a perfect introduction for the points he wanted to make: the story explained his customers' desire to display wealth, glamour, and Western-ness, the things that determined how they were treated in everyday life. The story also explained the other side of this coin, namely that there must be someone who helps these people fulfill their desire. He, Yavuz, was such a person. These were universal characteristics. However, it was worth pointing them out, for those who fiercely criticized the existence of imitations tended to overlook them. Fake brands existed because people of lesser means needed them to claim a position for themselves in our consumer society.

The other crucial element that needed to be taken into account was the local clothing manufacturers' attitude toward design and branding. For many years, the majority of these manufacturers had been fairly content with doing low-skilled manufacturing work for foreign brands and, truth be told, with selling the excess products and reproducing these branded products. In the past years, although Turkey remained an important manufacturing location in the production of foreign branded garments, Chinese manufacturers had become a serious competitor both on the legal and illegal side of the clothing manufacture. Things had been changing for the worse in Istanbul, and contracts with foreign clothing brands had become increasingly difficult to obtain. This situation, Yavuz believed, would force local manufacturers to establish their own brands. Some had already achieved that, and there were now many good garment brands on the market. Their success abroad was an entirely different matter. Yavuz doubted many foreigners had heard of Turkish brands, with the exception perhaps of Colin's Jeans and Mavi Jeans. The majority, however, lacked the financial capital this enterprise required. However, he had high hopes for himself, now that the local companies had discovered the importance of design. Fake brands existed because local manufacturers—other people of lesser means—earned enough from legally manufacturing and illegally reproducing foreign brands.

I met Yavuz one more time for a life history interview. He spoke at length about the many hours he spent drawing during his school days, about how he invested his pocket money in paper, pencils, and colors, and about how he got more money than his siblings because he was a good boy. At first, his parents were pleased to see him sitting quietly in his room and drawing. At least they had one child they did not need to worry about. His other siblings were having normal childhoods hanging out on the streets of their neighborhood until late at night, much to his parents' dismay. However, when he told them he wanted to be a painter, their attitude changed drastically. His soft-hearted mother kept saying that painters had always been starving and that she did not want her dearest child to be one of them. His father, who had carved his way out of a Kurdish village to a low-ranking officer position in the army, did not even want to hear about such plans. Good for nothing ideals, the father said over and over. He reminded him that they lived in a society where making money was highly prized. The man with no money in his pockets was not a man at all. The man with a business, a car, and a house was more of a man. His father tried hard to talk him out of this because this was not a profession. His parents eventually succeeded and put him off the idea. Yavuz did different jobs. Two in particular were worth mentioning. He worked in a printing shop and grew familiar with different types of paper. He worked in a café and managed to convince the owner to name it Van Gogh Café, after his role model. In this way, he earned his living. He also learned what it was like to not get to do the job you loved doing and be forced to do other things.

One day, a few years ago, somebody he vaguely knew through one of his brothers told him that a person with drawing skills could earn good money in the clothing industry. He saw an opportunity to do what he had always wanted to do and went for it. At first, one of his responsibilities was to accompany a man who combed the market in search of remains from the official production that could be reused in the manufacture of other branded garments. His job was to use his imagination and decide on the spot what could be combined with what. Moreover, he had to select whatever items he considered useful for drawing sewing patterns. The man taught him how to distinguish between fabrics and how quality feels, familiarized him with the local clothing industry, and introduced him to many people, now useful contacts for his own business. Then he spent most of his time in the office, drawing sewing patterns and trying his hand at his own models. Today he has a reputation in this market and his own office on whose door anyone can read "Fashion Designer."

As this last ethnographic vignette demonstrates, Yavuz uses a different strategy to legitimize his involvement in the market for fake brands. He presents himself not only as someone who copies and imitates, but also as someone who is copied and imitated. He introduces himself as someone who learned his profession on the periphery but could easily move to the center and put his designing skills to other uses. Like Kerim and Abdullah, he emphasizes the professional and personal investment in the trade in fake brands. He positions himself on the margin of this activity, not truly involved, but improving his designing skills. This double position not only affords him a different perspective, but also contributes to his indecision about how to explain and who to make responsible for the presence of fake brands.

LEGITIMIZING THE FAKE BRAND

The people introduced here, and many others I met during my fieldwork in Istanbul, argue that the fake brand has its own legitimacy. Their arguments are structured around the following themes: the materiality of objects, the morality of prices, and the social legitimacy of activities. These people point out that in a manufacturing site in the global brand economy the branded commodity comes in authorized and unauthorized versions and the illegal objects might be identical or almost identical to their legal counterparts. Moreover, they stress that the legal objects or at least parts of them might be incorporated into the illegal objects. On one hand, these possibilities demonstrate the limits of the legal understanding of these objects, in particular the claim that the illegally manufactured item is necessarily of a lower quality. On the other hand, the very possibility of manufacturing unauthorized products, which come dangerously close to the authorized versions, drives companies to pressure for the global recognition of intellectual property legislation. The law becomes the only means to separate identical or almost identical commodities. These possibilities show that the value of the fake is not only the unauthorized duplication of a brand name, but also a well-produced object. Therefore, materiality is invoked to support the argument that the fake brand has its legitimacy.

These lines of reasoning echo Baudrillard's (2001) discussion of the different "orders of appearance." Under intellectual property law, the fake branded commodity belongs to "the first order of appearance," its relation to the officially branded goods being that of a counterfeit to an original. The first-order simulacrum never abolishes difference, its main characteristic being an always detectable alteration between semblance and reality. My informants point out that the fake brands belong to "the second order of appearance," that is, the order of the serial production. The relation between the objects of a series is not that of an original to its counterfeit. It is neither analogy nor reflections, but equivalence and indifference. In a series, objects become simulacra of one another. In other words, the law delegitimizes these objects as illegal copies and these men legitimize them as licit copies.

Second, these people emphasized that, at least in the area they are familiar with, that is, the manufacture of standardized clothes, the high prices charged by brand owners are illicit. These garments are relatively easy and cheap to manufacture. However, the prices of originals are kept high to cultivate brands' prestige and satisfy consumers' desire for prestige commodities. These people emphasize that this situation affronts a sense of a moral economy. They discuss the presence of this diverse materiality in terms of fairness. The price of the inauthentic object is closer to the manufacture costs, better reflects the quality of the products, and clearly illustrates the ease with which brands can be reproduced at low costs. The morality of price further supports the argument that the fake brand has its legitimacy.

Third, these people stress that the inauthentic object has social legitimacy. The manufacture and trade in what are legally fake branded garments represent a viable outlet for their financial needs. Manufacture and retail are morally defensible activities because, unlike outright stealing, they require their own labor. Engagement with fake brands might be accepted and acceptable if it represents a reasonable means of alleviating poverty and a source for gaining advantages over the entrenched economies that exclude many. This logic was fully articulated by a brand lawyer I encountered in Istanbul. The lawyer recounted that shortly after he began working as a brand lawyer he raided the basement of a building on the periphery of the city. The cold, badly lit place served both as a living area and a workshop to a young man, his pregnant wife, and a small snotty boy. They had only one sewing machine and used it for sewing fake brand labels on plain T-shirts. Some three hundred pieces were found piled in a corner. "I pitied them," the lawyer confessed. He confiscated their products, but, impressed by their poverty, took no legal action against them, even proposed to personally compensate for the confiscated goods. Years later, he learned that counterfeits of a foreign clothing brand he was representing in Turkey had been located in a factory. He rushed there with a search warrant. A black Mercedes parked in front of the building and the sartorial elegance of the man who ran that business were, to his mind, clear signs of the large scale of that business. Some 20,000 pieces of counterfeited garments were confiscated. The real surprise was the identity of the man. He recognized the lawyer and reminded him that they once met in a ramshackle basement. This time, the lawyer fined him a significant amount of money and sentenced him to two years in prison. This story concurs with Hosein's argument (2009) that as well as formal law there is a general sense of fairness by which people see means as justified by ends. Moreover, they point out that the inauthentic object acquires a form of social legitimacy as a response to an unsatisfied market demand that brand economy has generated in the first place. This is in accord with Siegel's observation that producing and consuming fake brands is not about defying authority, but about "creating a sort of authority for oneself" (1998: 57).

Furthermore, they emphasize that the state also recognizes its social legitimacy and therefore only occasionally and situationally represses these activities. The way many of my informants talk about their work illustrates this conception. They describe it as a game of hide-and-seek. Most of the participants in this game hide. The manufacture and, to a certain extent, distribution, take place in secluded places. As happens in the game, someone has to go to look for people and objects. "Brand agents," usually former policemen, infiltrate the underbelly of the clothing industry and collect information about the level of accuracy, quality, quantity, production capacity, and locations. They also gather information about the unauthorized distribution of export excess, these products being originals, according to some definitions. They sell this information to intellectual property law enforcement agencies. "Small fish" would not do. "Sharks" doing large-scale business are hunted most. Moreover, as happens in the game, someone has to be the victim. Raids are organized, fines are paid, and sentences are served. Nevertheless, business is thriving, generating jobs and income, including in the less-privileged areas of society.

Keyder's discussion of the integration/exclusion of migrants in Istanbul provides more evidence in support of these claims. Those migrants who settled down in Istanbul during the national developmentalist period benefited from and, at the same time, were able to contribute to the rather smooth functioning of various formal and informal mechanisms of social, economic, and political integration. The crucial element was the possibility of acquiring a house. The moral economy of housing—access to land and housing, first as illegal squatter housing, later to be legalized in exchange for political allegiance—served as an "ersatz institution" that facilitated the integration. With the shift from developmentalism to neoliberal capitalism and the accompanying changes in the labor and housing markets, these mechanisms of integration lost their efficiency. Migrants were once seen as poor people. Since the mid-1980s, they have been portrayed as "invaders of public property and beneficiaries of unfair privileges" (Keyder 2005: 130). The ethnic composition of the recent waves of migrants played a role in the construction of this image too. Most of these people are unskilled Kurds from eastern and southeastern provinces of Turkey. The clothing industry, the largest manufacturing sector in Istanbul, is by far the most welcoming sector. It allows these people to earn a living through involvement in legal and illegal activities. This might be a reason behind the state's tolerance of these activities. To conclude, these are the main lines along which the people introduced here, and many others I encountered during my stay in Istanbul, legitimize the fake brands and, consequently, their engagements with these objects. They argue against the assumptions about objects and people who engage with them that the mainstream understanding of fake brand carries, that is, the ideas that the objects are inferior material forms and that people are deceivers profiting from the hard-won popularity of brands as well as consumers' naïveté.

CONCLUSION

In the legal understanding, the fake brand is not what it is claimed and presumed to be. Its existence is illegal and its materiality is deceptive. This chapter has shown how engagements with these objects are experienced and reflected on in relation to the fake-ness and the brand-ness in fake brands and, in the case of fake branded garments, their materiality as clothes.

The chapter has demonstrated that inauthenticity is an elusive attribute. It has illustrated when, why, and how the classification of objects as fake brands is opened to negotiation. Under the gaze of authorities, fake brands should become unauthorized, illegitimate and, therefore, inauthentic. However, for the right price, this transformation can be avoided. "Brand agents," brand lawyers, and various state agents might include or exclude certain objects from the category of fake brands, depending on how well this inclusion or exclusion serves the interests of various parties, theirs also taken into account. Moreover, it has shown that the characterization of objects as fake brands and the attendant assumption about their inferior materiality are contested and dismissed. In a manufacturing site in the global brand economy, the diversity of material forms of different degrees of similitude and various qualities is enormous. The law tries to squeeze this messy materiality into two categories, that is, originals and fakes, and to convince people that fakes are necessarily of an inferior quality. People familiar with the underbelly of the clothing industry strongly disagree. The variety of objects and the very materiality of particular objects might be at any time invoked to challenge the assumption that fake brands are inferior and, more important, to call into question the very category of fake brand. These people do not only bring to the fore these more or less identical objects, but also point out that originals are in many cases ordinary objects that can be easily and cheaply duplicated. They emphasize the paradoxes, anxieties, and elaborations inherent in the construction of mass-produced branded commodities as authentic objects. Therefore, fake brands are inauthentic only in the eyes of certain people and only in certain moments and contexts.

The chapter has also shown that in the underbelly of the global brand economy the realization of brand is seen as dependent on the materiality of the products. People who work in the clothing brand economy—they might be situated in its illegal side, but this does not prevent them from learning about and criticizing the workings of the legal side—argue for the importance of substance and materiality and not of semiotics and signification. They pride themselves in providing good quality, like the original. They urge consumers to focus on materiality. They teach consumers how to distinguish quality and to base their attitude toward brand on an appreciation of its material realization. They argue that the significance of brand is related not to the brand itself and the exaggerated claims, but to the attendant materiality that accompanies the brand. Moreover, through their encounters with customers from different strata of their society and various countries, these manufacturers and sellers play an active role in the constitution of the meaning of brand on the periphery.

The chapter has also offered examples of the meanings these fake branded garments might hold for the people who engage with them as producers and sellers. For Ismail, they could be cherished clothes in his own wardrobe, in models that suit his taste and materials that keep him warm. For Abdullah, they could be smart garments that help him stay in touch with the bright side of life. For Yavuz, they could be garments he himself has designed, evidence that he is finally doing what he has always dreamt of doing in life. However, the chapter has focused more on the efforts of such people to influence consumers' construction of the meaning of brand and on the justification of this role through their ability to look behind the glamorous façade of brand.

The Elusiveness of Inauthenticity, The Materiality of Brand: Fake Branded Garments in Romania

In Romania, branded garments can be purchased in locations other than brand stores and authorized outlets. These might be shops and booths in a commercial area on the periphery of the capital city, or market stands and shops in towns and villages all over the country. Many of these garments fall into the legal category of counterfeit. In this country, laws for the protection of different forms of intellectual property have been used since the late nineteenth century. After the Union of the Romanian principalities in 1859, the process of constructing a modern state included a thorough reform of the legal system. The first law regarding copyright was passed in 1862, as part of the newly introduced Law of Press. Trademark law was put in effect in 1879, Romania being the first country in Eastern Europe to introduce such a law (Romiţan 2010, 2011). More than a century later, Romania renewed its legislation on intellectual property. As an EU candidate state, Romania became subject to the "Copenhagen criteria." This involved the adoption of the Community acquis, that is, the entire body of EU law, including intellectual property rights legislation (see also Linden 2002). Harmonization of intellectual property legislation with EU laws has become an integral part of integration into the European Union.

This chapter demonstrates that inauthenticity is an elusive attribute: it might be recognized and refuted when it refers to objects; it might be recognized, negotiated, or feared when it affects the activities that circulate these objects; it might be acknowledged and agreed with when it refers to the illegitimate nature of the large-scale presence of these objects; and it might be recognized or not and might matter or not when it refers to the garments in one's wardrobe. Moreover, this chapter shows that the brand-ness in fake brands might prompt reflections on the nature of brand. These reflections demonstrate that the realization of brand depends on the materiality of the branded commodity and illustrate why this matters for people who construct their identities and articulate their notions of true self through engagements with garments that others might label as fake brands. The structure of this chapter is comparable to that of the previous chapter. In the first section, fake brands are situated within the political economy of their distribution and their presence is discussed in relation to local concerns about informal economy. In the second section, fake brands are situated within individual wardrobes and their acquisition is analyzed in relation to clothing decisions and consumption strategies.

The ethnographic material included in this chapter was collected in two different settings, a peripheral commercial area in Bucharest and a provincial town in south Romania. At the beginning of my fieldwork in this town, I tried to elicit local definitions of fake brands. The reactions were rather bitter. A young man, who wore a fake Calvin Klein jacket during our meeting, snapped at me: "So you came to research how we dress in Chinese and Turkish clothes! And to laugh because we tog up in fakes!" Another reckoned that counterfeited clothing "lacks beauty and cannot be loved. You can feel whether you are wearing a genuine or a counterfeited garment. Well, maybe you only subconsciously realise this," and concluded, "either way, people will not be eager to speak about this with you." A woman admonished me: "I can tell you what a counterfeit is: they copied the model, but they used low quality fabrics and accessories. But you know you cannot wander around the town and ask such questions, do you not?" These reactions were directed toward the insider/ outsider. My interlocutors imagined I was turning my nose up at the garments that predominated on the local market and deriding and judging them for their consumption of fake branded garments.

To avoid criticism and rejection, I presented an enlarged research agenda and declared an interest in clothing as an aspect of everyday life. I investigated sources of clothing, preferences, relationships to materiality, notions of quality, the dialectics between the aspirational and the actual, and the search for the normative in clothing choices. I gradually understood the importance these people attributed to clothing and the efforts they put into and the pleasures they took in dressing well. Many times fake branded clothes and accessories turned out to be possessions that people were willing to talk about. Once it was a pair of blue jeans that a mother bought for her daughter, reasoning that the words written in rhinestones added the touch of glamour a party outfit needed. The shop assistant told her the words were actually a brand name, but she was not impressed. For her, the rhinestones were the most important detail of that garment, and it was from this point of view that she introduced the story to this anthropologist. On a different occasion, it was a pretty Prada purse bought because of its good enough quality and good price. The owner found out from the anthropologist that the word was actually a brand name. At other times, fake branded clothes were included in the stories people told to make me understand the importance of clothing. To give an example, a fake branded item appeared while my interlocutor was explaining the importance of clothing in social interactions.

To illustrate his opinions, he recounted a failed attempt at passing as an orphan and, consequently, benefiting from travel concessions. He had a fake card that identified him as an orphan, but in the end could not fool the ticket inspector because of his good-looking garments. He wore a brand new jogging suit, but could not openly declare his clothes were fakes. He realized their cheapness could not be invoked as an argument in support of this claim. The inspector saw the good-looking clothes, not the fake branded garments. In these discussions, the fake brands, recognized or not, declared or not, were valued as "affordable brands" and "new clothes" and devalued as "cheap things that have invaded our market," depending on persons and contexts. From a different perspective, these stories revealed attitudes toward brand.

I also visited the commercial area in Bucharest that was the main source of clothing for the inhabitants of this provincial town. For two months, I often traveled to this area as the companion of a local petty trader, who supplied her shop from this place. I observed how the trade worked and how new arrivals were transformed into the latest fashion through the combined efforts of traders and sellers.[1] I stayed in Bucharest for a while and ventured on my own to research the area. I was not only lost in the hustle and bustle, but also rejected as a researcher. People working in this quasi-illegal place often had hostile attitudes toward me.[2] The few friendly and talkative traders pointed out that complicity in illegal activities "places all of us in the same boat" and that talking to me could be a risky enterprise for them. As attempts to engage vendors in longer conversations failed, I changed my research strategy to an unassuming one, wandering the area for hours and days in a row, and then writing down moments objectified by my anthropological gaze. These were fleeting glimpses of a hectic world, caught while I was strolling through the alleys, stopping to look at this and that stand, eavesdropping, and interviewing by comment. I pieced together various impressions, for example, different ways of exploring this commercial area, the garments of the visitors, ways of selecting the goods, retorts, exclamations of delight or disappointment, until I felt saturated in this experience. I also made extensive use of journalistic reports on this area.

As a regular visitor of the market, I became a source of information for people in this provincial town, who had neither time nor money to travel there. Cristiana, for example, who is introduced in this chapter, constantly wanted to be informed about new arrivals. On these occasions, she shared with me her considerations about this place, either positive images of a place full of desirable things or negative images of a dangerous place inhabited by villains of all sorts. I also shared my knowledge of the darker side of the market. The general opinion was that the place is somewhat "rotten." As the fires that frequently occurred in the area, especially in Europa market, were a topic extensively covered in the mass media, they were often the starting point in such comments. Interviews and casual conversations about clothing choices conducted in this provincial town also supplied a wealth of data, as the garments most of my informants wore originated in this commercial area.

FAKE BRANDS

In Romania, many of the people I encountered during my fieldwork indicated a huge commercial area on the outskirts of the capital city as the main source of counterfeited commodities. Official reports and journalistic investigations about this area and the presence of counterfeits in Romania suggested the same.

This area has grown in the vicinity of an open-air market named Europa, which was established at the beginning of the 1990s for the newly arrived Turkish, Kurdish, Arab, and Chinese petty traders. Europa market expanded rapidly, as tables and plastic sheets conquered meter after meter, inside and outside its designated perimeter, and enthusiastic traders made use of every nook and cranny to display their merchandise. In time, some of its parts have fallen into decay, consumed by fire, eaten away by rust, conquered by rubbish; others have been refurbished, the rusted booths replaced with standard stands and small shops and the alleys paved.

One of my informants, who has been coming to this market for many years, describes its transformation as follows:

> At the beginning, there were a few booths. People just spread plastic sheets on the ground. And people rummaged through these piles. The Gypsy sat on the edge of the pile, screaming "three pairs of underwear" for I do not know how much. I remember once I was looking for trousers but, because my size is so difficult, I thought I would better try them on before buying. This was a real problem back then. The Gypsy woman kept telling me not to be ashamed, take out my trousers and try on her pair. In the end, I gave up. I tried the trousers on, there, in sight of everybody. Women hesitated before doing this, looked behind those booths for a place to hide. Things have changed for good, the place is better now, even if newcomers find it hard to believe. Some parts are clean, with decent stands, some even have a dressing room. The stands run by the Turks. One can shop there and feel okay. One does not need to go to the huts and the Chinese sellers and muddy his shoes or have his wallet stolen.

Today Europa market represents only a tenth of an enormous commercial area. New commercial spaces were established in its vicinity, from rows of identical kiosks to container-like buildings divided into equal booths. Amidst them sit SamExpo, a two-story construction advertised as the biggest deposit of textiles in Bucharest; City Shoes, a long metal building, nowadays eaten away with rust, inside which the smell of shoes is stifling; and City Town, a narrow construction with one row of concrete tables on each side. The newest buildings are five red hangar-like buildings, named the Red Dragons 1–5, and the Megashop, a poor version of a mall, all part of the future China Town Romania. In spite of their names, they accommodate the same mixture of Chinese, Turkish, Kurdish, Arab, Romanian, and Gypsy shopkeepers and shop assistants and offer more or less the same merchandise but at higher prices. The civilizing crust added to justify these prices includes not only the resemblance to a supermarket, but also free shuttles connecting the area and the city, flower beds, benches, artesian wells, restaurants, dressing rooms, escalators and elevators in the Megashop, things inconceivable a few years ago. "You have made the right choice," a banner hanging from one of the Red Dragons informs visitors. Promotional materials claim that the Megashop is "the biggest commercial centre in Romania" and offers "the lowest prices on the market." Once I heard two visitors spelling out the naked truth. Stopping in front of such a banner, one of them commented: "the lowest prices on the market, indeed, and the worst goods in Romania." His companion agreed with him: "Indeed, you put it very well." Then he continued: "But still? Prices lower than in Europa? I do not think so," he firmly stated.

Since the early 1990s such commercial areas have flourished all over Eastern Europe and the former Soviet Union. They represent "a form of continuity between capitalism in the past, socialism in the past, as well as capitalism in the present" (Sik and Wallace 1999: 697). They incorporate the medieval tradition of agricultural and artisanal fairs and institutionalize the flight-ready markets of the socialist period, which were so important for

the distribution of goods during that period of shortage, but at best tolerated by the socialist state and ideologically condemned as places of profit making and criminal activity. In the postsocialist period, trading has become a more open and more acceptable activity, though "post-socialist societies still struggle to come to terms with the clash between deeply ingrained moralities and the daily pressures, opportunities and inequalities posed by market penetration" (Mandel and Humphrey 2002: 1). Various factors account for their development during the postsocialist period, from the dismantling of the socialist retail sector, the retreat of the state from its position as principal provider, and the sudden dismissal of the trade agreements between socialist countries to the opening of borders, the decrease of the standard of living, and the growth of consumer culture. These markets are characterized by different degrees of formalization and bring together traders of different ethnicities, resulting not only in new forms of interethnic relations, but also resentment and animosity (Czakó and Sik 1999; Hann and Beller-Hann 1992; Hohnen 2003; Humphrey 2002; Kaneff 2002; Konstantinov 1996; Pedersen 2007; Sik and Wallace 1999; Spector 2008; Yalçın-Heckmann and Demirdirek 2007). Though there is a growing regional differentiation, Sik and Wallace (1999) argue that these markets roughly play two different roles in the local economies. They might be a supplement to and a substitute for formal retail. In Central Europe, these markets have become increasingly regulated and restricted and have been normalized as a supplement to formal retail, more or less like their counterparts in Western Europe, some even turning into tourist attractions. In other places, where more people take the opportunity this trade offers for earning a living and more people are price-hunting consumers, these markets represent a substitute for formal retail.

This commercial area on the outskirts of Bucharest offers a wide assortment of goods of domestic and foreign origin. The following description includes expressions my informants used in our conversations about this place. These commodities range from clothes (including piles of "flawed T-shirts" and crumpled items that "smell like a soaked dog") for women and men of any age (including Romanian garments for old ladies, "a rare merchandise these days"), for any occasion (including funerals, "coffins next to bridal wear, for so it is in life anyway"), to household wares and interior decoration items (including "Chinese rice straw hats, as if we really needed them!"). There is a concentration of certain items in some places, for example the wedding articles manufactured in Romania and Turkey in a corner of Europa market or the Chinese home textile sectors. Prices are fixed, however bargaining and compliments as only the Gypsies can make are part of the specificity of Europa market. Boasting the Romanian and Turkish origin of the merchandise is a presentation strategy often employed by Romanian and Gypsy stand owners ("we have Romanian merchandise"; "factory price"; "we have only good

merchandise from Istanbul, branded goods"; "they are more expensive because they are better, merchandise produced by Turks, if you do not like it, go
and buy polyester from the Chinese"; "have a good look, my dear, the Chinese
do not manufacture such things, they make plastic, synthetic, they do not
have cotton"). This is a direct illustration of a hierarchy that places Chinese
commodities on the lowest level because of their perceived inferiority.

To evaluate the materiality of these goods, the visitor has to rely on personal knowledge, expectations of materiality, and knowledge that circulates
among fellow customers and petty traders. Discussions with sellers are not
the most informative, for the Romanian shop assistants are clueless themselves and reluctant to share opinions based on personal evaluation, and
the foreigners are hard to trust and approach given the language barrier.
In this respect, the area is indeed a bazaar, wherein, as Geertz writes, "information is generally poor, scarce, maldistributed, inefficiently communicated,
and intensely valued . . . The search for information one lacks and the protection of information one has is the name of the game . . . [T]he primary problem
is not balancing options, but finding out what they are" (1979: 124). There is
no information available on the quality of these products and, in the case of
garments, the size does not always follow the standards to which people are
accustomed. Therefore, customers have to find their ways of evaluating materiality. They value natural fabrics, consider them superior to artificial ones,
and thus stigmatize the latter and associate them to an inferior social status
(see also Schneider 1994). However, this is mainly at the aspirational level,
for finding such products is another matter, and most of them doubt such
things can be found here. The sellers in Europa market try to convince their
customers that they really have such products, screaming at the top of their
voice that they sell "good cotton." Nevertheless, in this impressive accumula-
tion of objects, there seems to be something for everyone.

Imported goods arrive here via various transnational trading routes. The
now limited "suitcase trade" and the more lucrative large-scale import trade
with Turkey are among them. The "suitcase trade" began in the early 1990s
with petty traders from the former socialist countries pouring into Istanbul in
search of merchandise, especially garments and leather goods. "The common pattern has been to engage in intensive, short-term, opportunistic and
hectic activity, often involving performative creativity yet hardly sustainable
through time" (Yalçın-Heckmann and Demirdirek 2007: 8). From the beginning, this trade has been based on a fiction. Petty traders pretended they
were tourists. At customs, they declared that the goods they carried were for
personal use or presents and the customs officers accepted this declaration
in exchange for money and goods (Eder 2003; Keyder 1999; Konstantinov
1996; Yükseker 2004). Today, this has been partially replaced by institu-
tionalized informal trade carried out by import and export companies and

travel agencies (Davidova 2010; İçduygu and Toktaş 2002; Pelkmans 2006).[3] However, as I could observe during my trips by bus, plane, and train between Istanbul and Bucharest, petty traders still travel to Istanbul. Bus drivers informed me that their number decreased dramatically at the beginning of the 2000s, when many Romanians could easily find work in other European countries. Then, when finding a job abroad was not that easy, some returned to this trade. They estimated that every day eight to ten buses traveled between different Romanian cities and Istanbul. Gypsy traders based in Europa market also claimed they traveled to Istanbul on a regular basis.

Every day except for Sundays hundreds of customers from all over the country pour into this commercial area. "People go in and out continuously. It is utterly crazy. It looks like a lunatic asylum," one of my informants emphasized. This image can be compared with that offered by Geertz: "to the foreign eye, a mid-Eastern bazaar . . . is a tumbling chaos . . . sensory confusion brought to a majestic pitch" (1979: 197). The pathways are thronged with people, to the point of becoming claustrophobic. The clamor is often pierced by deep cries. "Excuse me," pronounced in the Turkish way, with the accent on the first syllable, can be heard everywhere. Sellers in Europa market scream "cheap" in all possible tones. Gypsies cry out flattering descriptions of their wares. Turks cover everything with a thick smoke of cigarettes. Chinese give everyone broad grins. Every day this place accommodates a chaotic flow of people, parcels, and means of transportation. In postsocialist Romania, this area has become part and parcel of everyday life, an important source of consumer products and a resource for people who earn their living by engaging in shuttle trade.

As I could observe during my visits to this commercial area, fake branded goods, most of them garments, represented a tiny part of this material world. To give a few examples, on an alley in Niro market, I turned toward a shop-keeper who shouted at the top of his voice that he had fashionable garments for young women. When I approached his stand, his voice sank to a whisper and he began listing the famous brand names these garments carried. I told him it might be dangerous to sell these goods back at home. He assured me nothing would happen if I sold the clothes under the counter and to trusted customers. In a peripheral place, I chanced upon a booth crammed to the brim with "famous brands," as advertised by the smartly dressed seller. The offer included garments, perfumes, sunglasses, bags, wallets, belts, and shoes. The following branded names were available: Dolce & Gabbana, Versace, Calvin Klein, Gucci, Channel, Armani, and Victoria Beckham. The seller engaged in longer conversations only with smartly dressed customers and dismissed others as too poor or ignorant about brands. Annoyed at the way he treated her, a woman told him this was not a reasonable strategy in a place frequented by petty traders. "This is not a mall," she told him. "I left my home town at 3 o'clock in the morning and came all the way here to buy things for my shop. And here I find an idiot who looks down me because I wear tracksuit and running shoes! I wear real Gucci at home, you idiot." In a Red Dragon, I saw a shop assistant quickly filling a customer's bag with Louis Vuitton purses. He assured the woman these were all new models and there would be even more to choose from when his boss returned from his business trip to Istanbul. In front of a stand in Europa market, two young men laughingly asked the Chinese seller if he had Abibas sport shoes. When offered Adidas shoes, they insisted they wanted Abibas. Then they moved on to another stand, leaving the Chinese seller lost in translation. On an alley in Europa market, I followed a police team who checked the papers of the stand owners and informed them that they sold counterfeits and, therefore, another team would arrive in a short while to pick up the whole stock. Some of the sellers took this announcement lightly, while others defended themselves as poor people trying to earn a decent living. One seller of fake branded jeans annoyed the policemen with his laments. He was told to pay the fine and be grateful that the legal procedures against the selling of counterfeits were not entirely followed. The seller replied that two weeks ago they told him the same. He did pay the fine, but could not understand why he was punished on every occasion. His fellow traders, who also sold branded jeans, did not suffer. The policeman told him laughingly: "Because we like you!"

Fake branded garments manufactured in Istanbul arrive in this market too, sometimes in the parcels of petty traders. However, as I could observe during my trips between Istanbul and Bucharest, this journey is often problematic, the traders having to smooth their way across different border check points. To give an example, when the bus on which I was traveling from Istanbul to Bucharest approached the Turkish-Bulgarian border, a crew member announced that branded garments (*haine de firmă*) meant trouble. He was actually referring to fake branded garments, but called them branded goods like many other Romanians do when they do not intend to disparage objects or offend people. The attendant told us that the European Union regulations were stricter in the case of these goods. A passenger could cross the border with these goods, but he had to demonstrate that he bought them from authorized outlets. The attendant emphasized that nobody on the bus could actually meet this requirement. Therefore, he advised everyone to be honest about the content of their bags, so that the bus drivers knew the exact situation and acted accordingly. If the customs officers opened a bag and found branded garments there, the goods would be confiscated and the bus held at the border in custody for further investigations. The man informed the travelers that they expected a more substantial contribution to the collective bribe from the passengers with this type of goods. A heated debate began, for everyone more or less knew who had branded garments in their bags. Some travelers tried to avoid contributing a larger amount to the bribe. Others expressed their outrage. The debate continued after the safe border crossing, the ones who contributed more demanding a part of their money back. They voiced their doubts about the existence of stricter rules for branded garments. In their turn, the drivers and the other passengers argued that they could still create problems, for the Financial Squad often stopped buses from Istanbul before they arrived to Bucharest and checked papers and goods. On that occasion, nothing happened on the way to Bucharest either. I heard more arguments and counterarguments even in the bus station, while the petty traders were loading their parcels and preparing to return to their homes. It might not be a too far-fetched idea to assume that the transportation of such garments in large quantities from Turkey to Romania is even more challenging.

In this commercial area, these goods, especially the fake branded garments, did not form a homogeneous category, people distinguishing between the goods made in Turkey, of better quality, and those made in China, of lower quality. Moreover, the goods made in Turkey could be further differentiated. Gypsy sellers, for example, offered Nike, Adidas, Puma, Versace, Armani, Gucci, or Dolce & Gabbana and advertised them as "beautiful," "good," "cotton," "quality," "made in Turkey," "made in Turkey in the same factory in which Adidas makes its track suits," and "an incredible bargain." In contrast, Turkish and Kurdish shopkeepers had Dsquared, Abercrombie & Fitch, and G-Star Raw articles, but these brands were less known in Romania at that time and customers included them in the local category of "clothes with writings" or "clothes with wordings" (*haine cu scrisuri*). This is an understanding of brand that was formulated in the first postsocialist years. It is still used by less knowledgeable and/or older consumers or, as in this case, it is used to categorize unknown brands and, simultaneously, to signal that these might not be actual brands. Furthermore, categories overlapped. Such is the case with "Europa clothing" (*europenisme*) and fakes, and Chinese goods and fakes, on account of their perceived common characteristics, that is, illegal manufacture and low quality.

DELEGITIMIZING THE FAKE BRAND

For the casual observer who strolls into this area, fake branded goods make a sporadic appearance. However, in public as well as private accounts, this commercial area, especially Europa market, is presented not only as a place full of fakes, but as a sort of fake itself. I argue that it is not only their actual presence, but also the association between the objects and this place that brings the fake brand to the foreground and turns this commercial area into the main source of counterfeits on the market. The materiality of commodities might raise the issue of the inauthenticity of this area. However, in this case inauthenticity also means not being of Western origin. Many of my informants had confidence in their own assessment of the commodities they could find in this commercial area. They were also aware that that they could easily get things wrong, which was tantamount to being fooled and taking for the truth that which was false. This awareness was made explicit when my informants disparaged the quality of these goods; called them "plastic" (i.e., polyester), "rags," "disposables," and "rubbish"; and deplored the fact that ordinary Romanians, themselves included, have no choice but to use them.

Such disparaging remarks are common occurrences in postsocialist countries. Humphrey (2002) points out that in Russia people speak bitterly about the Great Trash Road that brings flimsy clothes and trinkets into the country from "Asia," a vague concept that includes China, Turkey, and the states of Central Asia. Patico (2005) presents the hierarchy that Muscovites use to classify the goods available on their market: Western goods are the most prestigious, followed by Russian goods and, on the lowest level of this hierarchy, the products of Asia, by which they usually mean Turkey and China. Pedersen (2007) notes that Chinese goods are considered of such low quality that they are not worthy of being sold in a "modern" Mongolian market. Creed (2002) observes the disappointment of his Bulgarian informants with the quality of the new market, which they see as being invaded by "garbage" from China and Turkey. Instead of the flawless Western material world they dreamt of for so long, the "current profile of goods ... is an indictment: cheap goods from marginal countries peddled by social inferiors" (Creed 2002: 5).

My informants articulated a feeling of betrayal of the promise of a Western material world especially in moments of anger at, for example, having to wear a T-shirt covered in bobbles, having to wash by hand most of their clothes because of their nondurable fabrics, although a brand new washing machine occupied half of the bathroom, or having to explain that one has the taste but lacks the money and so goes for Europa goods of dubious origin and fragile materiality. People judged these products as inferior in quality, style, and durability, a judgment that tended to imply a wider moral argument and that applied to all goods simply by virtue of the fact that they were sold in this area.

Moreover, the material culture of the location in itself might raise the issue of inauthenticity of the market. Despite the subsequent transformations, it is at a far remove from the shops that materialize European-ness, as people know or imagine it, and that represent the only legitimate present. Illustrative of this attitude are the following remarks. They belong to people I have encountered in the commercial area or accompanied on shopping trips to this place. Mirela, a woman in her early forties, a filing clerk in a Bucharester bank with a good income, told me that she liked to shop in the Megashop. She found it cleaner and safer than the neighboring areas. In addition, the

prices were attractive. However, she laughed at the garlands of artificial flow-ers, the rough pieces of concrete in the artesian well, and the Easter bunnies that greeted her in August. She reasoned that the model for this decoration must have been a mall, but the result was a cheap fake. To give another ex-ample, Maria, a divorcee in her early forties who visited the area quite often, emphasized: "I wander around and buy whatever I need or like. But there comes a moment when I feel disgusted by the dirtiness and shoddiness of this place and I have to leave." Andrei, a secondary schoolteacher in his late twenties who earned a modest living, pointed out that the efforts to refurbish Europa market would have been laudable, had it not been for the insistence to construct hangar-like buildings and give them ridiculous names, such as City Shoe and City Town. To give a final example, Mihai, a teenager who visited Europa market only once in the company of his parents, spoke about the overwhelming feeling of shame he experienced when walking around that dirty and disordered place. For these people, and many others, as I could hear numerous times in my conversations about this commercial area, this place was a false façade that occupied the space where a Western reality was expected. The place was an embarrassment that reflected Romanian society as a whole, now busier than ever with overcoming its ambiguous position between West and East.

This is, to a certain extent, a perspective shared by many postsocialist citizens. To give an example, in her study of an open-air market situated on the outskirts of the Lithuanian capital city, Hohnen (2003) notes that people who speak about the country's return to Europe try to keep this market on the margins of their society. With its products of Asian origin and resemblance to a bazaar, this market materializes the discrepancy between the imagined and the real. These areas are not welcomed in countries where a Western reality has been long expected. This perspective makes more sense when compared with the way Western commodities have been understood in the socialist and postsocialist world. To give an example, Rausing shows that, in a remote Estonian village, at the beginning of the 1990s when Estonia was no longer part of the Soviet Union, people consumed expensive Western branded household products in order to "return to normality." The concept of normality is related to the notion of Estonian-ness, which is, in every respect, opposed to the notion of Russian-ness. As she writes, "as a nation, the Estonians thought that they knew exactly what they would have been like if the situation had been 'normal'... Consumption of ordinary branded products in a 'normal' way could be seen as rituals of inauguration; signs of belonging in the West rather than the East, the 'normal' rather than the 'not-normal'" (Rausing 2002: 140). Therefore, such a commercial area cannot possibly relate to the notions of Romanian-ness and Romanians' legitimate longing for European-ness. Ordinary people like my informants admitted there were boundaries and that these needed to be protected, for at stake was their reputation and that of their fragile state that joined the European Union but, in a sense, still knocked at its doors.

Furthermore, beyond the inauthenticity of place and goods, there is another issue that pertains to this place as a whole. It is its association with a different kind of inauthenticity, that of crime. There are, within and in relation to this place, objects, activities, and individuals that ordinary people place beyond a boundary that they feel separates that which is legitimate from something else, murky and dangerous. My informants glimpsed what lay beyond not only from direct experience in the area as petty traders and consumers, but also from stories that circulated in the public space. The following account owes much of its substance to journalistic investigations and official reports. My informants had enough knowledge of these accounts, however, to confirm their own suspicion that this place had an illegal character.

Journalists reported that underworld characters, renowned for their criminal activity, were involved in the running of this area, either as managers or racketeers. The administrators' grip on the area was said to be tight, disciplining or scaring traders into a certain pattern of conduct. However, internal affairs surfaced spectacularly on a few occasions, proving that the power structure was contested. To give an example, in 1999, this peripheral area of Bucharest became a battlefield on which the bodyguards of the managers of two zones, the old Europa and the newer Niro, clashed. During that war, the manager of Niro market miraculously survived a violent attack. Apparently this was not just a war between the Romanian managers, but involved rival Chinese and Arab groups, which fought for their share of this lucrative business. Moreover, the administrators did not only control the inside, but also defied the authorities. Since its opening, building regulations and health and safety norms have been disregarded. Since 1993, no planning permission has been requested. Since 2001, thirty-eight trials have been opened, none of them yet finalized. Taxes have been only intermittently paid. For these reasons, this area, especially Europa market, was often described as a "state within the state." In different terms, this commercial area is illustrative of a more general phenomenon that has emerged throughout the former socialist space, that is, the parceling of sovereignty and consolidation of suzerainties (Humphrey 1991; Verdery 1996). Under this roof, petty traders ran their own profitable businesses. In mundane financial affairs, transgression was the norm: no bookkeeping, double-entry bookkeeping, the rental of stands to third and fourth parties, or the reselling of goods to other firms, at least according to the paperwork.

The cosmopolitanism of the area was often considered an element that contributes to its criminal character. The Turks, Arabs, or Chinese were not exactly the businessmen expected to invest in postsocialist Romania. The small-scale businesses they ran were not considered as representative of the real market economy, but façades for illegal activities. Xenophobic remarks were far from rare ("The booths should be all pulled down and the Chinese should be kicked out of our country!," "Europe does not want the Turks. Why should we let them prosper in our country?" "For how long are we going to tolerate this Chinese filth in our capital city?"). Moreover, the association between criminality and Gypsies, the outsiders par excellence, was well established, in Romania as elsewhere in Eastern Europe.

The state did battle against the criminal activities carried out in this place. To give an example, in September 2006, representatives of different institutions, among them the Metropolitan Police, the Civil Guard, the Guard for the Environment, the Metropolitan Sanitary Veterinary Directorate, the Financial Squad, and the National Authority for Consumer Protection, raided Europa market. The outcome was impressive: 138 offenses, 93 persons under investigation, 445 fines, seizure of goods, 24 foreign citizens without residence permits, and 11 illegal workers. However, the overall effect of such raids was rather insignificant. That year, authorities estimated that the annual tax evasion amounted to €300 million.

Journalists often portrayed this area as a case of gross corruption. They were exceedingly fond of juxtaposing official reports on the attempts to regulate it with scenes from the raids in the area. Their favorite snapshots were the empty administrative offices, the locked booths, the deserted alleys, and the groups of Chinese traders chit-chatting in the alleys, patiently waiting for the law to leave the place. These journalistic reports demonstrated that the state was not a unitary actor. Numerous individuals played their part in this "civilizing" project, their own interests often colliding with those of the state.

As I was able to understand from our conversations, many of my informants had some knowledge of the darker side of this commercial area. Moreover, on many occasions, talk of this darker side turned into talk of mafia. As Verdery argues, mafia is not only a real phenomenon, that is, "a group of people privatizing power along with state assets," but also an active symbol, "one that has spread because it symbolically expresses many of people's difficulties in the transition" (1996: 219). These people shared a feeling that there was more unknown and unknowable about this area, equally or even more dangerous than what they could gather from journalistic and official reports on the transgressions that occurred in the area.

In this way, the idea of the inauthenticity of this area is formulated in relation to the materiality of its commodities, the material culture of the location, and the falsehood of the criminal activities carried out in this area. Moreover, as the previous paragraphs demonstrate, facts and representations are effortlessly combined in these discourses. The area is thus understood as being itself a sort of fake.

Given the discrepancy between its bazaar-like appearance and its name, Europa market stands at the center of this portrayal of the area as a sort of fake. My informants emphasized that there was nothing European about Europa market. Journalists expressed this sense of falseness when they portrayed Europa market—and I combine in this paragraph the most frequently used images—as a grotesque place, where boorish and aggressive customers jostled and shoved, roared furiously, used coarse language, wandered lost in the hustle and bustle of the labyrinth of narrow, suffocating, dirty alleys and amidst heaps of rubbish sniffed at by stray dogs and traversed by rats, in search of cheap, low-quality Chinese and Turkish merchandise of any imaginable sort, displayed heaps on heaps, on tables and on the ground, and offered by dirty Chinese and persuasive Turks and their ostentatiously dressed and insolent Romanian assistants-cum-mistresses, inhabiting, together with pickpockets and other villains, this anthill, this wasps' nest, this boil, this infected area, this hotbed of business fraud, this battlefield of mafia clans, this absolute squalor, this lice house, this forest of hovels, this paradise of indifference and smuggling, this black market, this poorman's supermarket, this Oriental bazaar, this illegal Europe, this other Europe, this Chinese Europe, inhabited by genuine Europeans, such as Turks, Chinese, Arabs, and Gypsies. Many of my informants were familiar with such images and used them when sharing with me their opinions about Europa market.

A circular mode of reasoning brings together the fakes and the fake market: fake branded goods are thought of as an inevitable presence in the fake market. The following examples of the ways in which not only my informants, but also journalists and authorities linked the fake and the fake market support this argument. Again, it is Europa market that stands at the center of this line of reasoning. My informants, consumers of fake branded garments or not, journalists reporting on the presence of counterfeits in Romania, and representatives of anti-counterfeiting organizations lecturing on this phenomenon inevitably included a few thoughts about this market in their commentaries. To give an example, while traveling from a provincial town to this place in the company of petty traders, I heard a man telling his companion he wanted to buy an Adidas tracksuit for himself. The other replied, "then Europa is our next destination. We can find there what you want for a good price." To give another example, a journalist wrote a piece about changes in the legal system as part of the EU integration process, including a more comprehensive approach to intellectual property laws. He entitled the article "Europe demands that we give up Europa wholesale market." To give a final example, representatives of the Romanian Anti-counterfeiting Association REACT did not miss an opportunity to point out that 60, 70, or 80 percent of the counterfeited goods in the country were sold in Europa market and that the existence of such a breeding ground of law infringement was simply outrageous.

My informants, who prepared me for my first visit to the area; journalists, who investigated the underworld structure behind this thriving area; and authorities, who described the numerous transgressions taking place in the area—all referred to the commercialization of counterfeits. To give an example, one of my informants told me not to venture on my own to Europa market and definitely not to buy anything from there. As she put it, "they only sell counterfeited and smuggled things over there." To give another example, whenever the mayor discussed Europa market as the biggest problem in his borough, he mentioned the infringement of intellectual property law in his list of hot issues. To give a final example, a newspaper article, entitled "all roads of tax evasion lead to one place: Europa market," included a section on "'genuine' counterfeits" and presented the latest raid in the area and the seizure of counterfeited goods. In such a circular mode of reasoning, the inauthenticity of objects and the inauthenticity of the commercial area mutually reinforce each other.

Therefore, various observers, either ordinary people such as my informants or authorities and journalists, who use this circular mode of reasoning, tend to see inauthentic objects everywhere. They would describe this area as the main source of inauthentic objects on the Romanian market. This argument is not meant to dismiss official reports and journalists' investigations, which demonstrate that this area is an important source of counterfeits. It is rather intended to point out that other elements play a role in the crystallization of this idea.

This mode of reasoning invites the recognition of the legal definition of fake brand. This commercial area is considered an anomalous presence. It is a quasi-illegal venture with tax evasion and turnovers of millions of euros. Illegal economic activities might be accepted and acceptable, if they represent a reasonable means of alleviating poverty and a source for gaining advantages over the entrenched economies that exclude many. However, if these activities go beyond this purpose—and there is a general sense that in the case of this commercial area they do—then they are seen as criminal by the general public, not just the law.[4] In this case, the inauthentic market is condemned as illegitimate. Inauthentic objects are part of and partake in the illegitimacy of this commercial area. The inauthentic market and the inauthenticity of objects in it are united as areas of criminality. Consequently, the fake brand is condemned as illegitimate. These people draw a line beyond which fakes do not relate anymore with the compromises between right and wrong that characterize the actual world, but go beyond them and turn into something dangerous and scary. They take a public stand in areas where the inauthentic object lacks any form of legitimacy.

The characteristics of this commercial area affect not only public attitudes toward fake brands, but also private attitudes toward brand (see also Manning and Uplisashvili 2007). This commercial area is an important source of commodities. However, as the next section illustrates, there is a fear that some of these commodities are routed to shopping galleries and malls and even turned into branded goods through the fraudulent addition of brand names and logos. Many stories circulate in the public sphere. Knowledgeable consumers spot commodities from this commercial area in more prestigious locations. Badly paid students augment their salaries by secretively selling in posh shops goods they bought from this commercial area. Shop assistants speak about their bosses' habits of sewing brand names and logos onto cheap garments they bought from this commercial area. Developing skills for evaluating materiality and using them even when shopping in brand outlets are often seen as the best strategies to avoid being cheated by unscrupulous shop owners and assistants.

This discussion has referred to the abstract category of fake brand. The next section presents engagements with particular objects and focuses on the impact of these intimate relationships on the apprehension of fake-ness and brand-ness in fake brands and brands. If the previous pages discussed fake brands within the context of their distribution, the next section places fake brands within the intimate domain of consumption.

ENGAGEMENTS WITH FAKE BRANDS

As the previous section has demonstrated, in certain circumstances, people might recognize the legal definition of fake brand and might distance themselves from such objects. However, this is a partial recognition, the focus being on the element of criminality in an economy of scale, not on the characterization of objects as inferior and of people as deceivers. In other circumstances, the same people might engage with such objects. They find a place for fake branded garments in their wardrobes and reflect on or ignore their fake-ness or brand-ness from the vantage point of their intimate relationships with objects and sensuous apprehension of their materiality. Fake brands become garments and people select or do not select them in relation to concerns others than those circulated through the cultural and legal understanding of fake brands.

Garments have "an indisputable intimate relationship to persons" (Keane 2005: 183). They are the main medium between people's sense of their bodies and their sense of the surrounding world. They are an essential element in the construction of an image of the self for projection outward to the social world. Deciding what to wear is one of the most common means through which people try to control presentation as well as interpretation of the self (Banerjee and Miller 2003; Woodward 2007). A material culture perspective informs this discussion of clothing choices. Here garments are not treated as mere representations of inner selves and social relations, but considered in their own right by paying attention to the forms, qualities, and practical capacities through which they constitute persons and relationships (Küchler and Miller 2005).

The following ethnographic vignettes are constructed around particular shopping trips and present consumption activities through which commodities are singularized and appropriated by people pursuing projects of self-fabrication (Miller 1987). I also draw on information I gathered on other occasions, when I discussed those decisions in particular and clothing choices and consumption practices in general. Not all the vignettes focus on fake branded garments although the shopper has such types of clothes in his or her wardrobe. In this way I try to respect the local nature of these objects. They are garments like any other garments and are purchased for more or less the same reasons other items in the wardrobe were purchased. In some vignettes fake brands appear because these consumers mentioned them, not because I singled them out or asked about them in our conversations. They are part of these wardrobes and entered there for reasons and through strategies employed by that individual in other cases too.

These vignettes are based on conversations I had in a small provincial town in south Romania. The individuals I introduce here did most of their shopping in the town's high street and some adjacent commercial areas. The high street was lined with dozens of small shops, many of them rooms in ground floor flats and booths placed in courtyards and was connected to two other important commercial areas. At one end of the high street stood the food market, next to which stands and shops with other types of goods were built over the years. At its other end, there were two rows of standardized booths and the former socialist mall, now partly supermarket, partly clothing manufacturing workshop. The majority of these shops and stands offered goods that originated in the Bucharest commercial area presented in the previous section of this chapter. Fake brands were included in their stock of clothing, shoes, and accessories. To give a few examples, a discolored Dolce & Gabbana T-shirt hung in the window of a small shop as a means to attract young fashion-conscious customers; a pair of Columbia shorts carrying the label "authentic replica" was advertised by a stand owner as the best-selling item of that month; caps embellished with the Nike swoosh were displayed in a men's clothing shop; Adidas white socks were offered at a market stand; and bags and accessories carrying well-known brand names were sold under the counter in a shop with formal, evening, and cocktail dresses for women.

None of these individuals stands for a particular social category. However, they are typical inhabitants of this provincial town. Like many other inhabitants, they proudly report that people in their town put great store on clothes. This was often expressed through an idiom: "we might be poor but we are also proud" (*săraci, dar fudui*). Like many other inhabitants, they also criticize this preoccupation with appearance. Other idioms were used to convey disapproval: "Some wrongly believe that it is better not to have anything to put on the table than not to have anything to put on" (*mai bine să nu aibă ce pune pe masă decât să nu aibă ce pune pe ei*) and *sărăcie cu luciu*. The latter is a pun, coming from *sărăcie lucie,* a Romanian equivalent for dire poverty. The adjective *lucie,* which translates as "lustrous," indicates both lack of possessions and cleanness. The expression *sărăcie lucie* is used to describe dignified poverty. However, this expression is often transformed into *sărăcie cu luciu,* which translates as "poverty with luster." This second expression is used to express disapproval of acts of consumption that are improper for the relatively poor. In this context, "luster" stands not for emptiness and cleanliness, but for extravagance and excess. Like many inhabitants of this town, they wonder whether or not "clothes make the person."

Moreover, these individuals are typical in another sense too. Like many inhabitants of this town, they are aware that in the postsocialist period commodities have become an important medium through which people construct themselves and shape their social relationships (see also Caldwell 2002; Fehérváry 2002; Humphrey 2002; Patico 2002). However, they question the capacity of brands to play an even more important role in these processes. During socialism, by encouraging, but being unwilling or unable to satisfy the desire for consumption, the socialist regimes prompted an "equation of Western standards of living with self-value and dignity" (Fehérváry 2002: 369). Brand was an attribute of goods originating from the capitalist systems. Socialist citizens also learned about or imagined these Western standards of living through their sporadic engagements with branded commodities and their seductive forms and sensuous qualities. Socialist brands also existed, but their presence reflected particular politico-economic agendas. Branding functioned as a mechanism through which the socialist state controlled and guaranteed the quality of products. Moreover, branding did not really involve carefully appealing to consumers' needs and desires. Brand identity was not ready available, because branding and advertising were subject to particular economic and political conditions. "In the absence of these readily supplied brand identities . . . Eastern consumers frequently had to construct their own product identities, often in the form of 'product biographies,' based on their own particular experiences with the products" (Blum 2000: 235). The socialist state produced a range of branded goods, mainly common luxuries, but presented them as materializations of the socialist concept of cultured consumption (Manning 2009). Although appreciated, the socialist brands were nevertheless considered mere imitations of the capitalist brands, of which most socialist consumers had some knowledge.[5] Today, brands are no longer metonyms of the "Imaginary West" (Yurchak 2006). Branded goods are on display in luxurious retail oases, shopping malls, and supermarkets. They are attached to and differentiate real commodities, index specific producers, address certain consumers, and play a crucial role in strategies of social distinction. However, these objects, especially garments, are too expensive for many Romanians, the majority of the inhabitants of this town among them.

Like many inhabitants of this town, the individuals introduced here wonder whether or not "brands make the person more of a person."

MONICA

During our first meeting, Monica pointed out that she could not help me with my research. She thought her wardrobe was small, but contained all she needed. She had her own style and was not interested in the latest trends on the market. She wore her garments until they were worn out. In brief, she was someone who did not make "too much fuss" about clothes. Soon after this visit, I met Monica by chance in the high street. She wanted to buy a pair of denim trousers for herself and invited me to accompany her. We entered different shops, but she could not find the plain jeans she had in mind. Monica reminisced about the period when a friend with similar taste ran a clothing shop. She became a regular customer and filled her wardrobe with smart casual garments. She was still wearing those garments with great pleasure. That was the only period in her life when she really gave in the desire to wear beautiful things and bought more than she needed. Then the friend moved to another town and the person who took over the business changed the profile of the shop, much to her disappointment. While she was sharing these thoughts with me, we entered her favorite shop. The shop was run by a Chinese family and offered the same range of garments and home textile as other shops run by Chinese petty traders in the Bucharester commercial area. In this shop Monica finally found what she wanted: a pair of straight leg dark blue denim trousers. However, there was one detail that she did not like. Two letters, D and G, were embroidered on one of the back pockets. She hesitated buying the trousers not because of their fake brand, but because of their silver embroidery. To assure me that this was the case, she told me that she still had at home an old pair of Levi's jeans she bought from a market stand. The seller brought his merchandise from Istanbul, so those jeans must have been manufactured in some illegal Turkish factory. She bought them for their acceptable quality, and this proved to be a good choice. In the end, Monica found a solution to this problem and bought the trousers. She would cut a worn out pair of jeans and would cover both pockets with darker denim.

On this and other occasions, Monica declared that she wanted to be comfortable with her clothes and herself. This resonates with Woodward's definition of comfort as "incorporating both a physical sensation of comfort and, in a more nuanced sense, the notion of aesthetic fit: the wearing of clothes which are 'you'" (2007: 73). She dressed according to her heart. A university-educated women in her late thirties working as head clerk in a career reorientation center, Monica preferred to wear sports clothes. Instead of fitted garments and high heels, which objectified the predominant notion of femininity, she wore classically cut jackets, trousers and jeans, plain T-shirt and shirts, cardigans, jeans, and flat shoes. Her style was locally defined as "sport," if not "modest," as opposed to "elegant."

Moreover, she stated she was an "ordinary consumer." To better illustrate this idea, one day she focused on the striped cardigan she wore. It was most probably a Chinese product from the commercial area on the periphery of Bucharest. She bought it from a small local shop because she liked its color palette and its comforting wool. Some of her coworkers wore the same model, and a neighbor and her aunt had identical cardigans. Another example she used to illustrate this idea was the blue Lacoste T-shirt her husband had worn for a few summers. He bought it from a man who traveled to Istanbul regularly and peddled his wares in various local institutions. All his work colleagues bought at least one T-shirt from this peddler. Her husband liked it very much. "This is why I call myself an 'ordinary consumer.' I wear what ordinary people in my town wear." Monica pointed out that some of her friends and coworkers tried to avoid shopping in their town as much as possible. They preferred to renew their wardrobes with fashionable clothes from the shopping centers in Bucharest. For her, this was an unconvincing strategy of differentiation, the garment and not the person standing out, the outside and not the inside of the person being valued. This also demonstrated their incapacity to distinguish good fabrics and spot smart clothes in the places perhaps less prestigious, but more appropriate for their actual financial status. Much to her annoyance, these people labeled clothes available on the local market as "rubbish," even though many of the things they bought originated in the same peripheral market in Bucharest from where local shopkeepers supplied their shops.

One day, toward the end of my stay in this town, by way of conclusion, Monica recounted a heated argument she had with a good friend. She asked this friend to accompany her to the Chinese man's shop. The woman refused, reasoning that she would make a fool of herself if someone saw her entering such a low-profile shop; even worse, one ran by a Chinese man. Another time, when she dropped by at this woman's house and was shown the new things this friend bought from a shopping center in Bucharest, Monica could not keep her mouth shut anymore. She pointed out that the new pajamas and slippers were identical to the ones the Chinese shopkeeper sold for a far better price. She stood by her opinion that a smart consumer had to admit that the Romanian market had been invaded by Turkish and Chinese products. Instead of taking questionable decisions and spending money unwisely in shopping galleries and malls, this smart consumer learned to distinguish quality and explored the low-end market in search of wearable garments.

Monica reminded her friend that she herself thought that shopping galleries and malls did not guarantee the quality of goods and she herself feared that she bought counterfeits for the price of originals. So many rumors circulated in their town. People recounted how such and such acquaintances of theirs worked as a shop assistant in a mall and supplemented her income by selling in the shop articles she purchased from Europa market; or that they went to the basement of the mall to have their trousers shortened only to find the seamstresses busy with sewing brand name labels on nonbranded items. Moreover, brand did not guarantee the quality of goods. Their own experience with branded garments nourished this anxiety. Monica recalled their conversation about the difference between their Breshka tops, one bought in Bucharest, the other in Madrid. The first lost its shape and color quickly. Monica's top still looked brand new. When she washed and hung it on the line, the fabric turned stiff, as if washed for the first time. That day they reached a somewhat embarrassing conclusion: the branded goods available in the Bucharest shops looked like inferior counterfeits. Furthermore, Monica recalled what a neighbor, a seamstress in a local clothing factory, told them about counterfeits. The factory manufactured Benetton T-shirts and hoodies from synthetic fabrics, so the workers reasoned they were manufacturing counterfeits. There was no doubt about that, for a famous brand such as Benetton could only use high-quality fabrics made of natural fibers. Monica mentioned other disturbing facts: the carpet in front of their wardrobes, which was always full of bobbles; the fear of using the washing machine to clean many items in their wardrobes; and the fluff that gathered around the machine. She concluded by emphasizing that the friend spent money unwisely only to feed her sense of superiority and urged her to become a smart consumer and make her decisions based on her own evaluation of fabrics, not on price, location, or brand. The friend, in turn, disagreed on almost every point. Their friendship survived, but with a tacit agreement not to discuss consumption choices again.

This vignette shows that fake brands might enter a wardrobe for reasons other than the expected ones: in this case, it is not their brand-ness that motivates consumption, but their perceived quality; in one example, the brand name would be even covered, for it does not fit a consumer's preference for plain denim trousers; in addition, in this case, it is their affordability and availability that motivates consumption; fake branded garments are "ordinary" goods for "ordinary consumers"; fake brands are new garments for smart thrifty consumers. Moreover, in this case, the possible characterization of these garments as fake brands is acknowledged, but disregarded. The inauthentic object has a functional legitimacy. While others worry about the counterfeit, Monica evaluates its fabric, form, color, and style and decides whether or not it is worth buying. While others worry about being in fashion and dressing well to accrue prestige and the respect of others, she wants to be comfortable. The assumptions about objects and people that such a characterization carries are not taken into consideration when it comes to particular objects; however, the assumption about the inferior materiality of the counterfeit is recognized in relation to the abstract category of fake brand. Ironically, this assumption affects the understanding of brand. In this inverse logic, branded garments executed in synthetic materials are assumed to be counterfeits. This vignette illuminates local reflections on the nature of brand: its extraordinariness, when people believe there is such a thing, is located in their materiality. Brand means quality; however, it is the consumer who has to evaluate the product and decide if this is the case or not.

The vignette offers evidence in support of an argument that has gradually taken form in this and the previous chapter: the significance of brand is related not to the brand itself, but to the attendant materiality that accompanies the brand. The next vignette follows a similar strategy and presents particular clothing decisions and general reflections on the nature of clothing and the nature of brand. Fake branded garments make their appearance in a way that respects their place in the wardrobe. They are shown to be a matter of pride as well as a matter of embarrassment.

CRISTIANA

During one of my visits to Cristiana's beauty parlor, I briefly met an overly dressed woman. After her departure, I was told she had spent about an hour there and the only purpose of her visit was to parade her newest garments and inform the others about the new arrivals on the market and about her plans to buy such and such article. This was not the first time I heard Cristiana and her customers gossiping about this woman. However, this time Cristina used the occasion to reflect aloud on her own consumption practices and unfulfilled desires.

She confessed that she envied women who managed to buy something for themselves almost every month. She was particularly jealous of this client of hers, a housewife married to a policeman, who wandered around town all day long and bought on credit whatever pleased her heart. On payday, her husband went to the shops and paid for her purchases. Cristiana wished she were lucky enough to have sufficient money for herself, household, and business. The only thing Cristiana had bought for herself that year, and it was already October, was a pair of bleached jeans. She liked the way they fit her, their color, and the shining embroidery on the back pockets (i.e., a flowery model on the left side and D&G written in silver thread on the right side). While she presented us these trousers as the newest item in her wardrobe, Cristiana noticed the brand name inserted in one of the embroideries and pointed it out as another touch of glamour. Her customers admired the jeans and she was obviously pleased.

Cristiana stressed that she did not envy her sister-in-law, who also bought clothes quite often. Her sister-in-law, who lived in Bucharest, bought only branded clothes and bragged about this every time they met. She reproduced her sister-in-law's standard line, adding an affected tone: "I respect myself. I buy only quality things. I buy brands." Cristiana believed that one paid more for the name and fame attached to branded garments than for their actual quality. She often observed her sister-in-law's clothes and could say that not everything was of quality, not to mention extraordinary quality. The police-man's wife did not pretend she was superior, her sister-in-law did. Cristiana extrapolated from this example and declared that buying brands was all about status. People wanted to demonstrate that they had succeeded in life. People wanted others to see the labels of their clothes, but could not really support their arguments through the quality of their branded garments. The other women who took part in the conversation agreed with Cristiana and added their own observations about branded garments and their proclaimed and perceived quality.

On this and other occasions, Cristiana emphasized, as if to console her-self, that she did not really need many new clothes. She spent most of her time in the beauty parlor, wearing old items underneath her white overall. Moreover, occasions to dress up were rare in such a small town. Once she pointed out that her husband was of a completely different opinion. He in-sisted that she invest more in her wardrobe precisely because she ran a busi-ness. He though that what would really impress people, especially those with whom she planned to do business, was not her thriftiness, but the image of success that smart clothes permitted. Cristiana thought he was wrong. One day the husband came to the beauty parlor, joined the conversation and, at an opportune moment, voiced his opinions about her clothes and what a suc-cessful businesswoman in her late twenties should wear. Much to her annoy-ance, some of customers-cum-friends agreed with him. That day it dawned upon her that she had the reputation of a stingy person.

Cristiana could not say in front of everyone what came to her mind at that moment. Later she shared with me an embarrassing experience. Dur-ing their last holiday at the seaside, her husband's idea about clothes and success took a ridiculous form. He wanted to impress their new friends and thought that one way to do it was to wear branded clothes. He could not really afford the Adidas things these new friends wore, and therefore found a less costly solution. He went to the local market and bought a pair of shorts and two T-shirts, all bearing the Nike swoosh. One day, when they were playing vol-leyball on the beach with their friends, a peddler showed them his wares. The source of her husband's shorts and T-shirts became evident. The peddler told them that these good-quality garments were manufactured in Istanbul in the same factory that produces original Nike articles. Nobody said anything, but Cristiana still remembered their smiles and her husband's red face.

One day Cristiana asked me to accompany her. She was going to a wedding and needed to buy something new for this occasion. To avoid being looked down on or, even worse, being refused to allow to pay in installments, she changed her worn out clothes and put on her bleached jeans and a long coat. Before we set off, she warned me that she planned to enter every shop and check every booth and market stand. This strategy contradicted her opinion about the uniformity of the local clothing market. I often heard her complaining that shops and stands offered more or less the same merchandise. As she put it once, "a shopkeeper found that cardigan in the Red Dragon or Europa market and he presents it to us as the latest fashion and expects us all to buy it." In reply to my observation, Cristiana said that the prices of identical objects varied from shop to shop. One possible explanation was the time of purchase from the Bucharest commercial area: if a shopkeeper bought his or her stock when these goods were novelties in the area, then the price he or she charged at home was higher; if a shopkeeper bought the same commodities a few weeks later, then the prices were lower. Cristiana was after good prices. She did the same when she bought her newest pair of jeans. She wandered around until she found the best price for the model she fancied. Her only regret was that she could never find the time to go herself to Bucharest and buy good things for less money. "If it is true what people say, that Europa closes down because we joined the European Union, then we are in trouble. What on earth are we going to wear in this case?" Cristiana shared with me her concern.

Our first stop was Metropol, the shop where people in this town went when they wanted to dress up. However, nothing there fit her budget and taste, so we headed for other places. After two hours of walking up and down the high street, liking this and that, but thinking of dressing for less, she chose a bright blue pencil dress with a flaw in the fabric and, thus, a price reduction. Cristiana counted on her neighbor to fix it, for the woman was a seamstress renowned for her mending skills. For matching shoes, we went to Masai, the kind of "pile it high and sell it cheap" shoe shop with products manufactured in China and bought wholesale from Europa market. Beige pointed high-heeled sandals were exactly what she was hoping to find. Cristiana was over the moon. She got a new outfit for even less than she planned to spend. She reasoned that the beige satin shawl with yellow parrots and blue flowers that her mother found in a secondhand shop would go very well with the dress and sandals. She concluded, with a touch of regret in her voice, that "here we dress in beautiful, but cheap clothes." However, she was confident that she would come across very well in this outfit. "Here people judge you on what you wear." She dropped by a friend's place to show off her new dress and sandals and indulge herself with a café frappe and a long chat.

This vignette shows that fake brands might enter a wardrobe for the expected reasons, that is, their brand-ness and affordability. However, the risk of embarrassment is a component of this decision: people inside or outside an individual's social milieu might interpret this clothing decision in derisive terms. Moreover, this vignette demonstrates that fake brands might enter a wardrobe for reasons other than the expected ones: a pair of fake branded jeans is a new item in a wardrobe; it is cherished for this reason, not for its brand-ness; it is a new item that elicits intense joy and expands on the self; its fake-ness is completely disregarded. The fake brand has its functional legitimacy. In this case, for a woman who carefully budgets her money to expand her current business, fake brands as cheap clothes are a truthful choice. Furthermore, this vignette illustrates attitudes toward brand. For people of lesser means, consumption of brands is conspicuous consumption. This is understood as "an activity where the actors have a clear and specific goal in mind: to impress others and thereby gain their esteem or envy" (Rowlands 1994: 148). However, these people declare that they can be impressed if the garments are of good to extraordinary quality and emphasize this is rarely the case. For them, beautiful cheap fake branded clothes are just as good for objectifying the self and staging individual success, if this is what one wants. This is new evidence for the argument that the significance of brand is related not to the brand itself, but to the attendant materiality that accompanies the brand.

This vignette also illustrates positions on the nature of clothing. Cristiana wants to succeed in life, but longs for pecuniary solidness, not sartorial lightness. Clothing does not represent, for her, a form of capital. Money is, as she insists, "entombed in the wardrobe," instead of being put to good use. Clothing does not constitute the material culture of success. The next vignette presents a different opinion and shows how this works as a framework in which both fake brands and brands are understood.

BIANCA

Bianca invited me to keep her company during her walks around the town and, thus, learn for myself what she liked and how she chose her clothes. These were long walks, because Bianca took great pleasure in visiting shops and searching for what she called "beautiful things." Bianca had always wanted to dress herself in beautiful things and to have a big wardrobe. Being poor, she had to wait for better times. In a way, these times had come. Upon finishing her undergraduate studies in the capital city, Bianca returned to her hometown, got married, and found a good job. Since then, she had been play-ing a game. The main rule of this game was to buy clothes only on payday.

From time to time, this rule could be broken. There were days in which Bianca opened her wardrobe and found it was rather lacking. Her clothes—scarves hanging on the door, black pieces at the back, and colorful items at the front—remained mute, unable to express or create the desired frame of mind. "I open the doors of my wardrobe and look and look at my clothes, but nothing winks at me. I like nothing. Then I panic and on the first occasion I go out to buy something. Any small colourful thing does. Then I am over the moon." However, this only happened a few times.

On the other days, the "normal" ones, she visited the shops as often as possible and made a list with the things she liked among the new arrivals. Then she thought about how she could combine the clothes she had with the ones she liked and imagined places and occasions where she could use these outfits. She searched for tops, cardigans, dresses, and scarves in lively colors, as this was the part of the wardrobe that allowed her to experiment and combine. Everything else was black, the color she thought best suited her plump body. Upon seeing something she liked on the street, Bianca did not shy away from asking whether the item was bought from the local market. She did not like to buy her garments on credit, but preferred to play her game, dream about clothes before actually buying them, and buy them only on pay-day. "When I buy something new, I put it on the moment I get home. Then I lie in bed and let it become part of me. Then it is mine. I can smell myself on it, so to say." Bianca linked these practices to a childhood when clothes were never truly hers, but things her elder siblings wore first and then were passed down to her. The wish list was often long, and daydreaming in bright colors was a good way to spend the time in the dark corner where Bianca's desk was placed. Her main duty was to fill and register credit application forms, a good job were it not for the obligation to wear that brown shirt she deeply disliked. Glossy magazines lay on her desk, but she saw little point in studying them, for the clothes presented there hardly matched the local offerings.

Bianca included only things of "a little bit of quality" on her wish list. "We have not got, I and my husband, anything extraordinary, rather things of a little bit of quality." They were both pleased with what they could find on the local market. However, she admitted that they bought more than they actually needed and she did so more than her husband. "It does not bother me that my mother-in-law says I did not need another cardigan or that my mother is convinced I will dislike in three days the thing I say I adore today. What am I to do if I like it?" Bianca defended herself.

However, her definition of quality did not match that of other family mem-bers. Her mother advised her to buy a cardigan produced in Romania and not one produced in China, no matter how beautiful it was. Other family members

argued that the clothes available on the local market, most of them originating in China and Turkey, lose their beauty quickly, tight-fitting turning into
loose-fitting, thick fabric becoming thin and bobbly. Bianca found such comments curious, as those voicing them actually wore the clothes they said
they would rather not buy. From time to time, they were right. Once she had
to hide a blouse deep in her wardrobe, because she could not admit that her
mother was right and the blouse was indeed a bad choice. "I have only worn
that blouse twice and it has already begun to bobble. Mother told me this
would happen." Moreover, different family members urged her to buy branded
garments. If they really liked so much to be dress smartly and had money
to spend on their wardrobes, they could do this with a few good quality garments instead of many lesser-quality clothes from the local shops. They had
branded articles in their wardrobe, but they were not originals. They bought
them because they liked them and thought they were of "a little bit of quality." Bianca stressed that brand was not the main reason for buying them.
Many of their friends consumed the same garments and this put one of their
friends in a rather ridiculous position. He spent a fortune on his branded jogging suits and trainers and then told everyone that they are originals, for otherwise nobody would have noticed this. Their relatives believed that brand
guaranteed quality. Bianca did not buy this. Her classmates believed in this
myth and made an effort to clothe themselves from the malls, but also endlessly complained about the bobbles, loose trims, and falling buttons of their
branded garments.

When she finally got her monthly salary, only certain clothes were still available, only some items were still desirable to her, and only a few articles could
be acquired within her budget. Nevertheless, she was pleased. Bianca felt
good in her beautiful clothes. They gave her strength and a sense of fulfill-
ment. She could proudly stroll into the streets of a town in which people were
smartly dressed and attentive to the dress of others as well. "In this town we
think that it is better not to have something to eat than not to have what to
put on." She shrugged her shoulders.

This vignette focuses on an individual's relationship to clothes. In this
case, clothes play a crucial role in the conceptualization of a person's success in life. Dressing well is a means of amassing a sense of personal worth
and empowerment. As Woodward points out, in Bianca's case, "clothing, as a
material form, gives [her] the sensation of having a self, including a self with
agency" (2007: 150). As Rowlands emphasizes, in this case success does
not mean escaping from a set of conditions, but rather indicates "a choice of
a sense of self to be achieved" (1994: 147). Having grown up in a relatively
poor family in which clothes were not purchased solely for her, and having recently embarked on adult life as a married childless woman with a good job,
Bianca expands on the self through gifts of clothes that she buys with her

own money, a sign of maturity and prosperity. The vignette demonstrates that fake brands can enter a wardrobe if they fulfill specific criteria, and these do not have to be about their brand-ness or affordability. Fake brands are just as good as any other affordable beautiful clothes of "a little bit of quality." They objectify the "middle" economic and social position to which she aspires. The local market offers enough clothes, inauthentic objects amidst them, that satisfy her criteria. Bianca is confident that she makes truthful choices. She "looks good" and "feels right" (Woodward 2007). This vignette offers new ethnographic material about the interest in the materiality of brands. In this vignette, other Romanian consumers are shown as reflecting on the nature of brand and the nature of clothing and finding difficult to believe the common definition of brand as an extraordinary thing.

CONCLUSION

In the legal understanding, the fake brand is not what is claimed and pre-sumed to be. Its existence is illegal and its materiality is deceptive. This chapter has shown how engagements with these objects are experienced and reflected on in relation to the fake-ness and the brand-ness in fake brands and their materiality as clothes.

The chapter has demonstrated that inauthenticity is an elusive attribute. Objects are inauthentic only in the eyes of certain people and only in certain moments and contexts. It has exemplified how and when the classification of certain objects as fake brands affects the activities of people who trade them and has shown that this impact is rather sporadic. It has illustrated when and why the notion of fake brand is acknowledged and has focused on the local concerns and contexts that convince individuals to publicly distance them-selves from these objects. Moreover, it has illustrated whether or not this classification affects the consumption of these objects. Consumption of fake brands has been typically explained as status emulation. Brands are a status marker. People of lesser means use fake brands in their attempts to signal status. However, this chapter has shown that the affordability of fake brands might give rise to a range of implications and associations illustrative of a more complex picture than that of consumption motivated by mere economic rationality and social emulation.

Furthermore, this chapter has illustrated criteria at work in clothing con-sumption and has demonstrated that fake brands enter wardrobes as gar-ments that meet these criteria. Their brand-ness might be important, but it is not the main criterion; their fake-ness is sometimes acknowledged but usually ignored. Materiality, not only affordability, plays a crucial role in deci-sions to consume or reject these garments. The persons introduced in the last section of this chapter, and many other people I encountered in Romania, do not see them as "copies of things," but as "things" that they can engage with. They see them as garments they can judge in aesthetical and material terms. They regard them as material forms they would feel on their bodies. They picture them in combinations with other items in their wardrobe and evaluate if they can come up with socially successful images. The social and the material are brought together in the acts of choosing these objects. The value of the fake brand stems not only from the unauthorized replication of a brand name, but also from the materiality of the object itself. Together with the reflections on the nature of brand, the debates about the proclaimed quality of branded garments, and the meanings Romanian consumers attributed to brand, this chapter has also provided ethnographic evidence in support of one main argument of this book: the significance of brand is related not to the brand, but to the attendant materiality that accompanies the brand.

–5–

Inauthentic Objects, Authentic Selves

This chapter includes the fake brand in the larger category of inauthentic object. The common notion of inauthentic object implies an intention to deceive: this object is produced and displayed with the intention of making someone believe it is indiscernibly identical with another object. With the advent of modernity, this intention to deceive is further interpreted as an intention not only to deceive others, but also to deceive one's self. People who engage with these objects are portrayed not only as deceivers, but also as self-deceivers who hide from themselves and others who they truly are.

This chapter focuses on this second assumption: people who engage with inauthentic objects are considered self-deceivers. The chapter presents the conceptual links through which this assumption is formulated. However, as authenticity and inauthenticity are intimately bound up in each other's histories, this is just one side of the coin. The other side of the coin is the strong connection that exists between the authenticity of selves and the authenticity of objects: engagement with authentic objects is considered a privileged means to construct authentic selves. This chapter discusses the force that the notion of authentic self has in modern culture and details how the authenticity of self is linked with the authenticity of object. Moreover, this chapter argues that another conceptual pair plays a role in the consolidation of this assumption. These entangled concepts are the authenticity of the center and the inauthenticity of the periphery. This chapter presents this conceptual pair and shows that people on the periphery are inclined to respond to the accusation of inauthenticity implied in this assumption. These are analytic strategies similar to those employed in the second chapter: the aim is to further unpack the notion of fake brand and show the complex assortment of concepts, interests, and concerns at work in the common understanding of fake brand.

Furthermore, this chapter illustrates ethnographically that there are moments and contexts in which this assumption is recognized and experienced as an accusation of inauthenticity. This chapter analyzes the ways people who engage with fake branded garments in the same ethnographic locations introduced in the previous chapters deal with such grave accusations and the ways they authenticate their selves.

SELF-DECEIVERS

In the common understanding, inauthentic objects materialize an intention to deceive. This intention has always prompted moral condemnation. However, with the advent of modernity, this intention to deceive was understood as affecting not only others, but also selves. Engagement with inauthentic objects was an act of falsification, theft, imitation, and impersonation. However, the act also showed something about the actor: it betrayed an inability or unwillingness to create, demonstrated disinclination or incapacity to work and assume risks on the market, and revealed an attempt to construct a false identity through deceptive objects. This actor hid from himself or herself who he or she truly was. This actor deceived himself or herself. This act distanced the individual from the culturally, morally, and legally sanctioned means of living authentically. People who engaged with inauthentic objects were not only accused of deceiving others, but also derided for the deception they presumably worked upon themselves.

Different concepts and concerns played a role in the elaboration of this understanding. One was the valorization of creativity. Creative work was understood as a means to express the authentic self. In contrast, copying and faking were derided as activities that betrayed an incapacity or unwillingness to connect with and present this authentic self. As Baines notes, in eighteenth-century Britain, "copying began to be stigmatised in literary and artistic theory because it represented not only diminution of the original, but a loss of self, authenticity and spontaneity" (1999: 96). The faker could make claims about the authenticity of the object, but not about the authenticity of the self as a site of production. The faker had to repress the self, so that his or her productions could be taken as originals. He or she was derided for trying to conceal the authentic self. Moreover, this was considered a futile endeavor. Traces of the faker's own self were believed to remain legible in the object. These traces would eventually permit the identification of the inauthentic object and the punishment of the culprit.

Another was the valorization of labor. This was celebrated for its capacity to confer a sense of self-worth. Deferred gratification was proclaimed as the only means by which people could build meaningful lives. Fakers avoided this virtuous path for achieving self-integrity. As Kriegel points out, in nineteenth-century Britain, "pirates" were portrayed as acting with "avarice," "impunity," and "unscrupulous morality," as "servile copyists" who showed no respect for originality, as "parasites" who sat "lying in wait to assail their more virtuous competitors," and as "persons of very little character, who did not like to be seen in daylight" (2004: 252–253). As Malton emphasizes, "the forger emerged as an emblematic, if subversive, figure of social and financial relations in the Victorian period, the inverse, as it were, of the ideal embodied by *homo economicus"* (2009: 8). Fraudulent copying of valuable objects and involvement in unauthorized duplication were understood as obstacles not only for living within the boundaries of virtuous society, but also for constructing a righteous self.

This understanding referred not only to the manufacturers of inauthentic objects, but also to their informed consumers (as the second chapter has shown, the misinformed consumers, who were cheated into buying inauthentic objects, were seen as victims; laws were formulated to protect them from being cheated). The number of these consumers grew exponentially as modern commercial culture offered more and more possibilities even to people of lesser means (Orvell 1989). These consumers were derided and condemned for attempting to construct a false identity for themselves. From a different perspective, this criticism illustrated social anxiety about creative self-fashioning and the instability of social categories (Baines 1999; Briefel 2006; Malton 2009). The consumption of inauthentic objects was conceptualized as an act that diminished the possibility of living authentically.

Engagements with inauthentic objects were understood as attempts to live through means other than those culturally, morally, and legally sanctioned. They were believed to result in the loss of one's true self. People who engaged with these objects were accused of falsification, theft, imitation, and impersonation. These were also accusations of the attenuation, if not negation, of one's self. In this way, these people came to be portrayed as self-deceivers.

This understanding has remained with us. It has been circulated around the world through various discourses, from modern discourses about art and the market to contemporary discourses about intellectual property laws. As Dent remarks, "corporate dictums say that piracy in its intellectual and more material forms clearly leads to an inadequate form of consumption, and the repercussions for diverse forms of self-awareness and self-definition are immense" (2012: 660). Such concerned warnings target the consumers. Through their engagements with these objects, the producers have already demonstrated lack of personal integrity.

This conceptual link between inauthentic object and inauthentic self has its counterpart in the conceptual link between authentic self and authentic object. The next section focuses on the second set of concepts. This is another illustration of the idea that the notion of authenticity implies the existence of its opposite, that is, inauthenticity.

AUTHENTIC SELVES

In the modern world, to be authentic, that is, to be true to one's self, is a notion around which many people build meaningful lives. Trilling (1972) links the appearance of the interrelated notions of sincerity and authenticity in Europe with the changes and challenges of modernity.[1] Beginning with the sixteenth century, the view that organized the medieval world was gradually replaced with an individualistic worldview. Every individual could express individuality and not merely a social position. These ideas were elaborated at a time when the strictly hierarchical and highly personalized medieval world was disintegrating under the impact of industrialization and urbanization. In this new context, people could pursue personal dreams of a better life. These possibilities also generated anxiety as to who people really were and whether the roles they played in society corresponded to their true selves. In this context, the notion of sincerity, that is, to be true to one's self as a means of being true to others, was articulated. It became a major preoccupation, if not obsession, for the early moderns. However, this was gradually replaced by an acute awareness that the practice of sincerity as a social virtue inevitably led to insincerity. The privileging of social relationships was abandoned in favor of an intense focus on the self, not as it was presented to the others, but as it truly was, deep inside, apart from the roles people performed in their everyday lives.[2] This intense inward focus was believed to allow for the possibility of constructing a righteous self.

Taylor (1991) explains the crystallization of the notion of authenticity as a moral ideal. At a certain point in modern history, the notion that each individual was endowed with an intuitive feeling for what was right and wrong was put forward. Being in touch with the moral voice within was a means to act rightly. As the turn toward subjectivity grew stronger, this idea was further elaborated. Being in touch with the voice within was seen as something people had to do to be full human beings. In Taylor's reading, it was Rousseau who displaced the moral accent and proclaimed that every individual had to be in contact with his or her self to attain the "sentiment of existence." Moreover, in Taylor's reading, it was Herder who added the Romantic notion of originality in this conceptual chain. Herder argued that every individual had an original way of being human and insisted that each individual had to live his or her life in accordance with this very specific way, and not in imitation of someone else's way or in response to the demands of society. This understanding increased the moral dimension of this notion.

To be true to one's self has remained an important notion, guiding people in their efforts to make sense of the surrounding world and carve out a place for themselves. In the early modern world, the authentic self was conceived in essentialist terms, as an essence that the individual could discover deep within, though not without effort. In the late modern world, this essentialist view has been replaced, or at least counterbalanced, by a constructivist perspective according to which the authentic self is continually recreated by the individual. Either way, "as taken-for-granted meaning systems have been challenged from within and without, human beings everywhere have sought ways to recapture a degree of significance and stability, often enough by inventing or affirming a form of authenticity they can claim for themselves and share with others" (Lindholm 2008: 145).

AUTHENTIC SELVES AND AUTHENTIC OBJECTS

For modern individuals who seek to articulate their authentic selves, one path to achieve this goal is to engage with authentic objects and use them as tools for self-formulation and self-performance. In the common understanding, authentic objects are "original, real and pure; they are what they purport to be, their roots are known and verified, their essence and appearance are one" (Lindholm 2008: 2). The very notion of the authentic object appears with the advent of modernity.[3]

The formulation of the idea that the authenticity of the object merges with, supports, and enhances that of the subject begins with the Romantic conceptualization of the artist as the quintessential authentic being and of the work of art as the prototypical authentic object. Trilling spells out the expectations built around works of art in the modern period: "the work of art is authentic by reason of its entire self-definition...Similarly the artist seeks his personal authenticity in his entire autonomousness...As for the audience, its expectation is that through its communication with the work of art...it acquires the authenticity of which the object itself is the model and the artist the personal example" (1972: 99–100). Lindholm (2002) points out that these expectations incorporate the relationships people had with sacred objects. In the past, people maintained their spiritual connection to the sacred through objects such as icons and relics, which were believed to carry its traces. In the modern period, works of art replaced the sacred objects. People assumed that by engaging with them they could partake in their authenticity. Therefore, works of art exemplarily serve the goal of constructing authentic selves through engagement with authentic objects. They objectify the authenticity of their creators and allow their owners and viewers to partake in this authenticity and, consequently, articulate their authentic selves.

Furthermore, Lindholm argues that the ardent desire for authenticity led people to cast around for other material forms on which to work out their self-definitions. In Lindholm's reading, it was Herder who legitimized this search. Herder argued that traditional societies constituted "organic entities each animated by its own distinctive 'genius'" and, consequently, their material productions "could be appreciated [and, I would add, appropriated] as a reflection of its organic unity and authentic essence" (Lindholm 2002: 333). In this way, the category of authentic object was enlarged to include not only authored objects, but also objects created in places and epochs imagined as unspoiled, uncontaminated, pristine, and genuine, unlike the modern world. These objects had the capacity to bestow authenticity upon estranged modern individuals and generate a feeling of stability in otherwise unstable conditions. Spooner summarizes this modern belief: authentic objects allow modern individuals to "express themselves and fix points of security and order in an amorphous modern society"; moreover, they are used to negotiate "a quality of personality, or how one should be understood and appreciated as an individual by others, and on a scale that has significance only for an individual's sense of social identity, not for the structure of the society as a whole" (1986: 226–227). In this way, the search for the authentic within gradually merged with the search for the authentic without, across social, spatial, and temporal boundaries.

The possibility for owners and viewers to partake in the authenticity of these objects was further guaranteed through the rationalization of the Romantic conceptualization of the authenticity of objects (the second chapter described other elements that contributed to the articulation of this conceptualization of authenticity as inherent in objects; in that chapter the focus was on the proclamation of inauthenticity rather than the confirmation of authenticity). Authenticity was conceived as inherent in the materiality of objects. In other words, authenticity emerged as an objective attribute that could be subjected to scientific investigation and confirmed or infirmed through material analyses of objects in terms of their material properties, design, production, context, and use. In addition, the authority to pronounce such verdicts was granted to experts—connoisseurs, dealers, art historians, archaeologists, anthropologists, conservators, and heritage managers—whose legitimacy and neutrality was guaranteed by their in-depth knowledge and objective methods (Lowenthal 1996). Under the guise of scientific objectivity, the authenticity of objects could be more confidently affirmed. In this way, the belief that authentic objects allow people to articulate their own authenticity was further strengthened.[4]

In recent decades, the objectivist perspective on the authenticity of objects has come under close scrutiny. It has been argued that authenticity is a cultural construct. It has been shown that objects become embedded in various regimes of value, in which their authenticity depends as much on the observer's interest as the object of that interest. It has been proven that originals and their copies can elicit similar experiences of authenticity, as long as the true nature of the latter is not known to their admirers (Holtorf and Schadla-Hall 1999). It has also been demonstrated that the proclamation of the authenticity of objects is never a neutral process (a similar point was raised in the second chapter, although this concerned the inauthenticity of objects) (Bruner 2005; Errington 1998; Phillips 1997). In this understanding, objects have been deemed less significant. It has been argued that authenticity cannot be explained only by reference to the material attributes of the objects. In a constructivist analysis, they can even be ignored. "Having situated authenticity as a cultural construct, it is as if layers of authenticity can be simply wrapped around *any* object irrespective of its unique history and materiality" (Jones 2010: 183, emphasis in the original). Nevertheless, the objectivist perspective on the authenticity of objects as inherent in their materiality remains hegemonic in many contemporary institutions such as museums, markets, and courts of law (Handler 2001).

Capitalism has tapped into the relationship that has been forged between the authenticity of beings and the authenticity of objects and has put forward the claim that the authenticity of selves can be attained and maintained in relation to its authentic commodities. Different sources of authenticity have been drawn on for this purpose, from the materiality of the object itself, its manufacturing process, and connection to certain places and historical periods, to the personality of its creator/owner, the myth of origin, and the significance it holds for its consumers (Brooks 2000; Jenß 2004; Kapferer 2006). No matter what sources of authenticity are drawn on, companies suggest that "those who choose [the proclaimed authentic commodities] gain a real or authentic existence" (Handler 1986: 2). The marketing of commodities as the "real things" is one side of the coin. The other is the attempt to convince potential consumers that their very lives lack reality and their sense of self-truthfulness and self-worth can be gained only through the consumption of these authentic commodities.

Mass-produced commodities, most of them ordinary goods, are singularized through lavish advertisements and marketed as "more real" than the things of everyday life. However, as the material ordinariness of these products remains a problem, a more recent move is toward the "dematerialisation of brand" (Manning 2010: 35). The brand itself leaves behind "the dull, passive, generic, inert utility and materiality of the product" (Manning 2010: 36) and takes on "an enchanting, sometimes religious character" and adds a "spiritual dimension to what used to be 'merely a product'" (Askegard 2006: 96). In this way, authenticity is asserted at the level of brand. Consumers are encouraged to differentiate themselves from others by buying branded commodities that conjure imaginaries of authenticity, originality, and freedom.

A deafening chorus of claims and counterclaims reverberates across capitalist markets, for "consumption has become a way to clutch at the chimera of a genuine and compelling reality that always slips out of reach because there is always another, potentially even more satisfying and convincing reality up for sale" (Lindholm 2008: 57). Chasing this dream of the "really real," one consumes more and more. However, one also believes less and less. The realm of the commercial is forever "wedded to a dialectic between authenticity and imitation" (Orvell 1989: 299). "Consumption of various forms of commodified authenticity has provided anxious buyers with feelings of autonomy, control, community, as well as feelings of distinction, status and self-actualisation in a risky and anonymous society. There is a hidden psychic price tag, as pervasive mediation eats away at all unreflective immediacy, leading to more and more consumption in order to fill the inner void" (Lindholm 2008: 64). The contradiction that everyone faces, brand managers as well as consumers, is to reconcile authenticity and commodification. Thus, somewhat inevitably, one keeps piling up satisfactions and dissatisfactions about the authenticity of self as well as the authenticity of objects. This sense of inevitability and the perpetual oscillation between feelings of gratification and frustration reflect people's ability to endlessly see through the excessive claims for product authenticity, while still being driven existentially to seek their authentic selves in and through these commodities. These ideas have been explored ethnographically in the previous chapters of this book through ordinary people's reflections on the nature of brand and the nature of fake. They are further discussed in the ethnographic sections of this chapter.

PERIPHERAL SELVES

In the modern world, some individuals have been denied the possibility of living an authentic life. The entangled history of the notions of authenticity and inauthenticity contains one more episode relevant for a discussion about authentic selves. This episode refers to the interested overlapping of this conceptual pair with another set of opposites, that is, the center and the periphery. As Taussig (1993) points out, mimesis was projected onto the colonial Other to preserve the distance between the center and the periphery. As Bhabha emphasizes, colonial subjects and objects were portrayed as "almost the same, but not quite," forever trying to cover this distance, but failing each time (1994: 86). In this way, the colonizer proclaimed its own authenticity and the inauthenticity of the colonized. This discursive separation of the world into center and periphery has remained with us, ingrained in cultural logics and reinforced by political structures.

Before I discuss the recognition of this discourse on the periphery, one brief point needs to be made. In the postcolonial order, this discourse is turned upside down and the notion of mimesis is discursively and materially revalorized. Postcolonial critics focus on its metonymical movement and argue that the effects it generates have a negative impact on colonial hegemony (Bhabha 1994). Postcolonial subjects practice a new form of mimesis, that is, an illegitimate mimesis. They turn deception into a means of production and manufacture fakes of every conceivable sort. As Comaroff and Comaroff note, "post-colonies are quite literally associated with a counterfeit modernity, a modernity of counterfeit" (2006: 13). Postcolonial subjects attempt to partake in the magic of the global forms of hegemony on their own terms.

In peripheral settings, local observers themselves often derided efforts at mastering predominant forms of authenticity and lamented the "persistent lack, the irremovable deficiency, the unyielding inadequacy" of their cultures and societies (Gürbilek 2003: 599). To a certain extent, the discourse that proclaimed the center as the locus of authenticity was interiorized in the periphery. An almost automatic disposition to consider everything local as mere imitation of an original that existed in the center haunted the peripheries. A sense of peripheral selves burdened these people. A desire to have authentic selves and inhabit authentic nations mobilized these people.

Turkey and Romania are both "belatedly modernized" societies (Jusdanis 1991); however, they followed divergent paths toward modernization. Turkey embarked on an ambitious process of voluntary Westernization, a more intense process of the Ottoman Empire's engagement with the West. This has been a complex process, marked not only by the desire to be the other, but also the fear of losing one's self, the deep-seated mistrust toward the other and the rejection of the "other" Other—that is, the Middle East. The peculiarity of this process reflects particular circumstances. As Silverstein shows, "the sum of the later Ottoman experiences of strategic reform, peripheral incorporation into industrial capitalism, and nation-state formation has profoundly imprinted the Turkish present and experience of modernity" (2003: 513). The Ottomans took active part in the European transformations, and did not simply look in from a distance. Moreover, as Çağlar Keyder points out, unlike in colonial settings, the elites who envisaged this "modernization from above" "did not feel any colonial resentment; they did not see themselves as belonging to a world different from the one they sought to emulate" (1997: 42). One of the first ways to imagine the new Turkish national identity was through the formula of a synthesis, and not simple emulation. Turks, who had their own valuable culture, could and had to borrow from Western civilization. However, as Ziya Gökalp, one of the major architects of the project of modern Turkey, pointed out, form and method could be borrowed from the West, but not essence or content (Koçak 2010). This formula of *both-this-and-that* would later be replaced by a formula of *neither-this-nor-that*. Turkish national identity had to be a completely new formulation, one that best suited a proud nation, one that left behind its Ottoman past and critically engaged with the European model. As an artisan of Turkish modernization once pointed out, "we didn't want to be three things, we wanted to be one thing" (Koçak 2010: 319). Other ways of defining Turkish national identity were proposed too, representing, in analytical terms, forms of Orientalism-in-reverse and Occidentalism. These various articulations illustrate the central role that adulation of/confrontation with the center, and its proclaimed, recognized, or contested authenticity, has played in Turkey's self-representation.

Romania, on the other hand, has occupied a different type of periphery, developing as a nation not so much in the vicinity of Europe, as Turkey did, but rather in the shadow of Europe, at the juncture of four crumbling empires and through the unification of three distinct provinces, each having a different cultural and political relationship with these empires, alongside sizable groups of people with ethnic origins other than Romanian. As Antohi writes, "this situation translates in terms of symbolic geography as follows: fragments of Romania belong to different European symbolic and historic regions, while Romania as a whole has trouble finding a stable and clear-cut symbolic location, as well as the associated political, economic, and institutional arrangements" (2002: 14). National identity building was an effort at emphasizing the relationship to Europe, of which Romania imagined itself to be an Eastern outpost and, simultaneously, at repressing the relationship to the Levant, the European Orient, and at creating distance from the Balkans. Later, during the communist period, after the partition of 1945 that divided Europe into the capitalist West and the socialist East, such efforts became futile, as Romania was now behind the Iron Curtain. After the collapse of the communist regime, this identity-building process was reframed as "returning to Europe" and regaining its European destiny that communism had so brutally interrupted. As Antohi notes, in the project of modern Romania, "the West was to play a paramount role: irrespective of their various ideological creeds, political allegiances, and vested interests, [various groups] up to WWI, agreed on a program of systematic imitation of the West. Maiorescu's opposition to 'forms without substance' was not against imitation, but rather against superficial imitation" (2002: 18). However, this process of "horizontal escape" toward the West has its own peculiarity. Antohi calls it "geocultural Bovarism"; that is, "the deeply entrenched idea that this country is intimately connected to the West, especially to France, and more precisely to Paris." In the Romanian case, thus, authenticity seems to have a clear location. As in the Turkish case, these ways of imagining the nationhood, which also reverberated in the ways selfhood was envisaged, illustrate the enduring significance of the center in these peripheral locations.

These are oversimplified presentations of how these two societies fashioned themselves in relation to Europe—the center that produced and experienced modern regimes of knowledge and power as authentic and exported them to/imposed them on the periphery. The point here is to emphasize that in both cases the notion of authenticity, and the related concepts of original, copy, imitation, and fake, have long been used for imagining selves and others, have frequently shaped the constitution of selfhood and nationhood, and have often informed the desires, aspirations, anxieties, fears, envies, and resentments of the architects of modernization and ordinary people alike. The inverse of this is that in both societies, recent harmonization with intellectual property legislation—as well as the gradual familiarization of the public with its characteristic associations between ideas and property rights, between authors and owners—adds another dimension to existing cultural and moral dispositions to celebrate the authentic and deplore the inauthentic, in relation to people as well as objects.

Such historical contexts might increase the gravity of the type of accusation of inauthenticity discussed in this chapter. Many of the people I met in my field sites occasionally encountered adverse reactions to their engagements with inauthentic objects. As I was able to observe and discuss many times over a nineteen-month period, these people deciphered in these reactions implicit or explicit accusations of deceiving not only others, but also themselves. In the following sections I exemplify and analyze this common experience and the similar ways in these people deal with it, be they producers and traders in Turkey or traders and consumers in Romania.

ENGAGEMENTS WITH INAUTHENTIC OBJECTS IN TURKEY

As the third chapter of this book demonstrated, in Turkey, fake branded goods of domestic origin are a common presence. The liberalization of the economy facilitated the integration of local firms into the global economy. Today a well-developed clothing industry places Turkey among the top ten major clothing exporters in the world. This industry is located mainly in Istanbul. Here branded garments are produced in hundreds of places, from tiny workshops to large, all-inclusive factories. Moreover, this industry has its equally well-developed informal sector. Many of the people I encountered in Istanbul whispered that fake branded garments could be produced everywhere and, in some cases, official and unofficial production was carried out on the same premises. However, even in these cases, the fakes were produced "under the stairs," that is, secretly.

Different economic and political logics explain the significant presence of inauthentic objects. This can be described as a case of "ambiguous persistence," when an illegal activity is tolerated and only occasionally and situationally repressed, since the state recognizes its social legitimacy (Smart 1999). Raids are organized, fines are paid, and sentences are served. Nevertheless, business is thriving, generating jobs and income, including in the less-privileged areas of society. Profits are big enough for everyone, including various state agents, to take a share. My informants stressed that they bribed lawyers, judges, municipality employees, policemen, and customs officials to keep their businesses running smoothly. Moreover, this presence reflects the specificity of industrial manufacturing. Fake branded garments are easy to manufacture because standardized clothes are easy to produce. They are easy to manufacture because of the transfer of technology and knowledge. My informants pointed out that subcontractors use the infrastructure for their own benefit and transfer knowledge through their own social networks. Export surplus, refused stocks, rejects, and overruns from the official production are also traded in the underbelly of the clothing industry. Remains such as fabric and accessories are incorporated into the manufacture of what might be called the "half fake," as opposed to the "entirely fake." More branded objects result from the distortion and hybridization of original models. Well-equipped manufacturing sites no longer caught up in the official commodity chains, after-hours production, leftover materials, and flawed commodities are used for the production of unofficially branded forms, as I was told or was able to observe many times during my fieldwork in Istanbul.

In this context, any conceptualization of the inauthentic object and any reflection on personal engagement with these objects and its implication for one's own sense of self arise from these particular conditions and this multiplicity of material forms. This is elaborated on ethnographically through the portrait of an individual who encounters adverse reactions to his engagement with inauthentic objects. Mustafa is a typical Istanbulite trader in fake branded garments to whom I was introduced by a common acquaintance and whom I visited from time to time, whenever I happened to be in the commercial district where he was based.

MUSTAFA

Our first meeting was arranged by his childhood friend. As Mustafa is speaking about himself, his friend suddenly interrupts. "But these are fakes, aren't they? That's why they sell well" he says. Mustafa does not reply. Breathing in deeply, he continues recounting his life story. Misunderstandings with his brother have caused him great distress. When the family business was finally going well, after years in which both he and his brother rarely had time for playing and studying, Mustafa saw no other solution but to leave and start anew. Instead of a fair share of their now prosperous business in denim garments, his father gave him US$10,000. That drove him to the verge of despair. It took months to pluck up the courage to construct a business plan.

First he visited various textile districts and talked to workshop owners. Then he rented a small shop in the Laleli neighborhood, the center of the informal trade with Eastern Europe and the former Soviet republics, and invested a part of his money in "exactly 700 pairs of jeans." One month later, his shop was still crammed with the same cheap jeans. Mustafa told himself that "the time to play with fire had come." He went again to the textile districts, knocked on many doors, and asked complete strangers what they had for sale. A firm offered him fancy jeans that for one reason or another could not reach its European market. He seized the opportunity with both hands and bought five thousand pairs at a total price of US$25,000. He paid in cash and by credit card. Luckily, the firm's owner accepted his card too, so he could cover the entire amount. In four months, he sold everything and made a good profit. Ever since, he has been scouring the textile districts and has been selling at a good markup. His success, his decent behavior, and his habit of keeping promises and paying his debts on time have assured him a place on the market. He hopes that a day will come when he is the first point of contact for producers and distributors with something to offer. "I am thirty-two years old and run my own business," he concludes.

Mustafa says that he sells "branded jeans," thus answering the question posed by his educated childhood friend. He shows some of his goods, piling pair on top of pair on the counter. He then puts aside two pairs, one of them branded Levi's. Although their quality is similar, he insists, discussing fabric, cut, stitching, and dye, the branded pair sells very well, despite being more expensive than the nonbranded pair, which does not. His declares that his business is based on a simple principle, that is, a prompt response to market demand. He is, thus, somewhat obliged to imitate brand models or, at least, to use their names on local products. He explains that he "watches the market," learns what models are in demand in Laleli, and tries to offer fancier jeans to customers renowned for their preference for garments with "a touch of glamour," to be embodied not only in the famous brand names but also brightness and busyness. He further emphasizes that, rather than "playing the designer" and placing orders for specific models with clothing manufacturers, he searches for "novelties," visiting not only workshops manufacturing for Western markets, but also workshops producing for the "Russian market."

As I learned, during the conversations that followed our first meeting, Mustafa buys various types of goods from clothing manufacturers: export surpluses, acceptable rejects, nonbranded items on which labels are attached or shiny embroidery is added at his request, faithful reproductions of famous brands, and local brands inspired by famous brands. Therefore, according to him, fake is too narrow a category: it makes reference neither to this material diversity nor his intervention. Moreover, fake is an inappropriate label, for it implies material inferiority. Many so-called originals are not notably distinct from the so-called fakes. Their materiality is only slightly different. However, glamorous shops and famous brands transform the so-called original into something extraordinary, a transformation Mustafa finds simultaneously disturbing and comforting. As he made clear in our conversations, he does not feel guilty. He sells products of medium to good quality for a reasonable price.

Moreover, he insists that he does not try to cheat his customers. There is no point in trying anyway, for they know what they are buying for what money and in what sort of place. These are his arguments against those eager to call his goods fakes and his business nothing more than theft. Nevertheless, as there are many who think this way, Mustafa takes his precautions. He learned that lawyers and police are mainly interested in originals routed into the informal market, that is, refused orders and the "little bit extra" produced by subcontractors without their contractors' knowledge. Consequently, his goods hardly ever fit into this category. Moreover, in Laleli, raids rarely take someone by surprise, as local merchants, he among them, know how to cultivate good relationships with the authorities.

Therefore, for Mustafa, to deal in fakes means to be a clever businessman who feels the market, orients toward goods that are in high demand and, thus, consolidate his position and increase his capital. His legitimacy—the form of legitimacy that really counts for him—comes from being a hard-working person who assumes risks and rightfully enjoys the fruits of his success. He dislikes the negative way many, such as his educated childhood friend, view his job, seeing him as a false businessman. He is worried he might be caught and punished for infringing on the law. However, he is more concerned that he might not be able to sell a sufficient quantity of merchandise to turn a good profit and, thus, make a fool of himself in the eyes of his significant others, namely his family and fellow traders. In fakes, Mustafa found a niche that allows him to construct himself in terms of a notion of success he is familiar with. As commodities that sell well, fakes objectify his success. As commodities that partake in the value of brand, these inauthentic objects express his relationship to the world. He also takes advantage of any opportunity to carve out a place for himself.

ENGAGEMENTS WITH INAUTHENTIC OBJECTS IN ROMANIA

As the fourth chapter of this book demonstrated, in Romania, fake branded goods of foreign origin abound. A huge commercial area located on the outskirts of Bucharest is officially considered the main source of fake branded goods on the Romanian market. Goods, not only fake branded, but also branded or nonbranded, arrive here via various transnational trading routes. The now limited "suitcase trade" and the more lucrative large-scale import trade with Turkey are among them. Although located in the capital city, this commercial area literally overflows into the country and its affordable commodities find their way into many Romanian homes.

However, this is a grey area. Official reports and journalistic investigations stress that it is a quasi-illegal venture with turnovers and tax evasion amounting to millions of euros. Moreover, this is a place that betrays a promise of Westernization of all products and all shopping venues. Many of my informants, despite being customers, reasoned that such a place should not exist in a European country. This commercial area was seen as a false façade that occupied the space where a Western reality was expected; an embarrassment that reflected on Romanian society as a whole and that demonstrated its incomplete Europeanization. The area was considered not only a place full of fakes, but also itself a sort of fake.

Goods originating in this commercial area are often judged as inferior in quality, style, and durability. This judgment tends to imply a wider moral argument that applies to all goods simply by virtue of the fact that they are sold in this market. In addition, these goods are placed in particular hierarchy of value that is articulated not only around, to use Manning and Uplisashvili's words, "an orientalist imaginary of alterity (which privileges European foreign goods over Asian ones)," but also around a "socialist one (which privileges quality [essence] over packaging [appearance])" (2007: 639). Moreover, as different informants from my two Romanian field sites made clear in our conversations, in this hierarchy, goods from Turkey are situated on a higher position than goods from China, in terms of quality and fashionability.

In this context, any conceptualization of the inauthentic object and any reflection on personal engagement with objects labeled inauthentic and its implication for one's own sense of self arise from these particular conditions and these peculiar hierarchies of material forms. As in the previous section, this is elaborated on through ethnographical vignettes about three individuals who encountered adverse reactions to their engagements with inauthentic objects. Each portrait is constructed around reflections on this type of critical moment, reflections I heard and discussed with them on a number of occasions. Valentina, Liviu, and Florin are typical Romanian consumers of fake branded garments, neither poor nor well-off, but somewhere in between. They do not approach a fake branded article simply as a cheap item, but they legitimize their clothing decisions in relation to the way they understand themselves and their position in their social world. I encountered them in one of my Romanian field sites, that is, a provincial town south of the capital city. Foreign brand name garments were available in the shops and market stalls of this town. However, these three persons, like my other informants, assumed their provenance was the Bucharest commercial area, for shopkeepers usually supplied their stocks from there. In other words, they knew these objects were legally inauthentic. It is worth mentioning that during my stay in Romania, I often met with Valentina. I spent mornings or afternoons at her place and accompanied her on shopping trips to the high street or the Bucharest commercial area. We often chatted about the opportunities and constraints in her life. I met Liviu and Florin less frequently, in the role of a researcher and/or friend with whom they could talk about their clothing preferences and choices.

VALENTINA

Valentina rarely buys new garments for herself. An unemployed widow in her early forties, she lives with her teenage daughter on state benefits and substantial support from her extended family and worries that one day she will not be able to cover her expenses. Nevertheless, she does not hesitate to spend small fortunes on quality garments for her daughter, several times going as far as to buy branded clothes from the Bucharest malls, however showing extreme care in evaluating their materiality.

She points out that she can still wear many of the garments she bought in her happier times, when she and her husband were running a shop and she could dress after her own heart. Moreover, she emphasizes that these garments offer clear proof that she has good taste in clothing. To give an example, she once told me how good she felt when a woman admired an old sweater of hers, asked her where she bought it and, upon hearing that it was a very old piece, congratulated her for that choice. Furthermore, almost every time we go through her wardrobe together, Valentina first chooses one of these older items, patting the fabrics, describing the feeling of those soft cottons, velvets, and wools on the skin, and asking me to touch them myself to better understand what she is talking about.

When she really needs something new for herself, Valentina goes in search of cheap things. She explains that it is not so much taste, but a preoccupation with "a little bit of quality" that guides her. As I was able to observe many times, while accompanying her on shopping trips, she equally scrutinizes shops, market stalls, one euro and secondhand clothes shops. Sometimes she fancies "beautiful things." "I found a nice green coat in a shop. Then they put it in the window. I looked at it for a few months. You see, if all you do is look, if you can never afford anything, in the end, you give up looking too, you do not know what it is beautiful anymore, you grow stupid and put on whatever you can afford," she once bitterly remarked. More often than not she complains that "beautiful quality things" at acceptable prices are hard to find in the shops for new clothes. She points out that once there were more garments from Turkey on the market and many were affordable, but now people of lesser means have to make do with lower-quality garments from China, which frequently irritate their skin, make them sweat, and annoy them with their bobbles. She often ends up buying good but out-of-fashion garments from the secondhand clothes shops.

She recounted a humiliating episode that made her reflect more on her clothing choices. She bought a pair of trousers without paying too much attention to their fake brand. She happened to have these trousers on when a younger cousin, a student who had moved to the capital city, dropped by. Upon seeing them, the cousin burst into laughter. "Did you buy these Lotto trousers before they closed the market stalls?" she asked, referring to a raid she had witnessed in the market. Police officers had been telling passersby that the merchants were trying to cheat them. They sold them fakes. "Who is that stupid to believe that she is buying original Adidas socks from the market stall? Well, in this small town, there might be a few people who believe this and even try to make others believe it," the cousin reasoned. "These socks," she went on, "come from Europa market. Why is the import of these goods permitted anyway?" She, for one, thought the event was rather hilarious, with stall owners running away and passersby shrugging their shoulders.

Valentina pointed out that this was the first time she considered what type of image she might be projecting through such fake branded garments. "They might think I am an ignorant. And that's not a very flattering image." A few weeks later she had to throw away the "plastic" (i.e., the polyester trousers) anyway. Buying those trousers had been an unfortunate choice. The fabric not only quickly deteriorated, but also irritated her skin. "They looked nice for a short while and then they began to bobble. They are like me. I might 'unravel' at any point too! I dress nicely for my guests, but I might not have anything to put on the table next day," she explained.

Moreover, as I was able to understand from our conversations, for Valentina, the category of fake includes branded as well as nonbranded garments. It is not the material semiotic apparatus of brand that makes all these garments counterfeits, but their inferior materiality. As she puts it, "there are only goods from Europa market (*europenisme*) in our shops. And all of them are fakes!" Garments available in her town are reasonably fashionable, but not good enough in terms of quality. She reasons they are made of inferior fabrics to reduce production costs and, thus, make them affordable to the majority of Romanians, poor people living in an impoverished country, second-class European citizens, she among them.

Valentina dissociates herself from such inauthentic objects as much as possible. They are not true to who she was and still wants to be through clothing. Materiality is of crucial importance here. The garments she finds on the local market cannot easily be appropriated. Their materiality is somewhat hostile. These garments stand in contrast to cherished items in the wardrobe, which not only retain memories of happier times but also feel good on the skin, attributes that reinforce each other. Moreover, this materiality is fragile. These garments have a short life and their fragility reminds her of the precariousness of her own situation. With fakes, objectification is incorrect and unfair. Rejecting fakes, Valentina turns to secondhand shops, which, in this way, represent not lack of choice but greater choice, a chance to find affordable clothes onto whose better quality fabrics she can project her sense of self. Moreover, it is her daughter's wardrobe that expresses, in a way, the person she wants to be, and effort is invested in this act of creating both mother and daughter.

LIVIU

Liviu recounts how, during his undergraduate studies in the capital city, he used to go on the sly to Europa market in search of cheaper but fashionable enough garments. As he puts it, "I did not tell anyone. I was embarrassed. I felt I debased myself. Europa market was the last solution, the decline, actually." He remembers fancying fake branded jeans and sportswear, and there were plenty to choose from, differing in terms of similitude and quality, but also reasoning that it was too risky a choice. "Fake branded garments from Europa would have been a terrible mistake. Everyone knew I cannot afford to shop in the malls. They would have immediately thought that my garments were fakes and would have all laughed up their sleeves at my attempts to imitate them," he explains. In his circle, nobody ever mentioned Europa market or dropped hints about the provenance of his clothes. His friends and colleagues were either very polite or completely ignorant about the range of garments on display in the "poor people's bazaar." Liviu loved to wear smart clothes, but had to accept that many things were beyond his budget and often he had to compromise and go for cheaper items.

Now, in his late twenties, he does not "feel that despair anymore." He gets by on the modest salary of a secondary school teacher and lives in a provincial town where many people clothe themselves with garments originating in this Bucharest commercial area. The passion for clothes is still very much present, but somehow domesticated by the responsibilities that come with adult life. "This is my real level. I don't try to pretend something else. I have now got the confidence to point out the fact that I bought this and that article from Europa market, and that I was able to evaluate the quality, such as it is. I don't keep quiet about my shopping trips. I don't try to pretend that I am someone else," he points out. The limited budget prompts him to improvise and combine divergent approaches to choosing garments. Moreover, in the way he shops for his clothes—meticulously exploring every commercial space and taking advantage of the few opportunities available—his manner of embracing his town becomes visible.

Liviu often goes to the high street of this provincial town for his routine inspection of the shops, to see and sometimes choose from the "new arrivals."

He himself rarely visits the Bucharest commercial area, preferring local shops where he can pay in installments. Every now and then he buys good rejects and stolen articles from a friend who works in a local clothing factory. For him, the ideal clothes are made in durable fabrics and can be easily combined with many others, the resulting outfits allowing the wearer to be at least smartly dressed, if not in fashion. He stresses that, if opportunities present themselves, he snatches up affordable items that come close to this ideal, even though in many cases he has to deposit them in the wardrobe until he can find other items matching them in perfect combinations.

To better illustrate his approach, as well as the kind of debates he and his friends engage in, Liviu often focuses on some item or other from his wardrobe. While visiting a Transylvanian town, he bought a pair of branded Italian shoes. The sole of the left shoe cracked after two days. Fortunately, he got his money back. The story of the branded shoes that failed the wearer is now part of a collective repertoire of disappointing experiences invoked when people in his circle debate the topic of branded goods and their promise of quality. "We are often weighting up the pros and cons of shopping in the malls and investing small fortunes in branded stuff. In the end, we buy almost exclusively from shops in our town. This is the level at which we can dress," he points out.

Liviu found his newest tracksuit in the shop of a friend, in a stock of tracksuits, shorts, T-shirts, and fleece hoodies that the friend bought from Europa market. The friend told him the seller, a Gypsy, brought them from Istanbul. Moreover, the Gypsy's story that the garments were produced during the night in the factory that manufactured originals during the day was quite plausible. However, neither his friend nor he could tell whether they were identical copies or not. The garments seemed similar enough, with their labels and logos, and good enough, with their thick, durable, and shiny fabrics. The friend assumed that his customers, though many were familiar with the range of garments on display in the official brand shops in Bucharest, were not so fastidious as to ask for identical copies. The friend further reasoned that these clothes were imitations. None of them could label them fakes, because they knew what they were buying. However, they both reckoned that some defect in the fabrics or accessories made them cheaper. The friend defined the imitation as "a compromise, the middle way between beautiful and cheap." Moreover, they were both of the opinion that these garments were made for people like them who could not afford to buy from the official shops of those famous brands, but loved to dress smartly and were willing to compromise. However, they both emphasize the modern look these garments confer on their wearer. "We both know that this is our level, this is what we wear, this is who we are, and we don't try to pretend we are someone else," Liviu summarizes their discussion.

Therefore, for Liviu, these inauthentic objects are true to who he is. They act as a signifier of a claim to maturity and of a capacity to compromise.

Moreover, fakes are a medium through which he situates himself in his social world, a medium through which belonging is reiterated. Fakes are something "local" for the "locals." Beautiful, good and cheap fake branded garments represent reasonable choices for reasonable individuals living in a provincial town inhabited by people of lesser means.

FLORIN

I met Florin while I was carrying out a survey on clothing consumption habits at a high school in this provincial town. As he was one of the most articulate respondents to my questions, I told him that I would like to continue our conversation. A couple of weeks later, Florin invited me to accompany him on "a shopping expedition." He urgently needed to buy a new pair of denim trousers. Upon seeing the huge hole in his new branded jeans, his mother urged him to replace them before his father noticed he tore an expensive garment. Any pair of blue jeans would do, his mother insisted, for his father did not pay much attention to details. Florin promised to give it a try, but found little comfort in the fact that the jeans section of the local clothing market was more generous than the rest. He thought that this was a good opportunity to continue our conversation about clothing.

On that day, we first had a coffee and a chat. Florin pointed out that this was going to be a true expedition as he had not bought clothes from the local shops in more than two years. Around the time he turned sixteen, he managed to convince his parents he was old enough to buy his own clothes. His parents agreed with him. However, his mother continued to bring home garments she liked and to inquire if he would want her to buy them for him. She knew many shopkeepers and could bring home and present garments to her husband and son. If they liked them, she would then buy the clothes on credit. For a while, in an effort not to hurt her feelings, Florin found different ways to reject these garments, ranging from inappropriate color to uncomfortable cut. Later he plucked up the courage to openly say that he did not like those things. He nevertheless gladly accepted shirts, T-shirts, and tracksuits manufactured in the local clothing factories. They were fashionable items of good quality because of the European standards of production imposed in these places. His mother was pleased and tried to keep herself updated with what was available on this informal market. Florin also managed to convince his parents that he could not find the clothes that suited his taste on the local market and that he would have more chances in Bucharest. They permitted him to go to the capital city every once in a while to renew his wardrobe.

Florin complained that these one-day trips were very tiring. He had to move quickly from one shopping center to another, to search the shops, to select

smart garments, to try them on, fidgeting in front of the mirror to get used to the feel of these garments, to image circumstances in which they could be worn, to ask for his friends' opinions, and finally to make a decision. Nevertheless, these were rewarding trips. He felt he could now speak about his own style. His skills at evaluating fabrics had also considerably improved. Together with his friends, he visited middle market places, well-supplied with fashionable and affordable garments manufactured in Romania and Turkey. A middle market brand, Kenvelo, was the best thing he had been able to afford so far. As a side note, he confessed that he bought both original and fake versions of Kenvelo T-shirts. They all bore the brand name, but he and his friends knew the difference. He used the originals only for special occasions, and that was a common and acceptable practice in his circle. In addition, he asked his mother to be more careful when cleaning the originals. All these strategies were meant to prolong the lives of these precious clothes. On the whole, although only a few items in his wardrobe were branded clothes, Florin could describe his garments as "one level above" what was available on the local market. He pointed out that none of them originated in Europa market. Upon noticing my puzzled look, he explained he and his colleagues could not even bear the thought that their clothes originated in some Chinese factories and some dirty stands in Europa market. Moreover, they all derided local habits of describing dirt cheap merchandise from this place as the latest fashion.

To be able to go to Bucharest, Florin saved most of his pocket money and student allowance. To spare himself of arguments he considered unnecessary, he never told his parents the real prices of his clothes. He admitted that the sad part was that they were less often able to buy themselves something than their son. His father had even habituated himself to the idea that from now on he would renew his wardrobe with the clothes his son did not wear anymore. However, it was better not to remember this situation very often. Parents lagged behind in many areas anyway, fashion trends and brand knowledge included. Many inhabitants of this town seemed to do so too.

To illustrate this idea, he recounted some hilarious arguments he and his cousin had with their mothers about branded garments. Since his cousin moved to Bucharest for undergraduate studies, she had changed her style, giving up her black jackets and trousers paired with flowery scarves and opting for, as she defined it, "casual with a touch." She bought some branded items, especially for going out. The mother noticed a polyester top among her new garments and advised her to throw it away. The daughter was outraged and told her not even to dare touch her DADA top. The mother cried indignantly. "What da-da? What nu-nu?" (in Romanian, "da" means "yes" and "nu" is "no"; DADA is a designer brand). The daughter was taken aback. "Mother, do not tell me you have never heard of this brand?" she asked her, astonished. This time the mother flew into a temper. "No, I have not. But I do believe that brands are special things. This top has a label on which is written DADA. That is it. The quality leaves much to be desired. There is nothing special about it. I am sure you can find something like this at a market stand," the mother concluded, deeply disappointed. Florin's mother had also gotten really angry when she realized that his smart jacket, bought from a supermarket in Bucharest, was manufactured in China. She reproached him for kicking up a row about the local shops being crammed with nothing but Chinese goods yet buying the same things for more money in Bucharest. He had to explain to her that nowadays most of the branded commodities were manufactured in China, but production had to meet the high standards of the brand. To emphasize this idea, he reminded her that strict quality standards were also imposed in clothing factories in their town. Her friend, who worked as a technician in such a place, spoke about this at great length. His mother seemed to understand these nuances, but still glared suspiciously at the jacket.

These points being clarified, Florin felt that we were both prepared for the expedition, so we set off to the high street. We headed to the two shops known for their large selection of denim garments manufactured in Turkey. There he had a chance to something of acceptable quality and style. After a thorough inspection, Florin listed the details that put him off: golden embroidery, red flames, silvery stripes, asymmetrical pockets, rhinestones, white patches, flaps, huge logos, and metal accessories. In addition, these jeans were distressed, ripped, cropped, bleached, washed, faded, and so on. One word could describe the whole range of products—tacky. He for one looked for plain jeans.

In one shop, however, he thought for an instance that he found a pair that suited his tastes. Upon seeing their brand, he screamed bloody murder: "Armani! I cannot believe this!" In an exaggerated manner, he complained to me that the only pair he really liked happened to be the kind of fake country bumpkins loved to don. I reminded him that he also wore fake Kenvelo T-shirts. He insisted that I have to understand the difference. He could not possibly afford to buy real Armani jeans. Therefore, anyone would assume that he wore a fake and would most probably have laughed at him. However, with some effort, he could afford to buy Kenvelo garments. Therefore, not everyone could figure out that he used a fake. He made sure that this would not be the cases by wearing the fake only in a safe social milieu. He had had enough of shopping for jeans in his hometown. If his father asked why he had only one pair of blue jeans, he would simply tell him what happened. He ripped the brand new pair on a nail. We left the shop and went to another café for a concluding chat. Florin returned over and over to the image of a country bumpkin clad in Armani jeans.

This teenager aimed at the urban sophistication his cousin seemed to have taken on in the capital city, where he would also move for undergraduate studies in the near future. Obvious fake brands pointed to the opposite. They gave away the poseur, who hid who he truly was and could be giving his life circumstances. Having recently asserted his clothing autonomy, Florin oriented himself toward middle market and gradually developed the critical skill that Hansen (2000) calls "clothing competence." In this case, this included a preference for a simple style imagined to be appropriate for the sophisticated urban individual, knowledge of fashion trends and brands, and a nascent ability to evaluate fabric quality. This is the type of cultural capital that would prepare his acceptance by future peers, the university-educated youth. In urban Romania, especially in the capital city, the country bumpkin Florin mentions belong to a category called "cocalari." Gross manners, fake branded clothes, massive gold jewelry, a preference for Oriental-sounding music, called "manele" and usually performed by Gypsies, are the main identification criteria of this social category. The opposite social category is that of "urbani," the young urban people, the ideal member of this category being the smartly dressed university educated individual. Brandtstädter also emphasizes that in post-Maoist China fake brands are associated with "the bumbling peasant who does not know" any better, a clear indicator of parochialism and backwardness (2009: 142). Thus, a deficiency (in the case of "cocalari") and abundance (in the case of "urbani") of civilization characterize these opposing categories. Florin dreamed of becoming an "urbanite." He prepared himself for this identity by rejecting the (obviously) inauthentic object and cultivating his skill in assembling an "urban" wardrobe.

THINKING INAUTHENTIC OBJECTS, AUTHENTICATING SELVES

In situations such as those recounted here, people who engage with objects labeled inauthentic are accused of falsification, theft, imitation, and impersonation. These are also accusations of attenuation, if not negation of one's self. Consequently, they invite anxiety over the integrity and credibility of one's existence. One's sense of self is at stake. In response to such adverse reactions, the people introduced here, as well as many others I met in my field sites, reflect on objects and selves.

These people center on materiality. These objects are garments, perhaps the most common objects of everyday life. Their availability to the senses challenges any pregiven framework for understanding inauthentic objects. In addition, this is a nondangerous materiality and, consequently, does not pose the same moral issues as other forms of fakes do, for example fake medication. These people address what Keane calls "bundling," that is, the notion that in any object qualities are always bound up with other qualities and that the relationship of co-presence between qualities is mediated by the co-presence in the same object. "Material things always combine an indefinite number of physical properties and qualities, whose particular juxtapositions may be mere happenstance. In any given practical or interpretative context, only some of these properties are relevant and come into play" (Keane 2006: 200). "Bundling" gives rise to the contingency and variability of the value of objects. This notion explains why objects might simultaneously participate in different registers of meaning and various fields of action and why objects exceed particular concepts and remain open to new uses and interpretation. In their reflections, these people mobilize some of the qualities "bundled" together in an object and emphasize that they, and not others, are salient, valuable, useful, and relevant. These people point out that the material semiotic apparatus of brand might not always be the only desirable aspect of these objects. Instead durability, frailty, density, brightness, shininess, smoothness, roughness, and busyness might come to the foreground.

Moreover, these people point out that there is multiplicity in material forms and diversity in terms of material qualities, a messy materiality that defies the disparaging assumption that all inauthentic objects are inferior objects. The Turkish informants, in particular, insist on the enormous variety of garments that might be produced officially and unofficially in a manufacturing site in the global clothing industry through the incessant recycling of knowledge, technology, and materials. They point out that the result is a deluge of objects of various degrees of similitude and of different qualities. They bring to the forefront the possibility to acquire expertise in the industrial manufacture of garments and in the evaluation of the material properties of cloth, clothes, and other accessories and materials. The Romanian informants, in particular, stress that, given this multiplicity, one might select objects in which he or she finds the desired qualities. They invoke the sensual properties of these objects. Situated at the periphery of the body, clothes simultaneously touch it and face outward to the others. As feeling and social experience, clothes represent a "social skin" (Turner 1993), a peculiar medium for negotiating and expressing a sense of the self. Materiality plays an important part in their decisions whether to consume these garments. In addition, both the Turkish and Romanian informants stress that they approach these objects and evaluate them in relation to other things, which can be, depending on the context, products of the official manufacturer, other goods on display in local shops and markets, or other items in the wardrobe.

As discussed in the third and fourth chapters, by bringing to the foreground the materiality of the inauthentic object, meaning not only objects, but also retail spaces, these people question the recurrent claims that sellers cheat and customers are cheated. Based in modest shops, sellers rarely claim they are selling originals, but insist that their customers must understand the nature of industrial clothing manufacturing and realize that, in the case of mass-produced garments, originals and fakes might be only slightly different. Customers are rarely fooled into believing they are buying originals. They are more or less aware that fakes are the excess of brand economy, which satisfies a surplus of demand and allows people of lesser means to be consumers of branded and/or new garments.

These persons draw out the nuances of these material forms and bring to the foreground the "honesty" of a materiality that they, and many other people, can apprehend sensuously, beyond and against any derogatory mainstream discourse. They contest the assumptions about inauthentic objects and the people who engage with them. They call into question the presumption that inauthentic objects are invariably inferior material forms. They argue that their engagements with these objects are not to be understood in terms of falsification, theft, imitation, and impersonation. They do not try to cheat and they are not cheated. They are not the deceivers portrayed in the mainstream conceptual framework. Moreover, by stressing the possibility of investing themselves professionally and personally in these objects, as manufacturers, traders, or consumers, these people emphasize that they do not deceive themselves. They know who they are, who they could be given the wider circumstances of their lives, although not necessarily who they would have liked to be. These reflections show that the possibility for authentication lies in the materiality of these objects (the third and fourth chapters demonstrated that the possibility for legitimation in contrast lies in the materiality of these objects).

However, this is not enough to counterattack these accusations of inauthenticity. From objects that are a somewhat ordinary presence in their social milieu, these people turn to their own place in this milieu and ponder whether they are true or false to their selves in relation to the wider context of their lives. This is not a search for a fixed inner self, but an evaluation of one's self-integrity in relation to the opportunities and constraints that one's life has had to offer and in relation to what their significant others could achieve in similar circumstances. In the contemporary world, concerns over personal authenticity are common reflexive exercises. In Handler's words, "we moderns are characteristically anxious about being, about 'reality' or, more particularly, about our lack of reality, about our lives which seem... 'unreal'" (1986: 3). Modern individuals, those introduced in this book among them, reflect on their self-integrity. Moreover, in certain places people are culturally predisposed to question the authenticity of their selves, mores, and practices. In the contemporary world, still structured in center and periphery, people on the fringe of the center might permanently question the degree to which they are themselves culturally constructed as copies or fakes of a world that in some other place is genuine.

A particular theoretical approach of this reflexive process is useful for illuminating these reflections on personal authenticity. In this understanding, the self that one is true to is constructed by the individual, but he or she is guided and constrained in this process of self-formation by his or her culture and society. The freedom of constructing one's self is situated and manifests itself within certain societal limits. Authenticity is constructed through social experience, not only the lived interactions with other individuals, but also the larger social, economic, political, and historical factors that shape these interactions (Appiah 1994; Brown 2010; Jackson 2005).

The people I encountered in my field sites argue that engagement with inauthentic objects is truthful to who they are, to who they could be given the wider circumstances of their lives, even though not necessarily to who they would have liked to be. These inauthentic objects are a source of procuring advantages over an economy that excludes some and enriches others. These inauthentic objects are affordable garments for people of lesser means. However, as this ethnographic material suggests, and as I was able to grasp from other informants' reflections, there is a certain heaviness in the producers and traders' ruminations that contrasts with a sort of lightness in the consumers' reflections. Producers and traders interact with an image of themselves created by others and have to find ways of dealing with its constraints and arguing against its serious claims of illegality and immorality, which accounts for this heaviness. For these producers and traders, their working lives and the extent to which others identify them with this work is at stake. Consumers create an image of themselves with more freedom and choice in their relations to the issues posed by the inauthentic object, which accounts for this lightness. For these consumers, the issue merely centers on what they wear. An understanding of clothes as revealing who one is can be accepted, shared, or rejected, depending on the context, the clothes one can afford, and the positive or negative feelings one has about the particular garments one wears at that moment. Engagements with objects that for others are inauthentic—the assumptions about objects and people that this characterization carries also acknowledged, but not necessarily accepted—affect the experience of the self differently.

To counterattack accusations of inauthenticity, these people draw on the ideal of sincerity in their consideration of the degree of correspondence between principles avowed by their societies and actual conduct. In Istanbul, informants pointed out that lawyers pretended to defend foreign companies and the customers against the dangers of counterfeiting, but took bribes from those they called counterfeiters. In Romania, informants emphasized that authorities claimed to protect citizens' interests, but turned a blind eye to unauthorized markets and illegal business practices. These people enact dialectical modes of apprehending reality. They emphasize that the world in which they live is a place full of contradictions, compromises, and constraints. This is an understanding of the world constructed through people's own life experiences and the ways they assemble these experiences into particular narratives. If the world itself is not ideal, but comprised of constant compromises that only ever partially realize any ideal, then in some ways, for these people, the inauthentic object is true to the nature of the world as they see it.

Furthermore, to authenticate their selves, these people also reconceptualize the inauthentic object. This process of reconceptualization can be summarized as follows: the starting point is the concept of a copy. A copy is "sort of something." In contrast, in its common understanding, a fake is "something." A fake is a copy that denies that it is a copy and pretends that it is the original. However, for the people I encountered in my field sites, the fake is "sort of something," a copy that does not hide its true nature. Moreover, this "sort of something" nature is elaborated on, in light of individual agendas, social circumstances, and approaches to the world. These people point out that these objects are "similar enough," "good enough," "famous enough," and "ambiguous enough." Though they may not always succeed in becoming any of these things. The fake is, thus, "sort of something" or, in other words, the approximation of the ideal. Furthermore, if the world is a place full of half-truths and half-measures, then the fake is entirely truthful to how the world truly is. The fake is, therefore, "sort of something," as opposed to being "absolutely something" or, in other words, the objectification of the ideal. In this case, the fake/copy is valued for what it is. In this particular conceptualization of the "sort of something" nature of the fake/copy, the emphasis is on *sort of* rather than on *something*.

In this way, these people authenticate their selves. They do so because they like to regard themselves as truthful about who they are and how the world around them is. They do so because they see these objects as truthful to who they are and to the world as they understand it. They do so because they see themselves as they truly are in this peculiar material mirror.

This chapter has demonstrated that the Istanbulite man introduced in the first chapter of this book is not unique in his reflections on inauthentic objects. He is not unusual in the way he acknowledges the characterization of certain objects as inauthentic, and refutes its assumptions about these objects and the people who engage with them. However, as the concluding section of this book further demonstrates ethnographically, the centrality of these objects in his life, and their privileged role as instruments of self-articulation, make his case different. This life is the paradigmatic example that best supports one of the main arguments of this book, namely that the authenticity of selves can be maintained in relation to the acknowledged inauthenticity of objects.

–6–

Conclusion

AN ORDINARY DAY IN THE LIFE OF AN ISTANBULITE

It is eight o'clock in the morning, the time when the bazaar slowly wakes up. The apprentice opens the shop, sweeps the floor, and dusts the front table. Soon after a porter comes, panting and covered in sweat, and delivers a huge sack with new merchandise coming directly from the manufacturing site. Without zeal, the teenager begins piling up packages on shelves and the floor. About an hour later, catching sight of the shop owner at the end of the alley, Burak picks up the pace. Kerim is on his way to the shop, stopping here and there, greeting his neighbors and wishing them a good day. He is late today, and everyone knows the reason—too much drinking the evening before. Burak orders a tea for him. "Âdem abi, a tea," he yells, waving to a man standing further down the alley. "Bring a strong coffee too," a neighbor screams, laughing. While waiting for his drinks, Kerim pays attention to the way his apprentice goes about arranging the shop. He reminds him that each model should be placed on the front table, in as many colors as possible, and should be neatly aligned so that each brand is visible. On the whole, the shop should be always tidy and crammed with goods, proof that this shop owner is a serious wholesaler. As a last touch, Kerim places two pairs of the new model of boxer briefs, in white and black, with the brand name stitched in red on the thin waistband, on the edge of the table. Sitting on a stool at the entrance of the shop, Kerim drinks the tea and the coffee, smokes, and gets himself ready for a new working day in the bazaar.

The first customer who drops by to see him this morning is one of his regulars, an energetic young man, himself a bazaar shopkeeper. He has brought a significant part of the money he owes Kerim a few days earlier than the agreed date. Arif soon spots the new arrivals. He likes one of the models very much, and, knowing Ralph Lauren sells well, he decides to buy fifteen hundred pairs, on the condition that he can pay for them four months later. Thrilled, Kerim accepts. Apologizing for such a short visit, Arif leaves, for he has many things to do this morning. "I like this boy. So determined. So efficient," Kerim tells Mahmut, his neighbor and closest friend on this bazaar alley. He relishes this unexpected success. The new merchandise just arrived and already he has sold fifteen hundred pairs. He got €2 per pair that cost him €1. To his chatterbox of an apprentice, Kerim feels bound to say that doing business requires mind and moderation, permanent circulation of money, and respect for the customers, and that forgetting these principles might result in losing everything. In their world, a poor man is a nobody. Ideally, the trader must put his whole heart into his work and be honest and thrifty. Consequently, he will prosper, and his shop and deposits will be heaped to the brim.

In this cheerful mood, he welcomes the next visitor, Ali Bey, an acquaintance who would like to know how this business functions. Once seated, with a glass of tea in his hand, the man reminds him that he wanted to speak with a serious and knowledgeable producer and that their common friend arranged this visit some two weeks ago on the guarantee that he would not share this information with anyone. He assures him once more that this will be the case. Kerim agrees to discuss what one needs to do and to have to enter this business. He takes a pair of the new model in his hands and begins by emphasizing that this pair of seamless underwear, like most of the other products in this shop, is manufactured in his own workshop. Everything in there is expensive. The wonderful computer-operated and technologically sophisticated sewing machines, with their dozens of needles weaving fast, are the most expensive pieces of equipment he has ever used. These machines can only work with a certain type of thread, and that is costly, too. The chemical solutions necessary to soften the fabric are also costly. This is why, Kerim points out, the final product is so soft that one can find himself wondering whether he has underwear on or not. He bursts into a hearty laugh. His guest laughs too. A moment later, Kerim returns to his most serious expression and continues the explanation. This investment in technology and materials can be earned back in a year and a half, provided that one sells his product for twice its price and has a good distribution network. Ali Bey is impressed, if not downright overwhelmed. He keeps saying, "Maşallah."[1]

Besides the considerable financial investment, this business requires a particular arrangement, that is, a credible mixture of black and white. In his workshop, for example, subcontracted work for local clothing firms is carried out during the day and imitations are manufactured during the evening. All the papers related to this formal work are in order. In addition, all these formal products can be manufactured with the equipment available in the workshop. Having been in the clothing industry for such a long time, he personally has enough connections to secure this part of the business. Moreover, his workers are the soul of discretion. He trusts they will not betray him because he pays them more than they can get elsewhere.

In addition, Kerim explains the clever way he organizes his business, subcontracting various parts of the production process to workshops in different parts of Istanbul and depositing his products in secure locations. He takes a piece of paper from his notebook and draws five points. From his workshop, the first point, the soon-to-be imitation underwear is taken to be dyed in a different workshop, the second point, in another neighborhood on the Anatolian side. Once, a lawyer and two policemen knocked at the door of this workshop. They had a search warrant, so his employees could do nothing but let them inspect the place. They found the "skirts," but no brand name was imprinted on them yet. In the end, they left, having found no incriminating evidence. In the third location, in the same neighborhood, goods eventually become imitations, with the brand names imprinted on them. Once they are painted and imprinted with brand names, the last stop is a workshop on the European side of Istanbul, where the "skirts" are shaped into underwear. Labels, which were produced in a different place, are sewed onto them. A part of the finished product is sent to his shop, another goes directly to large buyers based in thriving trading districts, and the rest is deposited in storehouses. "A lawyer has to be Schumacher to move between the different workshops before we can hear of the visit," Kerim points out.

This side of the business clarified, Kerim invites his guest to take a good look at the kind of goods he manufactures. Choosing an older model of boxer briefs from a shelf, he offers some financial details. This pair has a wholesale price of €1.80. In other shops, the same product can be found at a cost of €1.30 or €1.60. "That is plastic actually, not microfiber," he insists. His products are of a better quality. His price is still a very reasonable one, in comparison with the price of the so-called originals, often identical items produced with the same technology and materials as the ones he has. Despite the common opinion that all imitations are of low quality, there are different types of imitations on the market and their quality is different, some better than the other.

The shop displays everything that can be manufactured in his workshop, that is, a large selection of microfiber seamless underwear, men's boxer briefs with thin or wide waistband, men's standard and hipsters' briefs, and women's boxer briefs, g-string thongs, and hipsters' briefs, in different nuances of yellow, red, orange, blue, green, brown, white, black, grey, mauve, and purple, far more than could be found in any official shop. Fancier models, men's microfiber seamless boxer briefs in delicate tones of buttery white, pink, grey, emerald green, mauve, and copper brown, are produced mainly for his buyers from outside Istanbul, who cater for sophisticated customers and tourists. At first glance, the only difference seems to be the brand name, but Kerim shows the detailing in the fabric that differentiates one brand from another. However, he cannot provide identical copies. For example, the exact dimensions of the letters E and A, standing for Emporio Armani, are hard to establish if one has no access to the pattern used in the authorized production, so his machines can only approximate. He presents his guest with almost all his models, rendering their features as attractive and desirable, specifying their availability, and often referring to how well received they have been by other buyers and how crazy customers in this and that location are about them. Kerim confidently claims that most of his rivals, for there are plenty in this business, cannot compete with him. As he puts it, "what most of them make is Volkswagen. Mine is Ferrari."

This conversation is interrupted a few times by agitated men, who ignore or cannot find Burak, so they rush into the shop, in urgent need of articles in certain colors, sizes, and brands. "Three black pairs, size XL. It does not matter what brand, just hurry up, I have a client in my shop," a fellow trader from a parallel alley utters, breathing heavily with effort, only to bring them back, a few minutes later, apologizing, again in one breath, for the client changed his mind. "Give me the sexiest colors you have, brother, but only Armani," orders another, in quite a humdrum manner. "Erdem abi sent me to take two pairs of white Hugo Boss," says a teenager, stopping respectfully near the front table. "Tell him I said to send you with the full list. He should write down number, size, color and brand. For the whole week! I have ten piece packages and will not open a few packages every day just because he wants to," Kerim gets rid of him. "Am I a secretary now? Do I have to write down ten times per day two pairs for Erdem, three pairs for Merdem? Paper costs too. Am I not right, Ali Bey?" he asks his visitor, breathing exaggerated anger. Ali Bey understands him very well, or so he insists. However, Kerim promptly serves a fair-haired boy. He explains to his guest that the boy works for Yavuz, one of his most reliable buyers in the bazaar. This Yavuz appreciates his products and tries to convince other bazaar shopkeepers to buy Kerim's products, and not the cheaper and lower-quality products of his rivals. Kerim points out that this man knows what quality is, just like his late father. "I was on very good terms with his father too, may God rest him in peace. We grew up together in this bazaar," Kerim recounts, with eyes full of memories of other times.

This is another type of information about this business that Kerim passes to his visitor. These customers, tradesmen in this bazaar and the surrounding commercial area, sell his products at a markup. Each of them has his own page in his notebook; the date and quantity are written down every time they take something. He welcomes any shopkeeper who wants to buy his goods on delayed payment, provided that this man has someone to introduce him and speak on his behalf, confirming that he is a trustworthy person with a well-positioned shop. However, these relations are short-lived, terminated either by him when the payment is endlessly delayed or the traders themselves when they change their supplier. In this business, one strives to find large-scale buyers, but these bazaar shopkeepers are also valuable, not only because they buy, but also because they spread the word.

Gradually, Ali Bey plunges deep into thought. He drinks his tea—the fifth—and declares he will consider whether this business is good for him or not.

It brings good money, indeed, but the capital investment and the organizing effort it requires are also considerable, he adds, his voice coming out louder than the previous approving mumbles and soft giggles. After Ali Bey's departure, Burak and Mahmut pop up. They have been dying of curiosity outside the shop for almost an hour. As none of them knew the visitor, they did not dare to stay very close and, thus, could only catch bits of the conversation. Now they want to know who the shifty-looking skinny guy was and what he wanted. Lighting his cigarette, Kerim grins at them absentmindedly. "A guy who wanted to do imitations. A nobody. We will not see again," he finally says.

During this sort of visit, Burak stays in front of the shop and serves the occasional customer. He welcomes them with honeyed words and encourages them to choose to their hearts' desire. "Look! Armani! Dolce & Gabbana!" some cry, thrilled. "I have sixteen colors and many brands," the teenager says, tempting them with more colors than those displayed on the counter. Occasionally, he goes into details about manufacturing, insisting these products are produced with the same technology as the originals and sometimes on the same premises. He reminds them that they can buy for €2 quality merchandise that in the official shop costs €40. Attempts at bargaining are rejected, for Burak thinks his price is more than fair. Moreover, from force of habit, he rarely forgets to emphasize that this is a special low price, "only for you, my friend, because I like you."

The bothersome customers, who imagine they can get a good discount for buying three pairs instead of two, are cut short and let alone to ponder whether they want to buy or not. "Bargaining, as if he buys a car," Burak bursts out and puts back on the table the things that seemed too expensive to this customer. Anyone who hesitates is shown different items in the hope that he or she will finally reach a decision, but many times the obvious pleasure in turning the shop upside down indisposes the apprentice. The few naïfs, who think that they made a lucky find, brands for a fraction of their price, are assured the goods are imitations, but quality products. During these encounters, without exception, there comes a moment when both parties stretch the underwear, the seller to demonstrate their resistance and quality, the customers to check whether they suit them or not. Rarely will one leave with just one pair, for there is no harm in buying more, things being dirt cheap in this shop, people often think aloud. "Come again. You can find me here any time," Burak says, instead of goodbye.

Because they sold such a large amount of goods this morning, Kerim sends his shop assistant to the nearby storehouse to bring enough packages to fill the empty space on the shelves and floor. He phones the manufacturing site and changes the instructions he gave the day before, during the weekly visit of his foreman. With cautious optimism, he requests the production of more items in the new model. Every week this trusted man comes to the shop to collect the money for materials, workshop maintenance, and wages and to report on that week's situation. These are very short visits, at the same hour of the same day of each week, the visits of a respectful employer who refuses tea and does not smoke, just waits for the money to be counted in his presence and listens carefully to any new instructions. Kerim rarely needs to visit his manufacturing site, as the phone is enough for keeping in touch with his foreman and for supervising the movement of the goods and placing new orders.

When Burak returns, almost an hour later, white-faced and empty-handed, Kerim is still on the phone, this time talking in an exalted voice with a buyer based outside Istanbul, who called to place an order. Wiping the sweat off his forehead, he writes down the requested quantities, brands, sizes, models, and colors, and the list is very long, all the while assuring the man that everything will be sent in a jetty this very afternoon. Although he does business with several regular bulk buyers—hard-earned relationships with a lot of effort going in to maintaining them, as they are essential for the distribution of a significant part of his merchandise—he rarely deals with two big orders during the same day. He recognizes at once the immense potential of the situation. His words come out faster and faster, louder and louder, some more intelligible than others—"original model," "nowhere to be found," "fabulous price," "available materials," "seriousness." He tries to convince his interlocutor to buy not only his new models of microfiber seamless underwear, but also the cotton boxer briefs he himself takes from other manufacturers. His effort is not in vain, the man is interested in receiving samples of these models, next to the twelve hundred pairs he just ordered. Upon finishing the conversation, Kerim beams with joy.

His face changes when he notices his apprentice. "My boy," he says, "I am going to ask you just once: what took you so long and why did you not do what I said?" Burak gives him a tired look. "It was really really bad this time, father," he sighs. He and his friend Ekin were smoking in the depot. Ekin's father does not allow him to smoke, so there is no better place to hide. Kerim rolls his eyes. Burak insists this makes them even more cautious. Every time they go there, they make sure the newspapers that cover the windows are always at their place. They had even glued on the door a paper saying the place was for rent. Then he continues his story. They were smoking and chatting about Ekin's new sweetheart when they heard the screams. Someone yelled at the top of his voice that the police were raiding their part of the bazaar. At first, they did not know what to do, to stay there or leave. In the end, they decided to leave. Seconds after he locked the door, police officers entered the inn's courtyard. When asked what brought him to that place, Burak said he came to have a word with his father's friend, the tea maker. Although they did not know each other, the tea maker said nothing and allowed Burak to stay in his tiny place and even answered his questions about the business the man and his father were supposedly planning. When a police officer stopped in front of the depot, he thought he was going to faint. An actual friend of his father told the police officers that a certain Mehmet they did not know very well rented the place some time ago, did bad business, and had been trying to sublet it for a year but without success. A police officer called the number posted on the door, but nobody replied. The law put all sorts of questions to the people they found in the courtyard. They checked carefully the papers and the merchandise in a towel shop and asked the owner if he sold fake branded towels.

"This time it could have been really really bad, father," Burak repeats. The law stood in front of a depot filled to the brim with the type of merchandise they hunted. Burak often hears his father explaining to his visitors the comical side of this business. He reminds him which are his favorite examples. The first involves police officers who come to the bazaar and look for a certain individual, but they are told the bastard has disappeared, so they write in the register "unknown address" and leave, happy to get off cheaply. The second refers to raids, but it is meant to emphasize something else. Kerim is fond of reminding people that when lawyers raid a shop a second later the whole bazaar finds out and the goods vanish in the blink of an eye. Burak insists that things are changing. The raids are more frequent and the police officers seem more determined to find and punish the culprits. In the eyes of the law, they are the culprits.

Kerim tries to calm down his son. He admits Burak is right, this is a serious thing, but they can find a way to deal with this problem. "Remember, if the worst comes to the worst, all you have to do is to go to court clean-shaved," Kerim says. Burak stares at his father, incredulously. "You have to put on a nice suit, button it on the front. Stand up like a soldier in front of the judge and never admit having sold anything," he goes on. He for one always does so. He goes to the court in his Sunday best, listens to whatever they tell him, but insists he has never sold counterfeits. "I can play it really well, believe me, but the judge knows me by now. I have been caught thirteen times. Even the judge says 'welcome' when he sees me. This is how corrupted the situation is," Kerim concludes. Now Burak laughs.

Shopkeeper and apprentice have their lunch in the shop, the former treating himself to a double portion of pastry filled with cheese, a moderate meal after the excess of the previous evening, and enthusing over the new products and their success, the latter taking delight in his kebab and slowly forgetting his adventure. Burak tells his father about Ekin's sweetheart. Apparently her cousin is also very beautiful and he can hardly wait to meet with them on Saturday.

They rest and focus now on the next thing on today's agenda, the big order Kerim has just received. Packets are bundled up, wrapped in plastic, fastened with rubber bands, and left in front of the shop, ready to be picked up by the transport company's porters. Kerim gives the company his full name and address, a habit many but him consider foolish. He reasons that, in case something does happen, everybody will become a stranger all of a sudden, denying all responsibility. Upon finishing, they are both dog tired.

Kerim suddenly springs to his feet, something else occurring during this movement, for he welcomes his next visitor in a different voice, in a cordial language. The tall, smartly dressed man replies in the same idiom, taking a seat on the chair that Burak offers ceremoniously. Sitting down on his short, three-legged stool, Kerim raises his left eyebrow in surprise. He is taken aback, for the small restaurant at the end of the alley is the only place with that type of chairs in their part of the bazaar. Cemil Bey deserves this special treatment, for he is not only the landlord of the building in which Kerim's manufacturing site is located, but also an educated person, coming from an old Istanbulite family with whom his father also did business.

The man has brought a bag full of samples of stretch cotton boxer briefs and offers them one by one, emphasizing material characteristics, price, availability, and delivery slot. Kerim listens with his most respectful expression and takes each item in his hands and evaluates their characteristics according to his own criteria. One item attracts his attention: navy blue ankle-length leggings, the upper part of a pair of jeans sketched on them in darker blue. He dresses a mannequin to better see the details and suggests the changes he would like for the goods produced for him. The brand name should be written in white—he agrees with his visitor, the tights are chic, but he knows the customers better; they would like the name to be visible. The labels indicating the size should be attached at the back—he understands they are one size, but people want certitudes. He would like the labels to indicate two sizes, M-L and L-XL. The 400 items he orders will be delivered in one week's time, his guest assures him.

The cotton boxer briefs do not interest Kerim. The print is accurately executed in good paint, the fabric is acceptable, but the cut is completely wrong. A good friend of his disregarded this aspect, produced a considerable quantity, and now needed to find ignorant buyers for this impossible to wear model. The man says nothing, just puts the boxers back into his bag. A part of the goods Kerim keeps in his shop, especially the cotton underwear, arrives here through this kind of arrangement, offered as samples by people he knows. Sometimes, he decides on the spot that they have potential. He keeps the samples in the shop and shows them to his visitors, in an attempt to evaluate their marketability, in terms of brand, model, and quality. Relationships with producers or distributors of cotton underwear are something Kerim needs to cultivate, for fashions are changing and soon the cotton will be more in demand than the microfiber.

The two men continue their whispered conversation, in their extremely polite manner, sharing the latest news they heard about people they know in this trade—who did what, who cheated whom, who picked a quarrel with whom, who made peace with whom, and so on and so forth—a fruitful exchange between two serious tradesmen. When there is nothing left to share, he gives the man a bundle of YTL100 notes, reminding him that they agreed that the rest of the debt will be paid in three days. The man counts the money, puts it in his pocket, thanks him for the tea, says his goodbyes, and leaves. Burak rushes to the restaurant to return the chair and then takes his position in front of the shop, waiting for the occasional customer. Now Kerim is in the mood for lecturing. He tells his apprentice that doing business requires careful thought and moderation, good cash flow, and respect for the customers. Forgetting these principles might result in losing everything. In their world, a bankrupt trader is a nobody. Ideally, Kerim insists, the trader must put his whole heart into his work and must be honest and thrifty. Then he will prosper and his shop and storehouses will be full to the brim.

Soon, another man visits Kerim. However, this visit touches a raw nerve. One of his regular customers, who recently bought a large quantity of vests from him, returns with the merchandise, profoundly disappointed. The man complains that he could never have imagined that he would be treated so badly. Like many others in the trade, he considers Kerim a just and fair man who in times of crisis and of dispute is called upon to give advice or arbitrate. Kerim begs him to explain what is going on. The man empties his bag on the floor and bursts out: "you sold me these crappy vests!" Kerim can see for himself that the goods are failures of the worst type, with wrong cuts, stitches, lines drawn in ball pen around the arms. It is his turn to burst out. "Traitor! Ungrateful! Son of a bitch! I trusted him! I told everyone this is my trustworthy man and I guarantee for him," he yells, ablaze with anger. The visitor gets his money back and, in his turn, tries to comfort his fellow. Kerim's cries attract his neighbors. They come to learn what happened and offer their moral support.

Thoroughly irritated, Kerim makes sure the story will circulate in the bazaar and beyond. Though there are thousands in the clothing trade in Istanbul, their world is small, in fact. People know each other and spread the news. All the stories and all the people are so entangled in this world, so that, as they say, "the liar's candle will not last forever." This is a way of saying that sooner or later wrongs and betrayals are discovered. Kerim shares with his fellow traders his opinion that business propositions need to be carefully pondered over, for everyone can be a cheat, everyone is in the habit of bragging and promising, only to forget seconds later.

When his main partner drops by about an hour later, Kerim relives the incident, showing the rejects his most trusted man lured him into buying with his story about the overstock products from his friend's workshop. Trusting him, he did not double check the story. His apprentice has to unpack those 100 packages and separate sellable items from total failures. The news astounds Rıfat, too. Kerim runs the workshop in which most of these goods are produced together with this man. This partnership is rather a "marriage of convenience," the two keeping an eye on each other, one day kisses, another day curses. Each of them takes half of the goods produced in a workshop working at its full capacity, targets different markets, and uses different networks of distribution and influence. However, they support each other in case one has not enough money to pay his part of the workshop's expenses. Although this incident does not affect Rıfat directly, it might have implications regarding the security of their arrangement. He believes that the most drastic measure, that is, dismissal, is the best course of action. Kerim agrees. He will do so, firmly but quietly, after the next week's payment.

Rıfat has come to propose a new business. He brings samples of microfiber seamless vests in different colors and brand names, which can be manufactured in their workshop after some small technical changes. Kerim takes every sample, stretches its fabric, and looks carefully at the weaving pattern. "I will think about it. But keep in mind that the thread is of lower quality than ours. We can produce them, indeed, but our price will be bigger," he finally replies, knowing too well his partner's habit of enthusing over every new model he comes across and rushing to produce loads before properly evaluating their potential.

To calm himself down, Kerim leaves the shop and joins Mahmut and a young neighbor, Deniz, who talk about important issues, such as football and women. Soon he is caught in a passionate argument about the merits of such and such a Turkish football player. As an ardent supporter of Beşiktaş, he feels duty bound to say his team's players are the best. From the risks in football, the shy Deniz moves the discussion toward the risks in trading in imitations of branded garments. He knows fashion is changing quickly and would like to learn how the trader copes with this. Kerim assures him that there is no such thing as out of fashion in this sector. What is fashionable in Germany this year will become fashionable in some Eastern European country in a year or two years and in some Central Asian country in three or four years. Traders from these countries will come to Istanbul and buy their products. The most important lesson he can give, however, is respect for one's work, products, and customers. Ideally, the trader must put his whole heart into his work, must be honest and thrifty. Consequently, he will prosper and his shop and depots will be heaped to the brim.

He urges his young neighbor to bring a pair of underwear from his counter. He wants to teach him what quality feels like. Deniz brings the pair and then follows the gestured instructions, rubbing the fabric between his fingers and stretching it. Burak is sent to borrow a few items from his main rival in the bazaar, the teenager's protests being ignored. He brings a few items, not because he manages to convince the competitor, but because the man knows there is no fooling with Kerim. Deniz is instructed how to compare products and understand quality.

The lesson is interrupted by the arrival of another guest, an elderly carpet seller whom Kerim knows and respects. Barış Bey tells him openly that the reason for this visit is rather hilarious. He came to ask whether the new name he heard from his young and smart nephews, Björn Borg, is a real brand name, the invention of some Turkish guy, or something they came up with to poke fun at him. He could not ask this on the phone, fearing that even Kerim will laugh at his problem. To his surprise, he discovers he came to the right place, for Kerim has recently become a supplier of this brand. He himself learned about it by chance, when one of his acquaintances came to inform him about what good stocks were available on the market. A few pairs of cotton boxer briefs branded Björn Borg remained in his shop for months, until he made up his mind and bought the whole stock of that factory. Had these cotton boxer briefs in bright colors been produced by a Turkish company, Kerim ironically comments, nobody would have even looked at them. "It is the brand name that thrills everyone," he remarks. "Boxer shorts with flowers and flies," he repeats several times, scornfully. As other traders claimed this brand sells well in the seaside resorts, he decided to manufacture it in his workshop too, embellishing his microfiber seamless boxer briefs with tennis balls. Moreover, he found a manufacturer who can produce colorful cotton boxer briefs, though not with flowers or flies, but curly lines in different colors.

Barış Bey, an old-fashioned trader who believes in the objects themselves and not in their brand names, is the perfect audience for his critical opinions about the craze for brand names. Kerim laughs at this, but also admits he capitalizes on it. He confesses to Barış Bey that he not only manufactures or buys from other manufacturers branded articles, but also turns whatever seconds and nonbranded goods he can find into imitations. Though a great deal of information about such opportunities can be found out in face-to-face meetings or by phone, he employs an experienced man to comb the manufacturing districts of the city in search of products that can be routed through his business. This man gives periodical reports by phone, keeping him well informed about novelties on the market and buys in his name whatever he knows will meet his employer's quality standards, be it thread, paint, fabric, labels, or finished products. Rarely does Kerim need to go in person to settle a deal that this man traced down, for, having been around for so many years, people know him, put stock in his words, and are prepared to do business with his employee. This man drops by and brings samples only when he needs his opinion and knowledge of fashion trends. Though Kerim does believe in and benefits from this man's ability to discern good things, in the end, only he decides which products are marketable and which have the potential to become convincing fakes that can be displayed in his shop next to the imitations he manufactures. Barış Bey congratulates him on his idea. He recalls the time when he first met Kerim, a little boy who ran errands on the alleys of this bazaar or cried to go home to his mother. To his great joy, Kerim turned into a real businessman.

On the alley, not far from the shop, Burak whiles away time in the company of other apprentices, shop assistants, and shopkeepers. The troubles of the morning now seem far away, a normal occurrence in such a business. The last to join them is Ümit, who came to spend some pleasant moments as well as to do business. He is one of Kerim's partners in the manufacturing of seamless underwear. The last stage of the production, namely the sewing of labels, is carried out in his workshop. Kerim shows him the long list of items he just sent to a distant location, proving thus the viability of their partnership. He reminds him that his honesty is his most important capital. He informs his visitor that he sometimes signs checks without really having the money to cover them. He declares that "if you saw my check list, you would say I have the courage of a crazy person or a fool. Actually, I have the courage of an honest person." Kerim knows that he can sell his products and covers his checks in time. "My experience, my investments, my honesty, the idea people have about me, these all make up my settled position in the business," he concludes. Kerim invites Ümit to his shop to discuss the possible production of new models. Burak goes to the depot to bring the samples. Kerim is thinking of producing these models and needs their opinions about design and marketability. The request excites a great deal of interest and everyone has something to say and much to laugh about as they picture each other wearing these fancy undies. However, Burak's opinion is the one that matters the most, for the teenager is fond of trying all these new products and gives feedback on his experience and details about their fit on the body. Moreover, as he likes to show off in front of his friends, he can report on their reactions too. They all agree to change the original design slightly, deciding on another color scheme, enlarging the front part, choosing smaller labels and more brand names, and also ordering button-fly boxer briefs in the same fabric. Ümit, who has an issue with the labels, will go to the manufacturer to explain what they should look like.

Kerim recounts to Murat the conversation he had with Barış Bey about brands and quality products. While speaking, it dawns on him that he could have given another very good example to support the critical position he and Barış Bey shared. Kerim tells this example to Murat. He reminds him how he always tries to convince bazaar shopkeepers to buy nonbranded but quality underwear instead of the local brand they request. As a friend of his is the actual manufacturer of these branded products, Kerim knows the label misinforms the customers about the actual percentage of cotton in the fabric. He urges them to buy this or that, it might not be the brand they want, but it is quality. His advice falls on deaf ears. "They want that brand. As if wearing branded boxers or nonbranded boxers is not the same thing. As if they do not serve the same purpose, to keep your buttocks," Kerim concludes. Murat shrugs his shoulders and asks him to concentrate on their game, otherwise he is going to win this game of backgammon too.

Kerim has one more thing to deal with before this day draws to an end. While drinking his tea, he checks every page of his notebook and lists the bad payers from the bazaar. Tomorrow Burak will go to their shops and pass his reminders and threats. He decides to call a particularly annoying buyer. His mobile phone is engaged, so he waits a few more minutes and calls again and again, pausing to light a cigarette or call a third party and share his indignation at that man's behavior. About half an hour later, the man finally answers, but Kerim flies into a temper upon hearing him promise that he will pay a visit shortly. The most galling part is that the man does not even bother to use different words. Every week, for a year now, he has been using the same lines. The man's attitude is unacceptable and a one-year-old debt of YTL10000 puts his business in peril. Deciding that this is the last straw, Kerim phones a friend, a real power broker in their world, and complains. His curses are so terrible that neighbors, who chat in front of his shop, scuttle away discreetly, waiting on the alley for the storm to pass away. Chain smoking, Kerim calms down, for sooner or later a solution will be found. To make sure the situation will not be repeated, he phones another bad payer, with a four-month-old debt, and warns him to pay it as soon as possible.

After this clamor, another bad payer pays such an unexpected visit that the shopkeeper is left speechless for a moment. "Here you are," Kerim huffs, seconds later, eyes red with fury, and briskly pulls the notebook he keeps on a shelf, under a pile of boxer briefs. "A two page long debt," he snaps at him and reads aloud the dates at which such and such quantity was purchased. After harsh remarks, the matter is solved and the pages torn from the notebook. A bit more confident, Mehmet asks what is new in the shop. Rapidly Kerim's face turns from sulk to cordiality. When he speaks again, his voice does not have the same coarse tone anymore. The newest and most expensive models are shown first, the classical models in daring colors follow, and so on and so forth, for many minutes. "How much is this?" "Does it sell well?" the man wants to know.

Kerim's offers are turned down, one by one, despite the effort he puts into talking up his goods. He firmly rejects attempts at getting a discount, but suggests an alternative, a different shop not far from this bazaar, with cheaper goods, YTL2.5 instead of YTL3.5, his price. However, annoyed again, the shopkeeper emphasizes those goods, though seeming identical, are made of polyester, in sharp contrast to his fine-quality things. "Force the fabric near the stitches and you will get a ladder in seconds," he frowns and purses his lips. "Besides, they cheat the customers, selling ten pair packets minus one or two, all sizes packets minus one size. It is up to you, my brother. I can give you their business card, you can call them right now, using my phone." Upon Mehmet's departure, Kerim mutters under his breath: "cheapness, this is what he wants, not imitations. At least I got my money back."

The alleys of the bazaar are now full of cries and laughter. Men chat, smoke, drink tea, and play backgammon. Little boys run up and down. Burak is the first to notice this sudden commotion, a clear sign that the day is over and it is the time to close the shop. Kerim lights a cigarette and tells his last companion, this anthropologist, that in spite of the adventures and the problems this has been a good day. Life offered him bad days too, but he regrets none, for in the end he has lived the way he always wanted.

This is an ordinary day in the life of a man who celebrates the fullness of life to which a commitment to fake brands gave rise. This commitment translates into a particular relationship to materiality that supports certain types of arguments and into living within a moral universe of his own construction that legitimizes specific forms of actions. However, this commitment also means that circumstances might at any time throw up a crisis in which the integrity of self is challenged. Not only the law, but also ordinary people might think of this engagement in disapproving terms, from derisive commentary about copying to condemnatory remarks about the illegal practice of counterfeiting. This is why Kerim relentlessly makes claims not only about himself, but also about his fake brands. The message he tries hard to convey in his social world is that these claims are of a kind: the way he is reflects on his fake brands and the way his fake brands are reflects back on him; his honesty reflects on his products and the honesty of this materiality throws back on him. These claims are illustrative of an existential project of living an authentic life by engaging with what for many are only inauthentic objects. I came to this understanding while I was keeping him company in a shop full to the brim with fake brands. This man appeared completely aware of the contradictions and compromises that marked his life and, even more incredible, seemed to inhabit them with great ease, to feel comfortable with himself and to celebrate the fullness of a life dedicated to fake brands. This was so, I later realized, because Kerim saw in these objects and their very materiality something I could not see yet.

CONCLUSION

The entangled discourses of brand and authenticity contain not only exaggerated claims as to what they are, but also derogatory claims about what they are not. At a very basic level, these set of claims can be summarized as follows: authenticity is claimed at the level of brand; brand is ontologically purified from its connection to the products; the branded commodity is defined in opposition to the fake branded commodity; authenticity is defined against inauthenticity; engagements with authentic objects guarantee the possibility of articulating an authentic; self engagements with inauthentic objects erode, if not erase, this possibility; the notion of authentic object implies its opposite, the inauthentic object; and the center as the locus of authenticity is defined against a periphery that cannot be more than a site of mimesis. In addition, these claims present branded objects and fake branded objects, and authentic and inauthentic objects in terms of different "degrees of materiality" (Rowlands 2005). The inauthenticity of objects is said to be inherent in their materiality: something in the materiality of the inauthentic object eventually betrays its true nature. More often than not, this materiality is described as inferior to that of the authentic objects. The inauthentic object comes to matter less; it becomes an object that does not matter at all and, in the end, an object that should not exist at all. Inauthentic objects are less material than authentic objects, an effect also achieved through the removal of these objects from the public space; pushing them into the shadows, if not destroying, and, thus, to a certain extent, dematerializing them.

This book has argued for interventions into these discourses from the peripheries of Europe. For the individuals who informed this ethnography of fake branded garments in Turkey and Romania, these are objects, as material as any other objects, as saturated with moral, emotional, and affective qualities as any other objects. These individuals engage with particular material forms and apprehend their material characteristics sensuously. The possibility of legitimation lies in this materiality. Second, for them these objects are garments. These people deal with issues of manufacture, retail, and wearing that are highly specific to clothing. They are preoccupied with fiber, fabric, pattern, form, cut, trimming, and bobbling. They are interested in the durability, frailty, delicateness, density, brightness, shininess, smoothness, roughness, busyness, ruggedness, coldness, and warmness of fabrics. Producers are concerned with finding the best suppliers of materials. Consumers are preoccupied with finding the best materials. These people immerse themselves in the intricacies of clothing production and the intimacies of clothing consumption. They focus on how clothes look and feel. They set great store by or completely disregard the accuracy of the material semiotic apparatus of brands that embellishes these objects. These garments are part of what constitutes and forms their professional and personal trajectories. This interest in materiality also structures discussions regarding the nature of brand and the pretentious appropriations of branded garments.[2]

To these objects, and to their particular material qualities and properties, and their mainstream conceptualization in relation to fake-ness and brand-ness, these people respond in their own ways. They attribute different meanings and integrate them in or separate them from their lives. These diverse responses are possible because of the inherent properties of cloth and clothing: they are vulnerable to formation, transformation, wear and tear, and the dictates of fashion; consequently, their capacity to carry individual and social meanings is as enormous as it is mutable (Keane 2005). Moreover, these various approaches are possible because these objects "remain objects of experience." They are "enmeshed in causality, registered in and induced by their forms," "persist across contexts and beyond any particular intentions and projects and, as material things, are prone to enter into new contexts" (Keane 2008: 124). As they go on with their lives, these people acknowledge or disregard the characterization of these objects as fake brands and their celebration as brands and condemnation as fakes. These peripheral engagements with fake brands afford a new perspective on brand. This book argues that the significance of brand is related not to the brand itself, but to the attendant materiality that accompanies the brand.

Objects cannot be reduced to whatever happens to be found in the concepts that attempt to order their existence. Nevertheless, in this case, concepts retain their importance too. These people might ignore or dismiss this conceptualization, but there are moments and contexts in which they are reminded that for many others these objects are inauthentic. One of the assumptions that this conceptualization carries in particular causes them to reflect upon their engagement. This is the assumption that people who engage with inauthentic objects deceive themselves too. This assumption is recognized in charges of theft, fraud, imitation, and impersonation and is understood as an accusation of personal inauthenticity. These individuals realize that they are accused of pretending to be someone else—someone they cannot possibly be, because they lack the cultural and financial resources the construction of that self is presumed to require. These people routinely engage in conversations about the nature of clothing as the surface that represents or fails to represent the inner core of true being or that can be manipulated to represent a false identity. They also engage in similar discussions about the nature of brand, itself understood as a surface that represent or misrepresent the true being. These people belong to the social categories that are most expected to engage with such objects and, as such, are sensitive to these accusations. They live in two belatedly modernized societies, Turkey and Romania, whose inhabitants are accustomed to questioning the degree to which they are culturally constructed as copies or fakes of a world that in some other place is genuine.[3] In such peripheral locations, the inauthentic object has the potential to confront those who engage with it and give rise to existential questions about being true to one's self in relation to the wider context of one's life, questions that might not otherwise arise.

These individuals experience a crisis of authenticity, however momentary. They assert their self-integrity in relation to who they could be given the wider circumstances of their lives, as well as to who their significant others could become in similar circumstances. They invoke the honesty of the material forms with which they engage in order to support their claims to personal integrity. They point out that everyone can apprehend sensuously these mass-produced objects and decide for themselves if they wish to engage with them or not, and if they think they objectify them or not. The tactile and emotional nature of people's relationship to these objects allows them to authenticate their selves. The integration of materiality with sociality permits them to authenticate their selves. To paraphrase Miller (2009), the way these people think about themselves also *feels* right. The accusation of inauthenticity can be dealt with as long as the experience of materiality plays an essential part in shaping and determining what the self is. The accusation can be confronted or refuted as long as the individual perceives the inauthentic object as a site of self-objectification. These peripheral engagements with fake brands afford a new perspective on authenticity. This book argues that the authenticity of selves can be maintained in relation to the acknowledged inauthenticity of objects.

The book has offered ethnographic evidence of a "good enough" relationship to authenticity and not of a heroic quest for an unobtainable ideal. The people who informed this ethnography do want to live their lives in "good faith." They do like to think of themselves as being what they regard as truthful about who they are and how the world around them is. They do want to believe that they have carved for themselves a position in life that is truthful to how the world really is. They do want to feel comfortable with themselves and the choices they make in their lives. They do want to live within the limits of what they find acceptable or reasonable as a "sort of" or "good enough" approximation of the ideals.

Moreover, the book has demonstrated that this relationship to authenticity becomes visible when the focus turns to the role objects play in constituting the experience of the self. This approach finds a precedent in Pinney's (2002) study of the flow of objects from the periphery to the center. Pinney points out that such a focus permits the reconsideration of the metropolitan discourse of the pure center. Instead of the pure Europe of this discourse, he uncovers a creolized Europe that has constituted itself though objects from the periphery. In a similar way, the present book deconstructs the claim that the periphery can only be the site of mimesis. This book argues that this 'good enough' relationship to authenticity represents a particular form of authenticity. This is an unheralded and unmarked sense of self-integrity. This is authenticity on the periphery. This is authenticity writ small.

Notes

CHAPTER 1. INTRODUCTION

1. All the names in this book are pseudonyms.
2. At the time of this research, the safest brands were considered Armani and Dolce & Gabbana, because their owners did not deploy lawyers to protect their interests. Other producers and retailers of imitations were of the same opinion, their main arguments being the quantity and variety of imitations of these brands on the local market. However, lawyers and local associations (e.g., United Brands/Birleşmiş Markalar Derneği) claim exactly the opposite and give examples of raids to protect these brands.
3. Kerim's recollection of his father is a typical description of the patriarch. As Joseph points out, "patriarchy entails cultural constructs and structural relations that privilege the initiative of males and elders in directing the lives of others" (1999: 12). Moreover, in a patriarchal system, before they themselves become patriarchs, men are sons who have to obey seemingly all-powerful fathers. Delaney argues children "owe their life to their fathers, and thus owe them obedience and respect. This relationship is particularly severe for sons . . . In adulthood, men must learn to combine the seemingly contradictory characteristics of authority and submission" in front of their fathers (1991: 171).
4. With broad appeal to conservative families, Imam-Hatip schools are state-run vocational institutions opened in the early 1950s. These schools prepare students to become knowledgeable about Islam and, preferably, to occupy religious functionary positions. "In such a setting, students are expected to develop a sense of comfort in resigning themselves to accepting conformity, rather than developing the ability to recognise and confront their own complicity in the construction of their identities . . . The opportunities for the playful experimentation of the cultural milieu that marks the adolescent years in regular schools are curtailed in this environment" (Pak 2004: 336–337).
5. The term *delikanlı* is applied with reference to youth and its trappings. As Neyzi notes, "Turkish society does acknowledge a stage of potentially unruly behaviour, particularly among young men, who are referred to as *delikanlı*" (2001: 145). In the characterization of a young individual as *delikanlı*, the implication is that social transgressions are to some extent forgivable at the community level, since they are part of the experiences one accumulates on the path to adulthood (see also Delaney 1991; Kandiyoti 1994).

6. My encounter with Kerim can be described as an instance of the "complicity of mutual interest between anthropologist and informant, subtly but clearly understood by each other, that makes rapport possible—indeed that constitutes, even constructs it" (Marcus 1997: 89).

7. Most of my data were collected through (participant) observation: I spent a long period of time in this shop, keeping Kerim company, meeting his friends, visitors, and business partners, sometimes helping with selling and packing goods. I visited his workshop only once, in the company of his shop assistant. I also conducted a few semistructured recorded interviews, mostly to clarify business-related aspects Kerim mentioned en passant during our conversations. In addition, I conducted two life-history interviews and also listened to stories about their childhood recounted by Kerim's elder brother, himself a bazaar shopkeeper, who occasionally sold some of Kerim's products and visited him quite often. On a few occasions, Kerim requested that I record the counterarguments about counterfeiting that suddenly came to his mind. I did so, using the voice recorder he knew I always had in my bag. To most of the visitors, I was introduced as a special friend, a student in London, who learns the language and writes about imitations (I was never introduced as a Romanian, for my nationality would have been interpreted as a sure indicator that I was in fact a sex worker, a Natasha, the Turkish way of calling sex workers from the former socialist countries, who worked in areas in which trade was also concentrated). When he needed to discuss important matters with his visitors and felt or it was indicated to him that my presence would disturb such conversations, Kerim politely invited me to help Burak outside the shop or go and eat an ice cream.

8. There are different words for *imitation* in Turkish, that is, *imitasyon* and *taklit*. Kerim prefers the former, a word of French origin, over the latter, a word of Arabic origin, a religious term that connotes the acceptance of past patterns of behavior and submission to the Qur'an and tradition. Moreover, among the different Turkish words for *original*, that is, *orijinal*, a word of French origin, and *özgün*, a word coined from the Turkic *öz*, that is, essence, Kerim prefers the former.

9. The Turkish phrase Kerim used to point out that he has acquired experience is *ben kaşarlıyım*.

CHAPTER 2. FAKE BRANDS

1. Benjamin notes that "man-made artefacts could always be imitated by men. Replicas were made by pupils in practice of their craft, by masters for diffusing their works, and, finally, by third parties in pursuit of gain" ([1936] 1999: 212). Schwartz explains their presence as follows: "we admire the unique, then we reproduce it: faithfully, fatuously, faithlessly, fortuitously" (1996: 16). Benjamin employs a similar line of thinking when he emphasizes that "every day the urge grows stronger to get hold of an object at very close range by way of its likeness, its reproduction" ([1936] 1999: 217). Fakes are ubiquitous. Moreover, depending on particular interests and circumstances, the category of inauthentic object

can sometimes be very large, including copies, imitations, pastiches, reproductions, and studio works. In addition, objects deliberately misrepresented as they change hands can be considered fakes. These can be misattributed works and works restored or assembled from authentic and inauthentic parts.

2. Jones believes inauthentic art objects can also play a positive role: "even if the errors of the past only provided lessons for the future they would be worthy of retention and study. But fakes do far more than that. As keys to understanding the changing nature of our vision of the past, as motors for the development of scholarly and scientific techniques of analysis, as subverts of aesthetic certainties, they deserve our closer attention" (1992: 16). Moreover, he seems to share, at least partially, the popular fascination with art forgers: "while as the most entertaining of monuments to the wayward talents of generations of gifted rogues they claim our reluctant admiration" (1992: 16).

3. For examples of ideological responses to this conceptualization, see Coombe (1998).

CHAPTER 3. THE ELUSIVENESS OF INAUTHENTICITY . . . IN TURKEY

1. A significant part of the Istanbul labor force consists of semiskilled workers with short work experience, which is nevertheless sufficient for performing the standard operations of clothing manufacturing. However, to function properly, any workshop needs a certain critical mass of skilled workers.

2. These transformative processes are reminiscent of those described by Norris in her ethnography of the transformation of cast-off clothes in India by entrepreneurs "who rely on invisibility and secrecy to produce valued new products from the heaps of unwanted stuff that they surreptitiously collect" (2005: 102).

3. State agents could be also threatened. However, my informants insisted this happened only occasionally and they held the last comers, usually Kurds, responsible for the violent side of the trade, for these individuals had not yet learned how to do business.

4. In Istanbul, copying successful business ideas is not something new. The best illustration for the existence of such a practice is the sign on a wall inside the Sultanahmet Köftecisi restaurant, famous for the meatballs it has sold since the 1920s. Copies of this restaurant exist all over the city, not only selling similar food but also including its name, in one way or another, in their own. This sign reads "imitations keep the original alive" (*taklitler aslını yaşatır*), a recognition of the existence of copies and a statement of authenticity. Some of my Turkish acquaintances read in this sign an utter condemnation of the practice of copying successful ideas and objects. For others, however, the sign indicated the contribution of the fake to the success of the original.

5. This resonates with Baines's (1999) observation about the mythology of fakery, forgery, and counterfeiting that courts of law have perpetuated. In court, only a certain trajectory is possible, that is, transgression, detection, confession, and punishment.

CHAPTER 4. THE ELUSIVENESS OF INAUTHENTICITY . . . IN ROMANIA

1. My research agenda was never disclosed. My companion, confronted with the curiosity of her acquaintances as to who her new fellow trader was, decided that this would be beyond their comprehension, and worse, that it could jeopardize her hard-won relationships. As she acquired most of her goods on credit, good relationships were a precious capital.
2. Journalists who approached shopkeepers and administrative staff for interviews reported similar reactions.
3. Arguably, other forms of commerce grow inside this infrastructure, as Istanbul is an important illegal gate toward the European Union (Içduygu and Toktaş 2002).
4. This resonates with Hosein's (2007, 2009) argument. She points out that, as well as formal law, there is a general sense of fairness by which people see means as justified by ends. This sense translates into boundaries beyond which something can be condemned and not just perceived as illegal. Moreover, this is reminiscent of Slater's (1998) observation. According to him, traders in pornographic images on the Internet try to keep their sexual transgressions within the boundaries of conventional pornography and rigorously exclude those that they consider as going beyond the boundary. They become active participants in the construction of a sense of acceptable morality.
5. Some of the socialist brands are now reinvented as brands in postsocialist Romania, a process in which nostalgia is mixed with self-irony to create the coolness of socialism (see also Berdahl 1999).

CHAPTER 5. INAUTHENTIC OBJECTS, AUTHENTIC SELVES

1. The conceptualization of this novel form of inwardness drew its strength from other social, moral, and epistemological phenomena that were developing during the same period. Lindholm points out that the notion of authenticity "ascended on the rising tide of individuality, democracy and equality in the 17th and 18th centuries, which, along to capitalism, mobility, the public-private split, Protestant faith and scientific worldview, presumed the existence of a universal moral self, hidden beneath the parade of social roles" (2009: 151) (see also Berman 1971; Sennett 1979).
2. "Which is not to say," Trilling explains, "that the moral temper of our times sets no store by the avoidance of falsehood to others, only that it does not figure as the defining purpose of being true to one's self" (1972: 9).
3. As Benjamin points out, "at the time of its origin a medieval picture of the Madonna could not yet be said to be 'authentic.' It became 'authentic' only during the succeeding centuries and perhaps most strikingly so during the last one" ([1936] 1999: 243).
4. As Paul observes, in analyzing some of the outcomes of the encounter between Westerners and the Other, such as Cuna curing figurines of "European types,"

the anthropologists encounter "our fascination with reproduction, their fascination with us, our fascination with their fascination with our reproductions, their fascination with our commodities that they hope to possess in the spirit world that reproduces this one, and so on and on" (1994: 467).

CHAPTER 6. CONCLUSION

1. "Maşallah" means both "wonderful" and "may God preserve him from evil."
2. In art, the materiality of inauthentic objects is often brought to the fore in discussions about aesthetics. Forgeries that can be distinguished from originals only through scientific tests raise the question of aesthetic importance. It has been pointed out that authenticity in itself does not guarantee the aesthetic merit of a work. It is rather the cult of the artist and the price an authored work has that turn authenticity into an essential attribute of a work of art (Dutton 1983; Kennick 1985).
3. For discussions of other societies and communities marked by such sensitivity, see Taylor-Atkins (2000), Patico (2001), or Rausing (2002).

References

Antohi, S. (2002). Romania and the Balkans: From geocultural bovarism to ethnic ontology. http://archiv.iwm.at/index.php?option=com_content&task=view&id=235&Itemid=411

Appadurai, A. (1986). Introduction: Commodities and the politics of value. In A. Appadurai (ed.) *The social life of things: Commodities in cultural perspective.* New York: Cambridge University Press. Pp. 3–63.

Appadurai, A. (1996). *Modernity at large: Cultural dimensions of globalization.* Minneapolis: University of Minnesota Press.

Appiah, K. A. (1994). Identity, authenticity, survival: Multicultural societies and social reproduction. In A. Gutmann (ed.) *Multiculturalism: Examining the politics of recognition.* Princeton, NJ: Princeton University Press. Pp. 149–163.

Arvidsson, A. (2006). *Brands: Meaning and value in media culture.* Oxford: Routledge.

Askegard, S. (2006). Brands as a global ideoscape. In J. E. Schroeder and M. Salzer-Mörling (eds.) *Brand culture.* New York: Routledge. Pp. 91–102.

Baines, P. (1999). *The house of forgery in eighteenth-century Britain.* Aldershot, UK: Ashgate.

Banerjee, M. and D. Miller. (2003). *The sari.* Oxford: Berg.

Barron, A. (2002). Copyright, art and objecthood. In D. McClean and K. Schubert (eds.) *Dear images: Art, copyright and culture.* London: Ridinghouse/ICA. Pp. 277–309.

Baudrillard, J. (2001). Simulations. In R. Kearney and D. Rasmussen (eds.) *Continental aesthetics. Romanticism to postmodernism. An anthology.* Oxford: Blackwell. Pp. 414–430.

Beebe, B. (2004). The semiotic analysis of trademark law. *UCLA Law Rev.* 51(3): 621–704.

Beebe, B. (2008). The semiotic account of trademark doctrine and trademark culture. In G. Dinwoodie and M. Jamis (eds.) *Trademark law and theory: A handbook of contemporary research.* Cheltenham, UK: Edward Elgar. Pp. 42–64.

Benjamin, W. ([1936] 1999). The work of art in the age of mechanical reproduction. In W. Benjamin. *Illuminations.* London: Pimlico. Pp. 217–252.

Berdahl, D. (1999). "(N)Ostalgie" for the present: Memory, longing, and East German things. *Ethnos* 64(2): 192–211.

Berman, M. (1971). *The politics of authenticity: Radical individualism and the emergence of modern society.* London: Allen and Unwin.

Bhabha, H. K. (1994). *The location of culture.* London and New York: Routledge.

Blakeney, M. (2009). International proposals for the criminal enforcement of intellectual property rights: International concern with counterfeiting and piracy. *Intellectual Property Quarterly/Queen Mary School of Law Legal Studies Research Paper No. 29/2009.* http://ssrn.com/abstract=1476964

Blum, M. (2000). Remaking the East German past: *Ostalgie*, identity and material culture. *The Journal of Popular Culture* 34(3): 229–253.

Bourdieu, P. (1984). *Distinction: A social critique of the judgment of taste.* Cambridge, MA: Harvard University Press.

Brandtstädter, S. (2009). Fakes: Fraud, value-anxiety, and the politics of sincerity. In K. Sykes (ed.) *Ethnographies of moral reasoning: Living paradoxes of global age.* New York: Palgrave Macmillan. Pp. 139–160.

Briefel, A. (2006). *The deceivers: Art forgery and identity in the nineteenth century.* Ithaca, NY: Cornell University Press.

Brooks, D. (2000). *Bobos in paradise: The new upper class and how they got there.* New York: Simon & Schuster.

Brown, M. (2010). Changing authentic identities: Evidence from Taiwan and China. *Journal of the Royal Anthropological Institute* 16: 459–479.

Bruner, E. B. (2005). *Culture on tour: Ethnographies of travel.* Chicago: University of Chicago Press.

Caldwell, M. L. (2002). The taste of nationalism: Food politics in postsocialist Moscow. *Ethnos* 67(3): 295–319.

Carrier, J. G. (1995). *Gifts and commodities: Exchange and Western capitalism since 1700.* London: Routledge.

Chang, H. (2004). Fake logo, fake theory, fake globalization. *Inter-Asia Cultural Studies* 5(2): 222–236.

Comaroff, J. and J. Comaroff. (2006). Law and disorder in the postcolony: An introduction. In J. Comaroff and J. Comaroff (eds.) *Law and disorder in the postcolony.* Chicago: University of Chicago Press. Pp. 1–56.

Coombe, R. (1996). Embodied trademarks: Mimesis and alterity on American commercial frontiers. *Cultural Anthropology* 11(2): 202–224.

Coombe, R. (1998). *The cultural life of intellectual properties: Authorship, appropriation, and the law.* Durham, NC: Duke University Press.

Creed, G. (2002). (Consumer) paradise lost: Capitalist dynamics and disenchantment in rural Bulgaria. *Anthropology of East Europe Review* 20(2): 1–6.

Czakó, Á. and E. Sik (1999). Characteristics and origins of the Comecon open-air market in Hungary. *International Journal of Urban and Regional Research* 23: 715–738.

Çınar, E. et al. (1988). The present day status of small-scale industries (sanatkar) in Bursa, Turkey. *International Journal of Middle East Studies* 20: 287–301.

Danto, A. (1973). Artworks and real things. *Theoria* 39(1–3): 1–17.

Davidova, E. (2010). Post-1989 shopping tourism to Turkey as prologue to Bulgaria's "return to Europe." *New Perspectives on Turkey* 43: 135–164.

Dedeoğlu, S. (2008). *Women workers in Turkey: Global industrial production in Istanbul.* London and New York: I.B. Tauris.

Delaney, C. (1991). *The seed and the soil: Gender and cosmology in Turkish village society.* Berkeley: University of California Press.

Dent, A. S. (2012). Understanding the war on piracy, or why we need more anthropology of pirates. *Anthropological Quarterly* 85(3): 659–672.

Dutton, D. (1983). *The forger's art: Forgery and the philosophy of art.* Berkeley: University of California Press.

Eder, M. (2003). From suitcase trade to organized informal trade? The case of Laleli district in Istanbul. Paper presented at the Mediterranean Social and Political Research Meeting, Florence, Italy, March 19–23.

Eder, M. and Ö. Öz (2010). From cross-border exchange networks to transnational trading practices. The case of shuttle traders in Laleli, Istanbul. In M.-L. Djelic and S. Quack (eds.) *Transnational communities: Shaping global economic governance.* Cambridge: Cambridge University Press. Pp. 82–104.

Entwistle, J. (2000). *The fashioned body: Fashion, dress and modern social theory.* Oxford: Polity Press.

Eraydin, A. and A. Erendil (1999). The role of female labour in industrial restructuring: New production processes and labour market relations in the Istanbul clothing industry. *Gender, Place and Culture* 6(3): 259–272.

Errington, S. (1998). *The death of authentic primitive art and other tales of progress.* Berkeley: University of California Press.

Fehérváry, K. (2002). American kitchens, luxury bathrooms and the search for a "normal" life in post-socialist Hungary. *Ethnos* 67(3): 369–400.

Foster, R. (2005). Commodity futures: Labour, love, and value. *Anthropology Today* 21(4): 8–12.

Foster, R. (2008a). Commodities, brands, love and kula: Comparative notes on value creation. *Anthropological Theory* 8(1): 9–25.

Foster, R. (2008b). *Coca-Globalization. Following soft drinks from New York to New Guinea.* New York: Palgrave Macmillan.

Frow, J. (2003). Signature and brand. In J. Collins (ed.) *High-Pop: Making culture into popular entertainment.* Oxford: Blackwell. Pp. 56–74.

Fournier, S. (1998). Consumers and their brands: Developing relationship theory in consumer research. *Journal of Consumer Research* 24(4): 343–373.

Gable, E. and R. Handler (1996). After authenticity at an American heritage site. *American Anthropologist* 98(3): 568–578.

Gaines, J. (1991). *Contested culture: The image, the voice, and the law.* Chapel Hill: University of North Carolina Press.

Geary, P. (1986). Sacred commodities: The circulation of medieval relics. In A. Appadurai (ed.) *The social life of things: Commodities in cultural perspective.* New York: Cambridge University Press. Pp. 169–194.

Geertz, C. (1979). Suq: The bazaar economy in Sefrou. In C. Geertz, H. Geertz, and L. Rosen (eds.) *Meaning and order in Moroccan society: Three essays in cultural analysis.* Cambridge: Cambridge University Press. Pp. 123–243.

Geismar, H. (2005). Reproduction, creativity, restriction. Material culture and copyright in Vanuatu. *Journal of Social Archaeology* 5(1): 25–51.

Geismar, H. (2011). "Material Culture Studies" and other ways to theorize objects: A primer to a regional debate. *Comparative Studies in Society and History* 53(1): 1–9.

Gereffi, G. (1999). International trade and industrial upgrading in the apparel commodity chain. *Journal of International Economics* 48(1): 37–70.

Grafton. A. (1990). *Forgers and critics: Creativity and duplicity in western scholarship.* Princeton, NJ: Princeton University Press.

Gregson, N. and L. Crewe (2003). *Second-hand cultures.* Oxford: Berg.

Groom, N. (2007). Romanticism and forgery. *Literature Compass* 4(6): 1625–1649.

Grosse Ruse-Kahn, H. (2008). A pirate of the Caribbean? The attractions of suspending TRIPS obligations. *Journal of International Economic Law* 11(2): 313–364.

Grosse Ruse-Khan, H. (2010). From TRIPS to ACTA: Towards a new "gold standard" in criminal IP enforcement? Max Planck Institute for Intellectual Property and Competition Law. http://papers.ssrn.com/sol3/papers.cfm?abstract_id=1592104##

Gürbilek, N. (2003). Dandies and originals: Authenticity, belatedness, and the Turkish novel. *The South Atlantic Quarterly* 102(2–3): 599–628.

Halstead, N. (2002). Branding "perfection": Foreign as self; self as foreign-foreign. *Journal of Material Culture* 7(3): 273–293.

Handler, R. (1986). Authenticity. *Anthropology Today* 2(1): 2–4.

Handler, R. (2001). Anthropology of authenticity. In N. J. Smelser and P. B. Baltes (eds.) *International encyclopaedia of the social and behavioural sciences.* Oxford: Pergamon. Pp. 936–967.

Hann, C. and I. Beller-Hann (1992). Samovars and sex on Turkey's Russian markets. *Anthropology Today* 8(4): 3–6.

Hansen, K. T. (2000). *Salaula: The world of second hand clothing and Zambia.* Chicago: University of Chicago Press.

Haywood, I. (1987). *Faking it: Art and the politics of forgery.* Brighton, UK: Harvester.

Hohnen, P. (2003). *A Market out of place? Remaking economic, social and symbolic boundaries in post-communist Lithuania.* Oxford: Oxford University Press.

Holtorf, C. and T. Schadla-Hall (1999). Age as artefact: On archaeological authenticity. *European Journal of Archaeology* 2(2): 229–247.

Hosein, G. (2007). *Everybody have to eat: Politics and governance in Trinidad.* Unpublished PhD thesis. University College London.

Hosein, G. (2009). Food, family, art and God: Aesthetic authority in public life in Trinidad. In D. Miller (ed.) *Anthropology and the individual.* Oxford: Berg. Pp. 150–177.

Howard, A. (1997). Labor, history and sweatshops in the new global economy. In A. Ross (ed.) *No sweat: Fashion, free trade and the rights of garment workers.* London: Verso. Pp. 151–172.

Humphrey, C. (1991). "Icebergs," barter, and the mafia in provincial Russia. *Anthropology Today* 7(2): 8–13.

Humphrey, C. (2002). *The unmaking of Soviet life: Everyday economies after socialism.* Ithaca, NY: Cornell University Press.

Humphrey, C. and V. Skvirskaya (2009). Trading places: Post-socialist container market and the city. *Focaal* 55: 61–73.

Hung, C. L. (2003). The business of product counterfeiting in China and the post-WTO membership environment. *Asia Pacific Business Review* 10(1): 58–77.

Içduygu, A. and S. Toktaş (2002). How do smuggling and trafficking operate via irregular border crossing in the Middle East? Evidence from fieldwork in Turkey. *International Migration* 40(6): 23–65.

Jackson, M. (2005). *Existential anthropology: Events, exigencies and effects.* New York and Oxford: Berghahn Books.

Jaffé, D. (1992). Peiresc and new attitudes to authenticity in the seventeenth century. In M. Jones (ed.) *Why fakes matter: Essays on problems of authenticity.* London: British Museum Press. Pp. 157–173.

Jenß, H. (2004). Dressed in history: Retro styles and the construction of authenticity in youth culture. *Fashion Theory* 8(4): 387–403.

Johns, A. (2009). *Piracy: The intellectual property wars from Gutenberg to Gates.* Chicago: University of Chicago Press.

Jones, M. (1990). *Fake? The art of deception.* London: British Museum Press.

Jones, M. (1992). *Why fakes matter: Essays on problems of authenticity.* London: British Museum Press.

Jones, S. (2010). Negotiating authentic objects and authentic selves. Beyond the deconstructing of authenticity. *Journal of Material Culture* 15(2): 181–203.

Joseph, S. (1999). Introduction: Theories and dynamics of gender, self, and identity in Arab families. In S. Joseph (ed.) *Intimate selving in Arab families: Gender, self, and identity.* Syracuse, NY: Syracuse University Press. Pp. 1–17.

Jusdanis, G. (1991). *Belated modernity and aesthetic culture: Inventing national literature.* Minneapolis: University of Minnesota Press.

Kandiyoti, D. (1994). The paradoxes of masculinity. Some thoughts on segregated societies. In A. Cornwall and N. Lindisfarne (eds.) *Dislocating masculinity: Comparative ethnographies.* London and New York: Routledge. Pp. 197–213.

Kaneff, D. (2002). The shame and pride of market activity: Morality, identity and trading in postsocialist rural Bulgaria. In R. Mandel and C. Humphrey (eds.) *Markets and moralities: Ethnographies of postsocialism.* Oxford: Berg. Pp. 33–51.

Kapferer, J. N. (2006). The two business cultures of luxury brands. In J. E. Schroeder and M. Salzer-Mörling (eds.) *Brand culture.* New York: Routledge. Pp. 67–76.

Kayaoğlu, T. (2010). *Legal imperialism: Sovereignty and extraterritoriality in Japan, the Ottoman Empire, and China.* Cambridge: Cambridge University Press.

Kaytaz, M. (1994). Subcontracting practice in the Turkish textile and metal-working industries. In F. Şenses (ed.) *Recent industrialization experience of Turkey in a global context.* Westport, CT: Greenwood Press. Pp. 141–154.

Keane, W. (2003). Semiotics and the social analysis of material things. *Language & Communication* 23: 409–425.

Keane, W. (2005). The hazards of new clothes: What signs make possible. In S. Küchler and G. Were (eds.) *The art of clothing: A Pacific experience.* London: UCL Press. Pp. 1–16.

Keane, W. (2006). Subjects and objects. In C. Tilley, W. Keane, S. Küchler, M. Rowlands, and P. Spyer (eds.) *Handbook of material culture.* London: Sage. Pp. 197–202.

Keane, W. (2008). The Evidence of the Senses and the Materiality of Religion. *Journal of the Royal Anthropological Institute* 14(1): 110–127.

Kennick, W. E. (1985). Art and inauthenticity. *The Journal of Aesthetics and Art Criticism* 44(1): 3–12.

Keyder, Ç. (1997). Whither the project of modernity? Turkey in the 1990s. In S. Bozdoğan and R. Kasaba (eds.) *Rethinking modernity and national identity in Turkey.* Seattle: University of Washington Press. Pp. 37–51.

Keyder, Ç. (1999). A tale of two neighborhoods. In Ç. Keyder (ed.) *Istanbul: Between the global and the local.* Lanham, MD: Rowman & Littlefield. Pp 173–186.

Keyder, Ç. (2005). Globalization and social exclusion in Istanbul. *International Journal of Urban and Regional Research* 291: 124–134.

Keyder, V. B. (1997). *Intellectual property rights and customs union.* Istanbul: Intermedia Publications.

Klein, N. (2001). *No logo.* London: Flamingo.

Koçak, O. (2010). "Westernisation against the West": Cultural politics in the early Turkish Republic. In C. Kerslake, K. Öktem, and P. Robins (eds.) *Turkey's engagement with modernity: Conflict and change in the twentieth century.* Basingstoke, UK: Palgrave Macmillan. Pp. 305–321.

Konstantinov, Y. (1996). Patterns of reinterpretation: Trade-tourism in the Balkans (Bulgaria) as a picaresque metaphorical enactment of post-totalitarianism. *American Ethnologist* 23(4): 762–782.

Krauss, R. (1981). The originality of the avant-garde: A postmodernist repetition. *October* 18: 47–66.

Kriegel, L. (2004). Culture and the copy: Calico, capitalism, and design copyright in early Victorian Britain. *The Journal of British Studies* 43(2): 233–265.

Küchler, S. and D. Miller (2005). *Clothing as material culture.* Oxford: Berg.

Latour, B. and A. Lowe (2010). The migration of the aura or how to explore the original through its facsimiles. In T. Bartscherer and R. Coover (eds.) *Switching codes. Thinking through digital technology in the humanities and the arts.* Chicago: University of Chicago Press. Pp. 275–298.

Lin, Yi-Chieh J. (2011). *Fake stuff: China and the rise of counterfeit goods.* London: Routledge.

Linden, R. H. (2002). *Norms and nannies: The impact of international organizations on the Central and East European states.* Lanham, MD: Rowman & Littlefield.

Lindholm, C. (2002). Authenticity, anthropology, and the sacred. *Anthropological Quarterly* 75(2): 331–338.

Lindholm, C. (2008). *Culture and authenticity.* Malden, MA: Blackwell.

Lindholm, C. (2009). How we became authentic. *Ethos* 37(1): 148–153.

Lippert, O. (1999). *Competitive strategies for the protection of intellectual property.* Vancouver: Fraser Institute.

Lowenthal, D. (1992). Authenticity? The dogma of self-delusion. In M. Jones (ed.) *Why fakes matter: Essays on problems of authenticity.* London: British Museum Press. Pp. 184–192.

Lowenthal, D. (1996). *Possessed by the past: The heritage crusade and the spoils of history.* New York: Free Press.

Lury, C. (2004). *Brands. The logos of the global economy.* London and New York: Routledge.

Luvaas, B. (2010). Designer vandalism: Indonesian indie fashion and the cultural practice of cut 'n' paste. *Visual Anthropology* 26(1): 1–16.

Malton, S. (2009). *Forgery in nineteenth-century literature and culture: Fictions of finance from Dickens to Wilde.* New York: Palgrave Macmillan.

Mandel, R. and C. Humphrey (2002). *Markets and moralities: Ethnographies of postsocialism.* Oxford: Berg.

Manning, P. (2009). The epoch of Magna: Capitalist brands and postsocialist revolutions in Georgia. *Slavic Review* 68(4): 924–945.

Manning, P. (2010). The semiotics of brand. *Annual Review of Anthropology* 39: 33–49.

Manning, P. and A. Uplisashvili (2007). "Our beer": Ethnographic brands in postsocialist Georgia. *American Anthropologist* 109(4): 626–641.

Marcus, G. (1995). Ethnography in/out of the world system: The emergence of multi-sited ethnography. *Annual Review of Anthropology* 24: 95–117.

Marcus, G. (1997). The uses of complicity in the changing mise-en-scène of anthropological fieldwork. *Representations* 59: 85–108.

Mazzarella, W. (2003). "Very Bombay": Contending with the global in an Indian advertising agency. *Cultural Anthropology* 18(1): 33–71.

McClean, D. (2002). Introduction. In D. McClean and K. Schubert (eds.) *Dear images: Art, copyright and culture.* London: Ridinghouse/ICA. Pp: 10–45.

McClean, D. and K. Schubert (eds.) (2002). *Dear images: Art, copyright and culture.* London: Ridinghouse/ICA.

Meneley, A. (2007). Like an extra virgin. *American Anthropologist* 109(4): 678–687.

Mertha, A. (2005). *The politics of piracy: Intellectual property in contemporary China.* Ithaca, NY: Cornell University Press.

Miller, D. (1987). *Material culture and mass consumption.* Oxford: Blackwell.

Miller, D. (1995). *Acknowledging consumption.* London: Routledge.

Miller, D. (1998a). Coca-Cola: A black sweet drink from Trinidad. In D. Miller (ed.) *Material cultures: Why some things matter.* London: University College London Press. Pp: 169–187.

Miller, D. (1998b). *A theory of shopping.* Ithaca, NY: Cornell University Press.

Miller, D. (2005a). Introduction. In S. Küchler and D. Miller (eds.) *Clothing as material culture.* Oxford: Berg. Pp. 1–29.

Miller, D. (2005b). Materiality: An introduction. In D. Miller (ed.) *Materiality.* London: Duke University Press.

Miller, D. (2009). *Stuff.* Oxford: Polity.

Moor, L. (2007). *The rise of brands.* Oxford: Berg.

Moore, R. (2003). From genericide to viral marketing: On "brand." *Language & Communication* 23(3–4): 331–357.

Myers, F. (2004). Ontologies of the image and economies of exchange. *American Ethnologist* 31(1): 5–20.

Nakassis, C. (2012a). Counterfeiting what? Aesthetics of brandedness and brand in Tamil Nadu, India. *Anthropological Quarterly* 85(3): 701–722.

Nakassis, C. (2012b). Brand, citationality, performativity. *American Anthropologist* 114(4): 624–638.

Newell, S. (2013). Brands as masks: Public secrecy and the counterfeit in Côte d'Ivoire. *Journal of the Royal Anthropological Institute* 19: 138–154.

Neyzi, L. (2001). Object or Subject? The paradox of "youth" in Turkey. *International Journal of Middle East Studies* 33(3): 411–432.

Norris, L. (2005). Cloth that lies: The secrets of recycling in India. In S. Küchler and D. Miller (eds.) *Clothing as material culture*. Oxford: Berg. Pp. 83–106.

Orvell, M. (1989). *The real thing: Imitation and authenticity in American culture, 1880–1940.* Chapel Hill: University of North Carolina Press.

Pang, L. (2008). "China who makes and fakes": A semiotics of the counterfeit. *Theory, Culture & Society* 25(6): 117–140.

Pak, S.-Y. (2004). Articulating the boundary between secularism and Islamism: The Imam-Hatip schools of Turkey. *Anthropology and Education Quarterly* 55(3): 324–344.

Patico, J. (2001). Globalization in the postsocialist marketplace: Consumer readings of difference and development in urban Russia. *Kroeber Anthropological Society Papers* 86: 127–142.

Patico, J. (2002). Chocolate and cognac: Gifts and the recognition of social worlds in post-Soviet Russia. *Ethnos* 67(3): 345–368.

Patico, J. (2005). To be happy in a Mercedes: Tropes of value and ambivalent visions of marketization. *American Ethnologist* 32(3): 479–496.

Patico, J. and M. L. Caldwell (2002). Consumers exiting socialism: Ethnographic perspectives on daily life in post-communist Europe. *Ethnos* 67(3): 285–294.

Paul, R. A. (1994). Review. *American Anthropologist* 96(2): 466–467.

Pedersen, M. (2007). From "public" to "private" markets in postsocialist Mongolia. *Anthropology of East Europe Review* 25(1): 64–71.

Pelkmans, M. (2006). *Defending the border: Identity, religion and modernity in the Republic of Georgia.* Ithaca, NY: Cornell University Press.

Peters, E. D., C. R. Duran, and M. J. Piore (2002). Learning and the limits of foreign partners as teachers. In G. Gereffi, D. Spencer, and J. Bair (eds.) *Free trade and uneven development: The North American apparel industry after NAFTA*. Philadelphia: Temple University Press. Pp. 224–245.

Phillips, D. (1997). *Exhibiting authenticity*. Manchester: Manchester University Press.

Pinheiro-Machado, R. (2010). The attribution of authenticity to "real" and "fake" branded commodities in Brazil and China. In A. Bevan and D. Wengrow (eds.) *Cultures of commodity branding*. Walnut Creek, CA: Left Coast Press. Pp. 109–129.

Pinney, C. (2002). Creole Europe: The reflection of a reflection. *Journal of New Zealand Literature* 20: 125–161.

Radnóti, S. (1999). *The fake: Forgery and its place in art*. Lanham, MD and Oxford: Rowman & Littlefield.

Rausing, S. (2002). Re-constructing the normal: Identity and the consumption of western goods in Estonia. In R. Mandel and C. Humphrey (eds.) *Markets and moralities: Ethnographies of postsocialism*. New York: Berg. Pp. 127–142.

Riddle, L. and K. Gillespie (2003). Information sources for new ventures in the Turkish clothing export industry. *Small Business Economics* 20(1): 105–120.

Romiţan, C. R. (2010). Scurtă retrospectivă a reglementărilor legislative în domeniul mărcilor (1879–2009). *Romanian Journal of Intellectual Property Law (Revista Română de Dreptul Proprietăţii Intelectuale)* 1: 129–141.

Romiţan, C. R. (2011). 149 de ani de la adoptarea în România a primei legi care a reglementat drepturile autorilor de opere literare şi artistice. *Romanian Journal*

of Intellectual Property Law (Revista Română de Dreptul Proprietății Intelectuale)
1: 18–35.

Rose, M. (1994). *Authors and owners: The invention of copyright.* Cambridge, MA: Harvard University Press.

Rowlands, M. (1994). The material culture of success: Ideals and life cycles in Cameroon. In J. Friedman (ed.) *Consumption and identity.* Chur, Switzerland: Harwood Academic. Pp. 147–166.

Rowlands, M. (2005). A materialist approach to materiality. In D. Miller (ed.) *Materiality.* London: Duke University Press. Pp. 72–87.

Russett, M. (2006). *Fictions and fakes: Forging romantic authenticity, 1760–1845.* Cambridge: Cambridge University Press.

Santos, F. J. and C. Ribeiro (2006). An exploratory study of the relationship between counterfeiting and culture. *Revista de Estudos Politecnicos/Polytechnical Studies Review* 3(5–6): 227–243.

Savage, G. (1976). *Forgeries, fakes and reproductions.* London: White Lion.

Schmitz, H. and P. Knorringa (2000). Learning from global buyers. *Journal of Development Studies* 37: 177–205.

Schneider, J. (1994). In and out of polyester: Desire, disdain and global fibre competition. *Anthropology Today* 10(4): 2–10.

Schneider, J. (2006). Cloth and clothing. In C. Tilley, W. Keane, S. Küchler, M. Rowlands, and P. Spyer (eds.) *Handbook of material culture.* London: Sage. Pp. 203–220.

Schwartz, H. (1996). *The culture of the copy: Striking likeness, unreasonable racsimiles.* New York: Zone Books.

Sennett, R. (1979). *The fall of public man.* London: Faber.

Şenses, F. (1994). *Recent industrialization experience of Turkey in a global context.* Westport, CT: Greenwood Press.

Sherman. B. and L. Bently (1999). *The making of modern intellectual property law: The British experience, 1760–1911.* Cambridge: Cambridge University Press.

Siegel, J. (1998). *New criminal type in Jakarta: Counter-revolution today.* Durham, NC: Duke University Press.

Sik, E. and C. Wallace (1999). The development of open-air markets in East-Central Europe. *International Journal of Urban and Regional Research* 23: 697–714.

Silverstein, B. (2003). Islam and modernity in Turkey: Power, tradition and historicity in the European provinces of the Muslim world. *Anthropological Quarterly* 76(3): 497–517.

Skeggs, B. (1997). *Formations of class and gender: Becoming respectable.* London: Sage.

Slater, D. (1998). Trading sexpics on IRC: Embodiment and authenticity on the Internet. *Body & Society* 4(4): 91–117.

Smart, A. (1999). Predatory rule and illegal economic practices. In J. Heyman and A. Smart (eds.) *States and illegal practices.* Oxford: Berg. Pp. 99–128.

Sodipo, B. (1997). *Piracy and counterfeiting: GATT, TRIPS and developing countries,* International Economic Development Law (5). London: Kluwer Law International.

Spector, R. (2008). Bazaar politics: The fate of marketplaces in Kazakhstan. *Problems of Post-Communism* 55(6): 42–53.

Spooner, P. (1986). Weavers and dealers: The authenticity of an oriental carpet. In A. Appadurai, (ed.) *The social life of things: Commodities in cultural perspective.* New York: Cambridge University Press. Pp. 195–235.

Stoller, P. (2002). *Money has no smell: The Africanization of New York City.* Chicago: University of Chicago Press.

Sykes, K. (2009). *Ethnographies of moral reasoning. Living paradoxes of global age.* New York: Palgrave Macmillan.

Sylvanus, N. (2010). The copy and its counterfeit: Anxieties over product authenticity in a West African marketplace. Paper presented at the 2010 American Anthropological Association Annual Meeting, New Orleans, Louisiana, November 16–21.

Taussig, M. T. (1993). *Mimesis and alterity: A particular history of the senses.* New York: Routledge.

Taylor, C. (1991). *The ethics of authenticity.* Cambridge, MA: Harvard University Press.

Taylor-Atkins, E. (2000). Can Japanese sing the blues? In T. J. Craig (ed.) *Japan pop!: Inside the world of Japanese popular culture.* New York: Eastgate. Pp. 27–58.

Thomas, K. (2009). Structural adjustment, spatial imaginaries, and "piracy" in Guatemala's apparel industry. *Anthropology of Work Review* 30(1): 1–10.

Thomas, K. (2012). Intellectual property law and the ethics of imitation in Guatemala. *Anthropological Quarterly* 85(3): 785–816.

Thomas, N. (1999). The case of the misplaced ponchos. Speculations concerning the history of cloth in Polynesia. *Journal of Material Culture* 4(1): 5–20.

Tilley, C. (2006). Objectification. In C. Tilley, W. Keane, S. Küchler, M. Rowlands, and P. Spyer (eds.) *Handbook of material culture.* London: Sage. Pp. 60–73.

Togan, S. (1997). Opening up the Turkish economy in the context of the customs union with EU. *Journal of Economic Integration* 12(2): 157–179.

Tokatlı, N. (2003). Globalization and the changing clothing industry in Turkey. *Environment and Planning A* 35: 1877–1894.

Tokatlı, N. and Y. Boyacı (1997). Internationalization of retailing in Turkey. *New Perspectives on Turkey* 17: 97–128.

Tokatlı, N. and Ö. Kızılgün (2004). Upgrading in the global clothing industry: Mavi jeans and the transformation of a Turkish firm from full-package to brand-name manufacturing and retailing. *Economic Geography* 80(3): 221–240.

Trilling, L. (1972). *Sincerity and authenticity.* London: Oxford University Press.

Turner, T. (1993 [1980]). The social skin. In C. B. Burroughs and J. Ehrenreich (eds.) *Reading the social body.* Iowa City: University of Iowa Press. Pp. 15–39.

Vann, E. (2006). The limits of authenticity in Vietnamese consumer markets. *American Anthropologist* 108(2): 286–296.

Veblen, T. ([1899] 1924). *Theory of the leisure class.* London: Allen & Unwin.

Verdery, K. (1996). *What was socialism, and what comes next?* Princeton, NJ: Princeton University Press.

Waite, N. (2004). *The future of anti-counterfeiting, brand protection and security packaging in Central and Eastern Europe: Strategic forecasts and expert insight.* Leatherhead, UK: Pira International Ltd.

Wengrow, D. (2008). Prehistories of commodity branding. *Current Anthropology* 49(1): 7–34.

Woodmansee, M. (1984). The genius and the copyright: Economic and legal conditions of the emergence of the "author." *Eighteenth-Century Studies* 17(4): 425–448.

Woodward, S. (2007). *Why women wear what they wear.* Oxford: Berg.

Yalçın-Heckmann, L. and H. Demidirek (2007). Encounters of the postsocialist kind: The movement of goods and identities within and beyond the former socialist world. *Anthropology of East Europe Review* 25(1): 6–14.

Yao, J-t. (2005). Counterfeiting and an optimal monitoring policy. *European Journal of Law and Economics* 19(1): 95–114.

Yörük, E. (2006). *Social relations of production within the workshop system in Istanbul's apparel industry.* Unpublished MA thesis. University of Bosphorus, Istanbul.

Yükseker, D. (2004). Trust and gender in a transnational market: The public culture of Laleli, Istanbul. *Public Culture* 16(1): 47–65.

Yurchak, A. (2006). *Everything was forever, until there was no more: The last Soviet generation.* Princeton, NJ: Princeton University Press.

Index